THE RISE AND FALL
OF THE
HIGH COMMISSION

BY

ROLAND G. USHER, Ph.D.

ASSOCIATE PROFESSOR OF HISTORY
WASHINGTON UNIVERSITY, ST. LOUIS

AUTHOR OF
THE RECONSTRUCTION OF THE ENGLISH CHURCH

THE LAWBOOK EXCHANGE, LTD.
Clark, New Jersey
2007

ISBN-13: 978-1-58477-733-5
ISBN-10: 1-58477-733-8

The quality of this reprint is equivalent to the quality of the original work.

THE LAWBOOK EXCHANGE, LTD.
33 Terminal Avenue
Clark, New Jersey 07066-1321

Please see our website for a selection of our other publications and fine facsimile reprints of classic works of legal history:
www.lawbookexchange.com

Library of Congress Cataloging-in-Publication Data

Usher, Roland G. (Roland Greene), b. 1880.
The rise and fall of the High Commission / Usher, Roland G.
p. cm.
Originally published: Oxford : Clarendon Press, 1913.
Includes bibliographical references and index.
ISBN-13: 978-1-58477-733-5 (alk. paper)
ISBN-10: 1-58477-733-8 (alk. paper)
1. Great Britain. Court of High Commission--History. 2. Ecclesiastical courts--England--History. 3. Great Britain--History. I. Title.

KD8682.U84 2007
262.9'8342--dc22

2006017625

Printed in the United States of America on acid-free paper

THE RISE AND FALL OF THE HIGH COMMISSION

BY

ROLAND G. USHER, Ph.D.

ASSOCIATE PROFESSOR OF HISTORY
WASHINGTON UNIVERSITY, ST. LOUIS

AUTHOR OF
THE RECONSTRUCTION OF THE ENGLISH CHURCH

OXFORD
AT THE CLARENDON PRESS
1913

OXFORD UNIVERSITY PRESS
LONDON EDINBURGH GLASGOW NEW YORK
TORONTO MELBOURNE BOMBAY
HUMPHREY MILFORD M.A.
PUBLISHER TO THE UNIVERSITY

PREFACE

THE judicial and administrative history of an ecclesiastical court abolished nearly three hundred years ago would seem, to most readers, a subject too technical and too remote from the great issues, whose breadth gives to institutional history its vitality and permanent interest, to make the results attained of value to any but a few specialists. Yet the intimate connexion of the High Commission's history with the growth of the nonconformists, with their struggle to find a place in the English Church, and with their determination to leave it; the important part in the history of the institution played by Thomas Cromwell, Richard Bancroft, Sir Edward Coke, William Laud, and other notable men of the period; the insistence of the Puritans and lawyers in 1640 that the illegality of the Commission, as well as its brutality, was one of the chief causes of the Revolution of 1640; the vital importance of a knowledge of the controversy between the common lawyers and the High Commissioners to a proper understanding of the development and meaning of the constitutional issues so prominent during the Stuart period,—all impart a significant and broad interest to the study of the Commission's history, and make any sound conclusions about it of real value to the general student and even to the casual reader of English history.

Divergent legal and theological views were responsible for most of the verdicts passed upon the Commission by its contemporaries, and the instinctive preferences and beliefs peculiar to each generation of men will, no doubt, in the future as in the past, continue strongly to influence the opinions of students. We are treating, in fact, issues which are still of vital consequence to a great number of earnest men to whom the establishment of the truth of their view of history still seems to be a significant part of their general position. The controversies over the Commission's legality, expediency, severity, are indissolubly connected with the justification of the Puritan revolt from the Established Church ; with the battle of the common-law judges against all other jurisdictions in England and their contention that the ecclesiastical jurisdiction was foreign ; with the rise and influence of what is now popularly called the High Church wing of the present Established Church. In attempting to discover and tell the literal truth about the Commission's history, I have been increasingly conscious that the whole truth will not be particularly palatable to any one of these parties, and that my attitude will, very likely, seem to each to be prejudiced in favour of the others. If the conclusions I have reached should seem valid to those competent to judge, a good many verdicts, long thought to be well established, will need to be considerably modified, if not altogether abandoned. Previous to 1640 the Court of High Commission seems to have conformed in its institution and practice with equity and justice, and with the law of the land, as it was then commonly interpreted. The 'law' pronounced by Chief Justice Coke and accepted by the Long Parliament, the charges of brutality so repeatedly made by the Puritans, seem not to be supported by the evidence now available. If this be true, it then follows that one count of the indictment brought by the Long Parliament against King and Church must be, for the present in any case, declared not proven. On the other hand, it has not been difficult to explain why the common lawyers believed the Commission illegal, and why the Puritans thought it brutal and an 'innovation'. The student cannot entirely agree either with the Commission or with its opponents; the study of its history does not *defend* any particular view ever taken of it; it *explains* the existence and character of the previous disagreements about it.

The use of the phrase 'the High Commission' presents issues of such importance that they have been treated at some length in a note appended to chapter i. The phrase seems to have referred to a court of law, in session at London between (approximately) the years 1580 and 1641, whose judges were about a dozen of the Ecclesiastical Commissioners appointed by royal Letters Patent. If this be its real meaning, it may seem curious to find interwoven with the history of this court a more or less lengthy account of all the ecclesiastical commissions issued by the Crown between the Reformation and the Civil War. It would seem more natural to treat them separately or to omit them altogether. The impossibility of otherwise tracing the origin of the court, and of explaining many facts of its working, and many misconceptions about it, must be a sufficient defence for this apparently serious inconsistency.

A small part of my material on this subject was utilized in an essay submitted to the Department of History of Harvard University in 1905 in part fulfilment of the requirements for the degree of Doctor of Philosophy, but the treatment of the matter in this present book differs radically, in substance as well as form, from my earlier attempt.

I am deeply indebted to Hubert Hall, Esq., of the Public Record Office, for indispensable assistance in obtaining access to much material in private libraries and collections. The fact that I have already acknowledged his most generous interest on more than one previous occasion only makes my present sense of deep obligation the greater. My acknowledgements and thanks are due to the following noblemen and gentlemen, who most kindly opened to me the archives in their possession or under their charge: His Grace the Archbishop of Canterbury; His Grace the Archbishop of York; the Bishops of London, Norwich, Ely, Peterborough, and Lincoln; the Earl of Leicester and the Marquess of Salisbury; the Keeper of the Privy Council Records; the Librarian of the Inner Temple; the Librarian of the Congregational Library; the Librarians of all the Oxford and Cambridge Colleges, in particular of All Souls, Jesus, and Queen's Colleges, Oxford, and Trinity College, Cambridge.

It is too much to expect that I have succeeded, even with so much generous assistance, in investigating and treating so technical and highly controversial a subject without the commission of many errors. I can only beg the reader to deal charitably with such failings of mind and hand as he discovers.

R. G. U.

Washington University,
St. Louis, Missouri.

CONTENTS

APPENDIX

CHAPTER I

THE ORIGIN OF THE HIGH COMMISSION

FIRST PHASE: COMMISSIONERS FOR THE ESTABLISHMENT OF THE ROYAL SUPREMACY IN CAUSES ECCLESIASTICAL, 1535–80.

IF we mean by the phrase 'The High Commission' the law-court for the trial of suits between party and party whose existence becomes clear about 1580 and which persisted till 1641,[1] we shall find its beginnings in the ecclesiastical commissions issued by Henry VIII and his children in the preceding four decades. The investigation of the origin of so important an administrative and judicial body as this court was, is at best a difficult problem, but is peculiarly complicated by the abnormalities of the period in which these first commissions appeared. Royal caprice, political expediency, religious upheaval, ecclesiastical reform, all played their part in tangling the threads of judicial and administrative history. We cannot assume that every slight modification of the mediaeval heresy trial,[2] every 'irregularity' in the

[1] The difficulties occasioned by the use of this term are discussed at length in the note at the end of this chapter.

[2] According to Stubbs, the mediaeval heresy trial broke down before 1500, and trials for heresy between 1500 and 1530 often did not materially differ from ordinary trials for other ecclesiastical offences. Ecclesiastical Commissioners' Report, *Parl. Doc.* 1883, xxiv, 52. This breaking down of the line so long drawn between heresy trials and ordinary trials cannot have lacked significance in the development of such a court as the High Commission eventually became.

visitation of sees and monasteries, nor every evidence of the exercise of the royal supremacy in ecclesiastical affairs before or after 1535 by commission or otherwise, were all steps in the development of the institution later known as the High Commission. Many experiments were made, many temporary devices were tried, which unquestionably led to nothing and which were not intended to be more than makeshifts.[1] Nor is it unlikely that a great deal was arbitrarily but secretly done by Henry and Cromwell by forms which would seem to be far from legal or judicial if we had fuller information. Ecclesiastical commissions and their acts must not be connected with a formal delegation of the Supreme Headship on no stronger evidence than the fact that such acts were arbitrary. Again, we must carefully distinguish trials of individual heretics, always more or less common, from a systematic attempt to exterminate heresy; for it seems clear that until at least Elizabeth's reign ordinary cases of doctrinal heresy were not regularly dealt with by commissioners, but were usually left to the bishops and the local temporal judiciary, all of whom were given plenary statutory authority to deal with them. A

[1] As early as 1521 the King directed the local officials in the bishopric of Lincoln to protect and assist the bishop in his efforts to clear his diocese of heretics (Wilkins, *Concilia*, iii, 698). Commissions were certainly issued in 1525 and 1528 to inquire into heresy at the universities, and the Oath of Supremacy seems to have been drafted by Cranmer and his colleagues sitting in commission at Lambeth in 1534 (Pollard, *Cranmer*, 20, 80). Certainly royal commissioners considered, if they did not draw up, the 'Institution of a Christian Man', and spent much time in revising ecclesiastical laws (Strype, *Memorials*, I, i, 550; II, i, 530. Oxford, 1822–8. This edition has been used throughout this volume). But that any of these commissions had any connexion whatever with anything we ought to consider the predecessor of the later High Commission is not probable, and certainly not demonstrable.

Statute of 25 Henry VIII, c. 14, allowed even sheriffs in their Turns and stewards in their Leets to inquire into heresy and present to the bishop, who should try the cases and hand over the guilty to the temporal power to be burned. The Act of the Six Articles, while providing that its penalties might be exacted by commissioners appointed by the King for the various counties or dioceses, conferred upon practically all ecclesiastical and temporal officials full powers for the execution of its provisions. Certainly, too, under Mary similar powers were exercised by the local temporal officials as well as by the clergy.[1] It is therefore reasonably clear that the body of men later known as 'the High Commission' did not originate in the necessity for the trial of doctrinal heretics by royal commissioners. We are dealing in reality with a systematic attempt to suppress a peculiar and novel type of heresy by a certain method, and, in the nature of things, neither the heresy nor the method could have dated much before the Reformation.

The procedure and organization of the many commissions granted by Henry VIII and his children are even more perilous criteria on which to base our notions of the origin of the law-court of later years. A certain variance from past traditions was to have been expected after 1533, above all in the treatment of heretics ; for the early reformers, if not Henry himself, desired some alterations in administration and law merely to show the people how different the methods and substance of the new régime were from those of the corrupt rule of the Bishop of Rome. That these newer activities and methods should bear some resemblance to the activities and procedure of the ecclesiastical commissioners of later years is

[1] See the cases in Foxe's *Martyrs*, v, vi, viii, *passim*. (London, 1838.)

not surprising,[1] but is not necessarily significant, for the early commissioners used all sorts of methods, very few of which had had in the past any legitimate connexion with heresy trials. Moreover, the use of a commission of ecclesiastics cannot be considered in itself significant in the light of the fact that it was a very old papal device, and that certain trials of Lollards, notably Oldcastle's, had been conducted by special commissions.[2] A commission of temporal lords for the dispatch of secular business was even older, while an administrative council composed of bishops, ministers of state, and lawyers was the oldest administrative body in England. In short, we shall find the origin of the later Court of High Com-

[1] For instance, Wolsey issued a commission in 1521 to the bishops by virtue of his legatine powers to search for heretical books: Strype, *Memorials*, I, i, 56. The commission for First Fruits of 1535 and 1536, and that for the valuation of benefices of 1535, bear certain casual resemblances to the later High Commission, but more still to the subsidy commissions of earlier date: *ibid.* 325, 426. The commissions for divorces, and for the collection of lead, plate, ornaments, and the like from the churches and chantries in 1551 and 1552 discharged duties later performed by the Ecclesiastical Commissioners: Strype, *Memorials*, II, ii, 204, 208, 210, 211.

[2] Harl. MSS. 421, f. 132, dated 1413. In 1432 a commission issued to the Bishop of Hereford 'ad inquirendum de personis suspectis super hereticam pravitatem': *ibid.* f. 121. See also royal Letters Patent issued in 1392 to the same, granting power to arrest heretics who had fled into Wales: Foxe, *Martyrs*, iii, 195–6. Harl. MSS. 421 contains also many documents relating to Lollard trials, including a great array of formal articles, depositions, and the like, drawn up in accordance with the strict canon law. No doubt the trials of Lollards furnished in some way precedent of some sort for the later ecclesiastical commissions, but whatever we find out about the Lollard trials goes to show that they were conducted by some regular procedure, and the lack of a definite procedure and the possession of complete discretion as to ways and means are perhaps the only thing we can positively assert about the early post-reformation commissions.

mission in none of these, but in the systematic attempt to suppress a peculiar type of heresy by the machinery of a commission in which ecclesiastics, ministers of state, and lawyers sat side by side, and whose procedure was a compound of the old heresy trial, the ordinary ecclesiastical procedure, and the judicial traditions of the Privy Council. This device of an ecclesiastical privy council dealing with heresy and the visitation of the Church had certainly not been many times employed when a commission was issued about 1535, investing Thomas Cromwell with the plenitude of royal authority in ecclesiastical affairs, and directing him to delegate part of it from time to time to such persons as he thought fit. This commission, of whose exact language, date, purpose, and origin we know almost nothing,[1] is the first clear evidence we have of the existence of that type of ecclesiastical commission out of which was gradually evolved the court later celebrated as 'the High Commission'. In all probability, this commission to Cromwell was only the final step in a comparatively long series of events, not now traceable, through which the notion had gradually developed. We cannot be certain, but it is extremely likely that such a commission was never, in any proper sense of the word, 'created'.[2]

[1] The paper which Burnet believed to be this commission is in Cotton MSS. Cleopatra, F. II, f. 131, printed in Pocock's *Burnet's Reformation*, v, 456 (Oxford, 1865); the earlier editions are all inaccurate. It is, however, only a bad copy of one of the minor commissions issued by Cromwell by virtue of the general commission. The original of the latter had disappeared by 1609, and Archbishop Abbott's strenuous efforts to find it were unavailing.

[2] Toward the end of Elizabeth's reign the prevailing ignorance of history (and the government was anxious for the people to forget as much as possible of the doings of the previous two generations) fostered a notion which the common lawyers found

The efficient reason for employing this peculiar type of commission lay in the existence of the breach with Rome and the assumption of the Headship of the Church by the Crown. A peculiar situation, entirely without precedent, had thus arisen, and its very abnormalities explain the type of commission developed to cope with its exigencies. First and foremost stood that ever-present necessity to the Tudors, the preservation of the dynasty itself. Henry staked his power as king on the maintenance of the new Church settlement, and the chief enemies of both King and Church were those 'blasphemous' heretics who denied the royal supremacy. The spectre of heresy at which the mediaeval man had so long shuddered took on new forms more terrifying to Henry and Elizabeth than those visions of 'tearing Christ's robe' and of destroying the unity of religion which had checked the aggressions of mediaeval kings and emperors. The Tudors' imminent personal danger far outstripped in immediacy of importance any theoretical danger to the Church from divergent opinion. The State was threatened by every assault on the Church so long as the Crown remained the latter's spiritual head.[1] To acknowledge

convenient, that the Commission was 'created' in 1559 by the Statute of 1 Elizabeth, c. 1. One of the counts against Nicholas Fuller in 1607 was that he declared it 'apparent that before the said Acte there was neuer any such commission nor Commissioners': Lansdowne MSS. 1172, f. 101 b. To have admitted that there was a legal commission before the Statute would have admitted that the Commission could be authorized by the royal prerogative, and would have destroyed Fuller's and Coke's logic. Their view of its origin has been usually accepted. On the strength of it, Stubbs declared that the Edwardian and Marian commissions were precedents for the court which Elizabeth 'created'! *Parl. Doc.* 1883, xxiv, 41, 49.

[1] For the administrative consequences to the Church of this step, see Usher, *Reconstruction of the English Church*, i, 1–21, 1–100, 233–9.

the Pope's authority was, therefore, heresy to the Church and treason to the State, and the safety of both demanded the prompt punishment of such a serious offence by any spiritual or temporal means at hand.

But the old courts and councils were quite helpless to punish that offence. To begin with, it was hardly heresy according to the old laws. In addition, the punishment of heresy had been peculiarly the province of the clergy, and laymen had rarely if ever presumed to decide what was or was not heresy. Yet here was an heretical tenet—allegiance to the Bishop of Rome—which every notion of expediency in statecraft required to be severely dealt with, and which yet found its chief believers in the clergy themselves. It was beyond doubt idle to expect them to convict each other of such a heresy, or to enforce efficiently upon the laity a tenet which they themselves secretly disbelieved.[1] Had the Reformation made heresy in fact a temporal crime to be defined and punished by laymen? It was easy to declare that those who continued to obey the Pope were not clergymen and hence not empowered to decide what was heresy, but others could not be found to fill their places who promised to be more obedient or compliant than they, even if the machinery of the Church should succeed under the circumstances in expelling the one and inducting the other. Until the Church had been 'purified', it was folly to talk of entrusting bishops and deans, abbots and priors, with authority over this type of heresy. And who was to purify the Church, and by what means?

It was clear to Henry and Cromwell that the Crown must perform all these difficult tasks by the exercise of that plenitude of ecclesiastical authority which it had reassumed after so long a usurpation by the Pope; but

[1] See Pollard's *Cranmer*, 130–6.

the method by which such untrammelled powers could be safely and efficiently exercised was not as clear. Henry seems to have viewed his new powers with complaisance, and would undoubtedly have enjoyed exercising them in person, had it been physically possible for him to do that work in addition to his already onerous labours as king. The natural alternative to his personal exercise of the supreme power did not, however, seem more expedient or desirable. Prudence and tradition alike urged the development of some organ outside the regular ecclesiastical hierarchy by whose means the royal Head might supervise and control the hierarchy itself. Moreover, the powers of archbishops and bishops had been so long curtailed by legates and commissions from Rome, that to increase episcopal authority, even in practice, by the addition of any considerable proportion of the powers long exercised by the Pope, would make precisely that violent breach with traditional forms which Henry was particularly anxious to avoid. Furthermore, the work of most immediate importance in 1535 was the visitation, regulation, and perhaps suppression of the monasteries, and to entrust this task to the monks' hereditary enemies, the bishops, was the surest way to sow the seeds of strife and dissension in the path of the new settlement. Most monasteries had been responsible to the Pope alone, and all had been eager to free themselves from any authority short of the highest. It was hardly likely that in the present exigency they would tamely submit to the ordinary episcopal authority, or afterwards admit that any reform executed by the latter had been legal. It was clear, then, that the attempt to increase the authority of any ecclesiastic or of any ecclesiastical body then in existence would be certain to foster charges of illegality against all acts done by virtue of it. Under these circumstances and moved by some such considerations as these, Henry named Cromwell his Vicegerent.

The real justification of such commissions as he was to issue from a moral and ecclesiastical point of view, lay in the psychology of heresy. Strangely enough, the split of the Christian world into several well-defined churches had intensified rather than lessened the mediaeval belief in the necessity for a spiritual unity of the world and in the desirability and possibility of uniformity of ritual and creed. The attaining of this unity and uniformity was the task to be entrusted to commissioners as soon as the existing Church had been purified. According to any precise analysis of the question, the really efficient cause of the regular use of such commissions lay in the conviction that heresy was abnormal and therefore weak; that it *could* be suppressed; and that a sufficient amount of coercion, properly directed by unlimited authority and untrammelled discretion in the choice of means, *could* accomplish the desired result. That the 'heretics' should refuse to accept any given opinion with the constancy of Huss before the Council; that they should be too numerous to suppress; that such unity and uniformity as could be attained by force were not in themselves desirable,—none of these facts were even dreamt of by the men of the sixteenth century. No one, Roman Catholic, Anglican, or Puritan, could for a moment conceive that the other was right; each was anxious to compel men to agree with him, and complained less because force was used to obtain his conversion, than because he was furiously opposed to the notion that he needed to be converted. Toleration, freedom of opinion and of worship, the notion of relative truth—all of these concepts the very bases of modern thought—were so foreign to the ideas of the sixteenth century that the modern student ought not to expect to find himself in sympathy with the High Commission, or to obtain from his own premises the conclusions of the High Commissioners on any subject. Nor were the ideals cherished by the latter's opponents essentially different, despite the modern sound of certain phrases and catchwords. Both commissioners and opponents had, in fact, the same premises: neither believed in freedom of thought, liberty of conscience, or the rightness of toleration; both believed in the necessity of obtaining unity and uniformity by force if no other means would prevail; both believed in the loathsomeness of heresy and in the duty of rigorous dealing with heretics. The only difference between them was that each believed the other to be the heretic in need of 'shrewd handling'. According to the premises of the twentieth century, the High Commission was tyrannical, barbarous, and oppressive. According to the premises of the majority of men then alive, it was beneficent, humanitarian, and necessary. We must constantly bear in mind these considerations if we wish to understand the High Commission at all.

The commission issued to Cromwell about 1535 granted him 'omnem et omnimodam jurisdictionem, auctoritatem, sive potestatem ecclesiasticam, quae nobis tanquam supremo capiti hujusmodi competit, aut quovismodo competere possit, aut debeat, ubilibet infra regnum nostrum Angliae et loca quaecunque nobis subjecta'.[1] Under it the Vicegerent issued minor commissions to several

[1] These words would seem to leave no doubt of the extraordinary and unlimited authority conveyed, and Stubbs so read them, op. cit. 39. Yet the most recent student of Cromwell, Professor Merriman, seems to regard this commission as sanctioning nothing more than a general visitation of churches, monasteries, and clergy: *Life and Letters of Cromwell*, i, 166.

men, often civil lawyers, limited in authority to some few matters specifically mentioned. At first they were directed to visit the monasteries; then were ordered to proceed against Anabaptists. Until Mary's accession, the actual work seems to have been chiefly performed by the smaller commissions, the general commission serving as a source of authority and as a sort of executive to direct their labours. They were temporary, and usually limited to one case; even the general commission was apparently not meant to permit the continuous exercise of authority. The real work of suppressing doctrinal heresy had, however, been placed by Statute in the hands of the bishops, assisted by the temporal officers of the realm, and Cromwell's commissioners seem to have been less active after the suppression of the monasteries was completed. After Cromwell's death, the general commission does not seem to have been reissued,[1] and the Privy Council seems to have appointed the special commissioners for such cases as arose from time to time.[2] The first general commission of this nature directed to a number of men was probably issued by Edward VI in 1549,[3] and was in substance and form clearly the first of the long succession of Letters Patent issued by the Crown up to the moment of the abolition of the Court of High Commission in 1641. Certainly, if the phraseology of the Letters Patent is to be the criterion establishing

[1] There seems to have been a vote in the Privy Council in 1543 which might be interpreted as a decision to issue a general commission: *Letters and Papers, Henry VIII*, XVIII, part ii, p. 327.

[2] e.g. *Ibid.* XVI, no. 8; XVII, no. 537; XVIII, part i, no. 500. *Privy Council Register, New Series*, i, 418.

[3] Printed in Rymer, *Foedera*, XV, 181. A bibliography of Letters Patent, general and special, has been placed in the Appendix. They will be referred to in the future merely by date.

the beginning of 'the High Commission', we shall be compelled to call the Commission of 1549 the first 'High Commission'.

As in later years, the Patent issued to bishops and a number of other clergy, to a few ministers of state, and to a number of civil and common lawyers. The powers it conferred were fully as broad as those of the later commissions, which differed from it chiefly in the greater precision with which they explicitly defined more and more of what had at first been implied by a few broad phrases. The commissioners were to examine and inquire concerning all heretics whatsoever, all heresies whatever, 'suspectos, detectos, denunciatos, inquisitos,[1] et accusatos.'[2] They were to proceed by witnesses examined upon their oaths, or by any other method of proof whatsoever, or 'omnibus aliis viis et modis et formis quibus melius et efficacius poteritis'. They might proceed also (quoting here verbatim the common mediaeval formula descriptive of summary procedure), 'etiam summarie et de plano ac sine strepitu et figura judicii cognoscendi, inquirendi, et investigandi.' They should receive back into the bosom of the Church those who recanted, and should eject from it those who refused to abjure; should punish all who condemned or opposed the Book of Common Prayer, and should deliver up all such persons 'et carceri et vinculis si opus fuerit'.[3] Further, they should receive all necessary aid in their duties from all ecclesiastics, civil lawyers, mayors, sheriffs, bailiffs, and all other officers whatever. In January 1550/1, this Patent was reissued

[1] In technical phrase, whose offence had been sought and discovered by the court itself.

[2] Technically, those indicted by another party who himself brought suit.

[3] The Edwardian patents contain no explicit reference to fine, which makes its first explicit appearance in the Marian patents.

with a few unimportant verbal additions [1] to an increased number of commissioners, thirty-one instead of twenty-five. Smaller commissions upon this model and upon the models used under Henry VIII were issued frequently by Edward.[2] Mary seems at first to have had recourse to the pre-reformation ecclesiastical authority; the Statute of 1 and 2 Philip and Mary, c. 6, revived much of the pre-reformation legislation against heretics, and was certainly interpreted by the bishops and local officers as conferring upon them full powers to try and burn heretics.[3] But Pole as legate at once granted a commission to certain bishops not unlike Cromwell's commission,[4] and he also instructed the bishops in January 1555 that their powers against heretics were restored 'maxime ut possint'. They were, however, allowed to use only ecclesiastical penalties.[5]

Both the substance and form of the Letters Patent, under which 'the High Commission' flourished during the whole of its long life, assumed final shape in the general Commission issued by Mary in 1557, to twenty-two commissioners 'for a severer way of proceeding against heretics'.[6] The Patent declared that divers false rumours and seditious books had been set forth, and that misdemeanours and enormities had been committed to the disturbance of the peace and disquieting of the people.

[1] The Patent of 1549 had read mostly in the singular; this read in the plural.

[2] See the list in the Bibliography in the Appendix.

[3] Pocock's *Burnet*, ii, 554; v, 427, 429; Foxe, *Martyrs*, viii, 213; &c. Strype (*Memorials*, III, ii, 129) says the Marian prosecutions were based on these old Statutes; whether to the exclusion of the commissions he does not say.

[4] Strype, *Cranmer*, i, 495.

[5] *Ibid.* ii, 951. Pocock's *Burnet's Reformation*, vi, 367.

[6] It is possible, as Burnet says (Pocock's *Burnet*, ii, 556), that this was only a reissue of one issued in 1556.

To prevent which, we 'by these presents do give full power and authority unto you and three of you, to enquire, as well by the oaths of twelve good and lawful men, as by witnesses, and all other means and politic ways you can devise, of all and sundry heresies, heretical opinions, Lollardies, heretical and seditious books, concealments, contempts, conspiracies, and of all false rumours, tales, seditious and clamorous words or sayings, raised, published, bruited, invented, or set forth against us, or either of us; or against the quiet governance and rule of our people and subjects, by books, letters, tales, or otherwise, in any country, city, borough, or other place or places within this our realm of England and elsewhere'. Then followed certain specific matters of which they were 'to enquire, hear, and determine': all offences committed in churches, or against church property, all refusals to attend any part of the service, the warding of all vagabonds and masterless men in London. Then as to the method of procedure, they were directed 'to use and devise all such politic ways and means for the trial and searching out of the premises as by you or three of you shall be thought most expedient and necessary; and upon enquiry, and due proof had, known, perceived, and tried out by the confession of the parties, or by sufficient witnesses . . . or by any other ways or means requisite, to give and award such punishment to the offenders by fine, imprisonment, or otherwise; and to take such order for redress and reformation of the premises, as to your wisdoms, or three of you shall be thought meet and convenient'. In express language they were directed to use the *ex officio* oath: 'to examine and compel to answer, and swear, upon the holy evangelists, to declare the truth in all such things whereof they or any of them shall be examined.' They should fine and imprison all who refused to obey their decrees or orders, take bonds for appearance or for performance of decrees, and certify all fines into the Exchequer for collection. They should appoint a receiver of fines, and such messengers and officers as might be necessary; and in the execution of the premises receive the aid of all temporal officers. And further, in the said execution they should proceed, 'any of our laws, statutes, proclamations, or other grants, privileges, or ordinances, which be, or may seem to be contrary to the premises, notwithstanding.'

This form was a very considerable extension of the commissions of Edward VI, though it included little that was not implied by them. Like most early ecclesiastical commissions, however, it was temporary, and, though probably meant to be renewed, was granted only for one year. Until well into the reign of Elizabeth, all ecclesiastical commissions bore this temporary aspect. Moreover, as each was issued to the commissioners by name, a member's death, without invalidating the whole commission, created a vacancy which could not be filled and which did seriously interfere with the commissioners' efficiency. It was of course only a question of time when the death of its members would invalidate the Patent. In the later Elizabethan commissions the chief commissioners sat *ex officio*, and thus until revoked the Commission was permanent.

The chief work performed by these ecclesiastical commissioners had been thus far the suppression of heresy and the maintenance of a particular church settlement. The form of the Patent itself remained much the same, and the commissioners proceeded under it against Lollards and Roman Catholics, or against Lutherans and Anglicans, without hesitation. Henry VIII had considered it to sanction the suppression of heresy according to the

Canons of the Roman Catholic Church ; Edward VI had used it to deprive the priests and to uphold the Book of Common Prayer and the Forty-Two Articles ; under Mary, it had been employed to deprive the Edwardian bishops, reinstate the priests, and banish the Book of Common Prayer in favour of the mass and images. Elizabeth now used the selfsame forms and methods to upset the work just executed by Mary, and reinstated by them the Book of Common Prayer, and enforced her Acts of Supremacy and Uniformity and the Canons and Orders of the Elizabethan Church. On her accession, however, the new queen had recourse at first to the form of the early visitatorial commissions issued by Cromwell against the monasteries, and on that model, though probably with very considerable alterations in the exact wording, issued her first commissions [1] 'visitatoribus suis in partibus borealibus'. She adopted this form probably more from necessity than from choice, for the Edwardian and Marian forms of Letters Patent were essentially ecclesiastical, to be executed by clergy and civil lawyers under the canon law, and at the moment of her accession Elizabeth found so few clergy and civil lawyers openly in favour of her policy that she found it difficult to secure trustworthy men of sufficient importance to execute such a commission. The form of commission employed by Cromwell as Vicegerent, on the other hand, was in essence a secular form, to be carried out chiefly by secular officers acting under extraordinary royal authority, where lesser ecclesiastics could serve very well for the actual work if shielded by great civil dignitaries. It was in fact far better fitted

[1] Strype (*Annals*, I, part i, 245) says there were several. There is one in S. P. Dom. Eliz., 4, no. 62 ; printed with corrections of the extremely bad Latin in Pocock's *Burnet's Reformation*, v, 533–7.

for the purpose of ejecting the hostile clergy than the newer Marian form. While the commissioners were depriving the Marian clergy, Parliament passed the Act of Supremacy, affirming once more the annexation of the ancient jurisdiction ecclesiastical to the Crown, and containing a clause (viii) expressly authorizing the delegation to ecclesiastical commissioners by Letters Patent of powers almost as broad as those conferred by Henry VIII upon Cromwell.

In July 1559,[1] therefore, the Queen issued Letters Patent which were, with some changes of importance, practically a repetition verbatim of the Patent of 1557.[2] Of seventeen articles only four were new, and of those only one was of importance. In membership the two were strikingly similar,[3] and several of the members had already sat on the Marian Commission. The chief provisions concerning jurisdiction and procedure, though the wording differed slightly, were not essentially altered. Most changes of importance were aimed at reducing the commissioners' power, and though one new article possessed great significance its full meaning was not appreciated for nearly a score of years. It contained a repetition of the clause of the Act of Supremacy, 1 Eliz., c. 1, in which had been incorporated the phrases of the first Act of Supremacy, 26 Henry VIII, c. 1, and granted the Commission power 'to visit, reform, redress, order,

[1] According to a tract later published, and cited by Cosin, *Apologie*, part i, 114, the Commission was not actually signed by the Queen till November.

[2] See Appendix for a detailed comparison of the two.

[3] In each, two bishops, one other clergyman, four ministers of State. In Mary's, one serjeant-at-law, against two in Elizabeth's; six civil lawyers, against five in Elizabeth's; and eight without rank as against five without rank in Elizabeth's commission.

correct, and amend, in all places within this our realm of England, all such errors, heresies, crimes, abuses, offences, contempts, and enormities, spiritual and ecclesiastical whatsoever,[1] which by any spiritual or ecclesiastical power, authority, or jurisdiction can or may lawfully be reformed, ordered, redressed, corrected, restrained, or amended . . . and according to the authority and power limited, given, and appointed by any laws or statutes of this realm '. Other additions were of more immediate consequence : clause vii giving authority to deprive, restore, and appoint the clergy ; clause viii giving jurisdiction over moral crimes, and clause xiii appointing a registrar.

Compared with its predecessor, the Elizabethan Patent was conservative. The number of members was reduced ; the quorum necessary to act was doubled ; the Commission ran only to England, where the Edwardian and Marian Commissions had run to the whole of the Crown's dominions. Moreover, clause v required the commissioners to proceed ' according to the authority and power limited, given, and appointed by any laws or statutes of this realm '. To be sure, clause xv repeated the sweeping Marian *non obstante* clause, dispensing with all statutes or ' other grants ' which contravened the Letters Patent, and it was hardly to be supposed that any commissioner would attempt to proceed otherwise than by some warrant of law. Nevertheless, the very existence of the enabling clause in the Act of Supremacy was a limitation, though it is extremely doubtful whether Elizabeth or her counsellors regarded it in such a light. At the same time, the addition to the Henrician Statute of a few sentences permitting the delegation of the

[1] The original reads ' wheresoever ', a manifest error, which has been corrected wherever the clause has been quoted.

authority already assumed could hardly make legal what had been illegal before.

In the history of these commissions, there was no important change at either the year 1559, when the Statute of 1 Elizabeth, c. 1, was passed, nor in 1565, when the Elizabethan religious settlement became firmly established. We find in the language used by contemporaries no consciousness of any change, and no especial significance attached to the existence of the Statute which seemed, fifty years later, of such portentous importance. From 1557 to 1601 the form of the Letters Patent, and consequently the legal authority of the commissioners, was not essentially altered; the personnel of the commissioners remained much the same after 1559 as before; the authority and procedure actually employed were not (as far as we can tell) different; the relation of the commissioners to the Privy Council was precisely the same after 1559 as before. Nor can we truthfully say that institutional strength began to be acquired then, and that the Statute gave birth to the law-court later known as 'the High Commission'. The Elizabethan Commissioners of 1559 seemed to later generations the first High Commissioners, because they were the first empowered by a religious settlement which was itself permanent, because they were the first who had an opportunity to turn their attention to anything but the maintenance of the Royal Supremacy and the pressing needs of a new religious settlement. After 1559 the commissioners held office for the first time by a sufficiently permanent tenure to enable them to establish those traditions and judicial forms which, in time, caused contemporaries to call the sessions of Her Majesty's Commissioners in Causes Ecclesiastical 'the Court of High Commission'. But of this the efficient cause was the permanence of the Elizabethan settlement, and not the Statute; and the former merely provided the opportunity for growth. The growth itself and its peculiar forms were the result of other influences than Statutes and Letters Patent. 'The High Commission' was an evolution and not a 'creation', and there seems to be no valid reason for dating that evolution from 1559.

A new phase does seem to begin about 1565 which unquestionably contributed to the process of growth, already no doubt somewhat advanced. The completion of the work connected with the establishment of the Elizabethan settlement left the commissioners free to turn their attention to other work. Instead of a body of men exercising visitatorial authority in emergencies, the Commissioners for the Province of Canterbury became a sort of administrative organ for the performance of such routine business as the Privy Council saw fit to entrust to them, and began for the first time to devote their whole attention to a task which, in its own nature, was something more than confessedly temporary. Some faint adumbration of such routine work can be seen even during the lifetimes of Henry and Edward, but the paramount necessity of first ridding the Church of the dissentient clergy had prevented its development. From a body of men gathered together for the accomplishment of an object in its very nature temporary to a body of men entrusted with the performance of routine duties was not perhaps a very radical step, but it was one absolutely essential to be taken before 'the Ecclesiastical Commissioners' could become a permanent body or begin to develop the jurisdiction and formal procedure which is a prerequisite of a court of law. This step, moreover, was in all probability purely the result of circumstances, and not of a decision made after due deliberation and publicly announced by Statute or executive ordinance. Administrative and judicial convenience was the efficient cause of the growth of the High Commission, and it is impossible to connect either with a definite date.

One other change did take place soon after Elizabeth's accession. Special commissions for the trial of, or even for inquiry into, one case had been usually issued by the general commissioners; Elizabeth began the practice of issuing them herself, and apparently rescinded the power to delegate authority which earlier commissioners had so freely exercised. Under Cranmer and Pole, the general commissioners had themselves performed some of the duties assigned them in their Patent, though usually only after the receipt of explicit orders from the Privy Council. Under Parker, they regularly performed in person everything done by virtue of their Patent. After 1559 special commissions for the trial of a single case were rare, and commissions were issued instead to some bishop whose diocese was particularly in need of discipline, conferred on him and some others authority over certain classes of cases, and were rather intended to relieve, or perhaps supplant, the authority of the general commissioners than to perform the work allotted to them. Probably this subdivision of the visitatorial power can be explained more readily as a change in the general policy of ecclesiastical administration than as an intention to alter in so radical a fashion the organization of the ecclesiastical commissions, as the 'creation' of a court of law would suppose.

NOTE

The Accuracy and Validity of the Phrase, 'The High Commission'

When the acrimonious controversy between the common-law judges and the civil and ecclesiastical lawyers reached its climax in 1609, and had thoroughly enmeshed the High Commission, the proper interpretation of a part of the Elizabethan Act of Supremacy was clearly seen to be very closely related to the question of the origin of the Commission, to the method of its 'creation', and to the date and the authority by which it was accomplished. An examination of the accuracy and validity of the words 'the High Commission' as employed to describe the various commissions issued by different sovereigns between 1535 and 1641, similarly raises the issue of the legal controversy of 1609 and 1641. Indeed they are complementary. Whether we conclude that those words are accurate and valid, or that some more indefinite phrase must be substituted for them, our decision will be the result of a consideration of the character and legality of the institution itself, which will involve nearly every judicial and historical issue connected with it. We are asking, in fact, whether there ever was an institution sufficiently permanent and well-recognized to be called 'the' High Commission; whether 'it' was ever a law-court or was merely a body of men who exercised more or less frequently judicial functions under a temporary grant of authority from the Crown; whether 'it' or 'they' exceeded the bounds of the Statute 'creating' 'it' or 'them', and was or were accordingly abolished as an illegal usurpation of authority by the Act of 1641.

To the common lawyer of the period the answer was easy. He could not conceive of the legal existence in England of any court or permanent judicial organization outside the common-law hierarchy which was not explicitly 'created' by Statute. Upon the Statute of 1 Elizabeth, then, the answer to every question depended. It spoke of 'commissioners' and of 'a' commission, but said nothing about 'The High Commission', and nothing at all about the permanence of such 'a' commission. The Statute, therefore, they concluded, established nothing; it merely permitted the temporary delegation to commissioners of a limited part of the ecclesiastical authority vested in the Crown as Supreme Governor.[1] Upon these premises the proceedings against 'the Commission' in 1640 and 1641 were based, and the Act of 1641 abolished the so-called Court of High Commission on the ground that it was and had always been illegal and oppressive. This position, so authoritatively enounced under such dramatic circumstances, has been accepted without hesitation by judges and historians. The loss of the records of the so-called court, the inaccessibility till recent years of any evidence about it except the Statutes and the writings of the common lawyers and Parliamentarians, of course left the presumption in favour of the accuracy of the views expressed by those contemporaries whose opinions were on other points most in harmony with the ideas of later generations. To admit the propriety of the words, 'the High Commission,' for designating a judicial institution with a continuous and legal existence for at least sixty years before the meeting of the Long Parliament, involves, then, the denial of the historicity of the position assumed in 1641 by the Long Parliament, and a modification of the conclusions of lawyers and historians based upon it.

The ecclesiastics and civil lawyers, who were members of the Commission, declared that the Statute of 1 Elizabeth merely confirmed an authority already exercised by High Commissioners since 1535, when the first High Commission

[1] Nicholas Fuller is supposed to have said before the King's Bench in 1607: 'his Majestie's Commission, which they terme High, is by the true intent of the Statute only a Commission executorie, but for so long time onely as shall please the King, and is no setled court for continuance for ever; as they would haue it, comparing the authority thereof with the King's Bench and preferring it aboue it': *The Argument of Nicholas Fuller* . . . , 23 (1607). This tract was reprinted in 1641 and was apparently widely circulated. Fuller declared the tract to be a speech which he prepared but which he did not actually deliver.

was granted to Cromwell by Henry VIII. If the view of the common lawyers was unquestionably the result of an assumption that the Commission must have been created by Statute, the view of the ecclesiastics was no less the result of a belief that the Commission was created by the royal prerogative, and was legally invested with such authority as could be inferred from the broadest interpretation of the words of the Letters Patent. The ecclesiastics had no doubt that the Commission was a court and believed firmly in its continuous and legal existence since the days of Thomas Cromwell.

Strictly speaking, neither view is historically and legally correct. An absolutely accurate legal statement can say no more than that the Crown granted authority by Letters Patent to certain men for an indefinite length of time; that a new Patent from time to time conferred somewhat different powers upon substantially the same men; that as the new Patent invalidated the old, so it might be superseded in turn by another. Nor was there, until 1611, any explicit or formal statement that any commission had ever been issued before, or that the existing Patent would ever be renewed when the death of all its members had allowed it to lapse. It cannot be claimed that the Letters Patent before 1611 provided for the continuous exercise of authority; and it is unquestionably true that between 1535 and 1641 commissioners performed a great variety of functions. There is, in addition, no evidence to *demonstrate* an identity of procedure in enforcing the pre-reformation heresy Statutes, the Act of the Six Articles, the legislation of Edward, Mary, and Elizabeth. If identity of duties, of authority, and of procedure from 1535 to 1641 be essential to the correct use of the words 'the High Commission', the phrase can never be properly employed, for the facts do not fit such a definition. Behind these words, moreover, is the clear assumption that one particular commission existed. It is easy to say that the words always refer to the Commissioners for the Province of Canterbury; but it is impossible to deny that many commissions existed in England between 1535 and 1641 outwardly similar to the Commission for the Province of Canterbury in all but membership, and in the degree of authority conferred.

Yet, in the face of these facts, there can be even less doubt that in 1609 men who must have been familiar with every technicality of language possible at common, civil, or ecclesiastical law did *assume* the legal existence of 'The Court of High Commission', and conceded 'its' possession of a jurisdiction, a regular procedure, and an unquestioned judicial position of unusual dignity. Both parties to the bitter legal controversy conceded the continuous existence of this Court for decades. They differed chiefly as to the source from whence its authority came and as to the date of its inception; the one claiming its continuous existence since 1535, and the other denying any legal existence prior to 1559, but both unquestionably assuming it after that date. The history of contemporary usage is the most important evidence we possess for the decision of this perplexing problem.

Usage was at first confused and contradictory. Previous to Elizabeth's accession, we read most often of 'commissioners' or 'the ecclesiastical commissioners' when we are sure the writer meant the Commissioners for the Province of Canterbury, and of 'a commission' or 'commissioners' when the writer had in mind another body of men acting under a similar Patent. The words 'the Commission' and 'the Commission Ecclesiastical' occur rarely at first, but with increasing frequency as the year 1570 approaches; but they usually apply, without much room for doubt, to the Letters Patent themselves, to the document rather than to the members of the Commission or to the authority conferred upon them or to their sessions. About 1570, however, usage becomes less confused and begins to employ the singular number and the definite article more and more frequently to designate the men acting under the Patent. The word 'high' now appears—'the high commissioners,' 'the High Commissioners,' 'the High Commission'—and after 1580 popular usage regularly employs the phrase 'the High Commission' (not yet 'The High Commission') to denote a body of men with residence at London engaged in the trial of suits between private individuals. Probably the phrase was at first intended as a sort of nickname, but it was gradually adopted by lawyers and litigants, by the commissioners themselves, then by the common-law judges, and finally was used in the Letters Patent of 1613 as the official title of the Court. The importance of this matter of usage makes a few illustrations apposite.

A Puritan, writing in 1584, 'The Commission Ecclesiasticall requireth their warrants to be made,' &c., referred to the Patent (Morrice MSS. C, p. 652. See also other instances of Puritan usage in this same year to the same effect: Petyt MSS. 538. 36, f. 319, petition of the House of Commons; ibid. f. 324, Puritan tract). But this phrase written in the same year, 'the manner of proceedinge in the Commission is fownde to be greevous to the subjects,' refers to the action of the commissioners (Harleian MSS. 358, f. 224). Penry, in his tract, *Th' appelation of Iohn Penri unto the Highe Court of Parliament*, published in 1589, wrote of 'the Archb. of Canterb. and other his colleagues of the high commission'; and 'whence the highe Commission deriueth al the prerogatiue it hath'. Cosin, in 1593, wrote in his *Apologie*, part ii, 48, of 'the Court of Ecclesiasticall Commission', and of 'the Commission Ecclesiasticall'. This use by a commissioner of the singular number, the definite article, and the word 'Court' is significant. The common-law reports and treatises until about 1607 consistently employ the plural, 'Commissioners' (Coke, *Reports*, v, Cawdry's case; Fuller's tract; the judges' reply to the Articuli Cleri, 1605; the consultation in Fuller's case, Lansdowne MSS. 1172). Stoughton, in his *Assertion for True and Christian Church policie* (1604), p. 333, wrote: 'what a good manner of discipline and moderation it was for a Bp and his associates to make an act in the High Commission Court.' Barlow, in his official report of the *Summe and Substance of the* (Hampton Court) *Conference*, Third Day, wrote, the King 'fell into discourse about the High Commission'. Coke reported a speech by the Lord Chancellor at an informal conference in May 1609, and we still have in his holograph copy the words, 'The High Commission did fine one for committing incontinence' (Holkham MSS. 677, f. 252). In his treatise defending himself, written in 1609, Coke wrote 'euery man will come to the high Commission Cort'. Attorney-General Hobart, in his speech defending the Commission before the Privy Council in July 1609, entitled it 'the Grounds of Prohibicons to the high Commission', and employed the singular number (Stowe MSS. 420, f. 18). In the *Commons'*

Journals, i, 387 (1607) and 430 (1610), the phrase 'the High Commission' occurs. Clause iii of the Letters Patent of 1613 reads 'our said Court of High Commission'. The 'Orders for the regulation of the duties of the Registrar of the Court of High Commission' certainly shows official usage (S. P. Dom. Car. I, 339, no. 70).

The use of the word 'high' is further illustrated by the following cases. It is to be found in Cartwright's *Admonition to Parliament*, 1572, Division II, chap. i, tract. viii; the Privy Council used it in 1576, *Privy Council Register*, New Series, ix, 155; Chief Justice Wray used it in a letter in 1581 (Tanner MSS. 79, f. 153); the commissioners themselves used it in the title of the Articles Original for Cawdry's Case in 1586 (Morrice MSS. C, p. 790), and in a formal order to the London ministers in 1587 (Morrice MSS. C, p. 653); one of the Exchequer clerks employed it in 1592 (Exchequer Doc. Q. R. Eccles., bundle 12, no. 1).

Such usage of these words makes it clear that contemporaries employed 'Commission' and 'Commissioners' as the equivalents of 'court' and 'judges', and understood them to connote a permanent institution of so settled a character that it could properly be spoken of in the singular number. Indeed, it is hard to understand why this change in contemporary usage should have been made had it not been descriptive of a change in character which had actually taken place. If 'the Commission' was only a temporary delegation of authority, why should its contemporaries have persisted in the face of its own formal usage and the language of the Statute in ascribing to these men a name which implied a permanent membership, well-understood duties, and a definite place in the judicial hierarchy? Why should the debaters in 1609 have attempted to define its position and authority instead of contesting its right to exist? Why should the King, the Commissioners, the Lord Chancellor, the Lord Chief Justice, and the House of Commons employ language which accorded neither with strict law nor with the actual facts of the case? The strongest point, indeed, in favour of the correctness of this usage is the very fact that they, one and all, assume its correctness as a matter of course.

Further, if the passage of the Statute in 1559 was intended by its framers, as Coke claimed, to be the definite beginning of this new court, why do we find in contemporary usage no record of that fact? Neither the Queen nor the commissioners, neither official nor private papers, alter their earlier practice. The mere fact that the usage of the phrase 'the high commission' begins about 1570 and is well established by 1584 proves, in the absence of explicit evidence to the contrary, that the usage marks the moment when the public became conscious that a change had already taken place rather than the moment when the change actually took place. In fact, the institutional strength of the Commission, which made the phrase 'the High Commission' truly descriptive of its position, was a slow growth of which contemporaries could have become conscious only after it was in great measure complete. That these suppositions are true, a history of the Commission must demonstrate by other evidence than popular hearsay. Yet, in matters of this sort, is it not probable that the universal contemporary belief that the Commission was 'an' institution and not merely a temporary delegation of authority to a few men, is more trustworthy than any deductions we can now draw from such documents as are still available?

The question, however, can never be settled beyond dispute. The one thing indispensable to the demonstration of the truth of this difficult matter, one way or the other, is the evidence of the official records, kept (as we know) by the various Registrars of 'the Commission'. These would at once reveal by the presence or absence of regularity and continuity, and by the date at which they began to be regular and uniform, whether and when there were various bodies of commissioners or one Court of High Commission. But the records have disappeared. That they were accidentally lost during the seventeenth and eighteenth centuries seems improbable. Surely mere accident can scarcely account for the disappearance of registry books, act books, immense files of pleadings and lawyers' briefs, and bales and sacks of papers similar to those which the Commissioners left at Durham; in short, of every scrap of evidence great and small connected with the Court, except a couple of volumes of the Act Books containing the cases of Bastwick and Burton—needed of course as evidence in the proceedings in the House of Commons to annul their sentences—and a few score formal papers which happened to be in the bags of miscellaneous letters and petitions at the Tower. So large a bulk of papers, as the records of the Commission must have been, would, if merely mislaid, hardly have escaped the notice of the Historical Manuscripts' Commissioners in either public or private archives; and if they were hidden at any time, there would seem to be at present no reason for longer concealment. The Great Fire, which destroyed the documents collected at St. Paul's Cathedral, might explain the loss of the Commission's records if it could also account for the disappearance of the archives of the Bishop of London at Fulham Palace, which must have been extraordinarily rich in material connected with the Court. But the records seem to have disappeared before 1645. Laud complained of their seizure by his enemies in 1640; at his trial he pleaded for their production and claimed that they would completely vindicate him; from that day to this they have never been heard of. All this lends colour to the hypothesis that they were destroyed by order of the Long Parliament, together with all the papers of the High Commission that could anywhere be found.

This is confirmed by the logic of the situation. Is it probable that the Parliamentary lawyers would have destroyed evidence telling heavily in support of their chief contention—that the law-court they declared illegal was a recent innovation? Would they have lost or mislaid the records if they proved that 'the High Commission' had never existed and had shown that only temporary grants of authority had been made from time to time to various men? Had they not every reason to destroy evidence that would conclusively demonstrate the continuous existence of a law-court for more than a century? The Puritans and the common lawyers united in the passage of that Act not only to abolish the Court which then existed but to make impossible its revival at any future time. They well knew that the Act of one Parliament could not bind its successor; and how could they hope to be permanently successful in securing their object, if they left behind them a voluminous series of records, showing that a law-court had been in operation for at least half a century, not only with the full approbation of the King and of the ecclesiastics, but with the acquiescence of the common lawyers, and, what was worse, of the general public? Such a set of records would then be precedent for the institution of a similar court when the enemies of the common lawyers and Puritans should regain the ascendancy. The contravention of the historical propositions in the Statute of 1641 must be made impossible. Of course, it is easy to exaggerate the importance of a series of conjectures like these, especially when we have not yet demonstrated that the records were destroyed, but, considered in the light of the history of the Commission, they certainly provide a plausible explanation of a good many facts not otherwise easy to reconcile.

An added reason for writing about 'the High Commission' is the fact that such has been the ordinary historical and legal usage since 1640. It should be said, however, that historians and jurists have applied the term without discrimination to all the commissions subsequent to the Statute, and have either paid no attention to the earlier Patents or have considered them interesting precedents of little intrinsic value. As the first few chapters of my text attempt to show, there seems to be no valid reason for considering the year 1559 a turning-point in the Commission's history, and if we deny the validity of the use of the phrase 'the High Commission' for the years previous to 1559, we must also decline to employ it before 1580, when the transformation of a true commission into a court was publicly recognized by contemporary usage. The date when the process began is so uncertain, that if we must make any distinction at all, and not treat the whole subject as the history of 'the' High Commission, it seems better to be conservative and employ contemporary usage with exactitude, even though we may be conscious that it followed the real march of events at some little distance.

There is, indeed, much to be said in support of the use of the phrase throughout the whole course of the history of these commissions as one essentially true to fact. There can be little doubt that there was for nearly a century a practically continuous exercise of the supreme ecclesiastical authority by a single body of men whose personnel changed so little that it may fairly be said to have been as permanent—after 1549 at least—as the membership of any administrative body requiring the co-operation of many individuals. After that date there can be no doubt of the practical identity of the authority and procedure the various Letters Patent conferred upon the commissioners. It is hard to see why the Edwardian and Marian Patents should be considered merely precedent for the Patent of 1559 when the bulk of that document was composed of phrases taken verbatim from them and when several of the members named by it had been among the Marian Commissioners. Naturally, the whole question is one of the point of view, but are we not going out of our way a good deal and closing our eyes to a much simpler deduction by treating the Marian Commissions in any such way ?

CHAPTER II

THE ORIGIN OF THE HIGH COMMISSION

FIRST PHASE (*continued*): THE ACTUAL WORKING OF ECCLESIASTICAL COMMISSIONS, 1535–80.

UNTIL 1565 the chief work performed by these commissions was visitatorial, and their functions, authority, and personnel were dictated largely by expediency. They were intended to cope with such cases as might need the supreme authority of the Crown, and were to lapse as soon as their work was done. Nor can there be much reason to doubt the ubiquity of the Commissioners for the Province of Canterbury from 1549 to 1565. While it is impossible to demonstrate definitely what part they played, they probably had a share in everything of importance and in much that was not important. But the growth of such an institution as the Court of High Commission must be sought in the procedure, jurisdiction, personnel of these commissions, rather than in a list of monasteries dissolved, heretics tried, and bishops deposed, even could we positively identify all the cases.

We know little of the methods employed by these commissioners. We can often learn what they did, but rarely, if ever, find out anything definite about the way they did it. In the accounts of trials for heresy, no mention is usually made of the authority under which the judge or judges were proceeding, nor of the form and limitations of their commission, nor even whether they sat by commission at all.

So many kinds of commissions, general, special, local,

and those for the trial of a single case, existed at the same time, and so few details of any heresy proceedings are preserved, that it is practically impossible to distinguish the acts of one from those of another with any approach to certainty. Disciplinary authority over heretics, moreover, was by no means delegated exclusively to commissions, and was even granted to grand juries, justices of the peace, and mayors of towns by letters from the Privy Council,[1] as well as by the Statute of 1539. Contemporaries (and indeed most Church historians) were interested in doctrinal discussions, and recked little of procedure and jurisdiction, so that the accounts of the inquiries and trials we can identify contain little of any service to us. The name of the judge tells almost nothing, for the mere fact that he was a member of a general or special commission by no means proves that in a particular case he acted under that authority.[2]

[1] *Letters and Papers, Henry VIII*, XVII, no. 537 (1542); *Privy Council Register*, v, 63 (1554).

[2] The sort of provoking vagueness with which we have to cope appears in the case of Robert Wisdome, who was arrested by the apparitor of the Bishop of London, and then examined by the Privy Council (1543): *Letters and Papers, Henry VIII*, XVIII, part i, no. 539. In 1555 Rogers and nine others were examined for heresy by some of the Privy Council, and were tried by commissioners appointed by Pole as legate: Pocock's *Burnet's Reformation*, ii, 482. Lord Darcy in 1556 arrested heretics by direct order from the Council, which issued another special order to Bonner for their trial: Strype, *Memorials*, III, i, 552. Three heretics were tried in 1556 by a bishop's chancellor, a sheriff, and some parish priests, and were executed by the sheriff: Foxe, *Martyrs*, viii, 103–4. Another in the same year was tried at visitation by some minor ecclesiastic and burned by virtue of a writ *de haeretico comburendo*: Strype, *Memorials*, III, i, 483. Still another was examined by the Mayor of Reading and three justices of the peace, who then presented him at the regular visitation to the bishop's chancellor, who tried him by virtue of some commission: Foxe, *Martyrs*, viii, 213.

At the same time the Letters Patent and commissions are so vague in wording as to place beyond doubt the fact that the commissioners were little restricted in their choice of procedure or penalties. Their discretion was infinite and their decision final. The Marian Commission explicitly allowed them to use the *ex officio* oath, by which the accused swore to tell the whole truth before he learned with what he was charged. But it is not likely that this oath, later so prominent in controversy, was of much importance at this time. Indeed the heresy trials of which we have record reveal few marks of anything we should now recognize as procedure, and were chiefly acrimonious debates, freely interlarded with insults, between the judges and the prisoners.[1] During the first years, too, the commissioners seem more often to have inquired into the existence of heresy than to have tried heretics; some bishop conducted the trial by episcopal or statutory authority and handed the heretics over to the local temporal authorities (in most cases) for execution. Though the commissions issued by Cromwell in 1535 permitted the imposition of fines 'ac alia juris hujus regni nostri remedia', such cases as the commis-

[1] Good examples of heresy trials are to be found in Foxe, *Martyrs*, v, 229; viii, 109, 715; and *passim*; Pocock's *Burnet's Reformation*, ii, 483. Few, if any, of these can be connected with the High Commission. Articles Original were frequently offered the accused, and his answers often made in writing. We have mention of two men proceeded against *ex officio*, Pocock's *Burnet*, ii, 501; and others were presented with articles and condemned upon their answers, *ibid.* ii, 501; iii, 415. But it is sufficiently clear that we have here merely the continued use of the old canonical forms always employed at ecclesiastical law. All these officials, ecclesiastical as well as temporal, regularly imprisoned the culprits at discretion. Nothing was usually said about fines, for the guilty were burned and the innocent freed altogether.

sioners did themselves try seem to have been punished by ecclesiastical penalties only.

Under the Act of the Six Articles and the other reformation Statutes, a great variety of penalties were put at their disposal, though there is no reason to believe that they ever were able to use torture, or mutilation, or the penalty of death. The Letters Patent of Edward VI expressly directed them to imprison at discretion; those of Mary directed them to impose fines; and those penalties were very soon almost exclusively employed.

The one provision of the organization of these commissions which we can be sure was observed was the double condition to be fulfilled for a valid 'quorum'. Only a part of the commissioners named in the Patent were expected to sit on any particular case, and to allow any man or any two men to exercise the untrammelled authority accorded by the Letters Patent was clearly dangerous at a time when every one's loyalty was justly suspected. The Edwardian commissions,[1] accordingly, named three as the minimum number who might transact business, and imposed a further condition by requiring that one of the three should be one of certain specified persons, who thus came to be described as 'of the quorum' or even as 'the quorum'. Thus the Patent of 1549 named twenty-five men, eleven of whom were 'of the quorum'—seven bishops, two other ecclesiastics, and two ministers of state. One of the eleven and any two other commissioners thus might legally exercise the full powers vested in the twenty-five. This provision made possible the subdivision of the commissioners, and therefore

[1] The loss of practically all the Henrician patents makes it impossible to state definitely that this practice began earlier. Such a provision regarding a quorum was not uncommon at the time: 31 Henry VIII, c. 14, and other Reformation Statutes provided for it; see also Strype, *Memorials*, I, i, 426.

allowed them to prosecute several cases at the same time Mary did not name any quorum, and hence permitted any three of her commissioners to transact business. Elizabeth, ever cautious, required the presence of six commissioners for the transaction of business, and reduced the quorum to seven—two bishops, one minister of state, and four lawyers.

This untrammelled authority, this absolute discretion, made the personnel of the commissioners exceedingly important. Indeed, before 1580, it can hardly be claimed that 'the' Commission existed as an institution: a body of men was invested with authority for the execution of certain administrative duties, and upon their personality depended organization, procedure, and efficiency. A kindly, temperate, tolerant man like Cranmer would choose entirely different means for attaining the same object from a vigorous but intolerant man like Bonner. The early Ecclesiastical Commission was not an institution but an instrument, beneficent in good hands, savage and cruel in bad hands, and easily capable of abuse and oppression; and there can be little doubt that in the reigns of Henry and his children the instrument was often (and perhaps at times systematically) used for what we should now regard as the worst purposes. Unquestionably, the notable efficiency which became at once the chief characteristic of the commissioners' work was due to the eminence and ability of its members rather than to any merits of organization or procedure. If the leading bishops, the ablest privy councillors, and the most capable civil lawyers could not accomplish a given purpose with unlimited authority and discretion, it was because the best brains in England, coupled to the plenitude of the royal authority, had failed. Then the large number of men appointed commissioners, ranging from twenty-five to thirty; the fact that three members might act; the large quorum, only one of whom must be present, quite freed the commissioners from such hindrances to members' attendance as sickness or interference of other business. There would always be enough men free to attend to affairs with dispatch.

Until about 1580 [1] this flexible and adaptable instrument, though ecclesiastical in name, was entirely controlled and directed by the State. A commission was a tool, a machine, without institutional life or continuity of its own, and the elasticity of its composition, its broad indefinite powers, and its discretionary procedure made it an able servant skilled in many tasks. Between 1535 and 1540 these ecclesiastical commissions were controlled by Cromwell, who was probably personally responsible to the King; then, on his fall, they began to be dominated by the Privy Council. We find the latter deciding in September 1540 to 'send a commission to Calais for inquiry of the Six Articles and certain heresies of Thos. Dynton'.

The Archbishop was to name a commissary who should be the quorum.[2] Apparently, while several men would be named, the actual execution of the commission was to be entrusted to one. A couple of years later the Council ordered the sheriffs and justices of Coventry to return a grand jury to inquire into heresy under the Act of Six Articles: [3] clearly commissioners were not at this time the Council's only agents. At the Council meeting of May 4, 1543, even more explicit directions were issued.

[1] The considerations advanced in the following chapter will make clear the reasons for considering this date extremely approximate.

[2] *Letters and Papers, Henry VIII*, XVI, no. 8. Sept. 2, 1540. The Council was also personally examining priests.

[3] *Letters and Papers, Henry VIII*, XVII, no. 537. July 27, 1542.

'It was thought if the King should so please, "that a general commission should be sent into Kent, with certain special articles and generally all abuses and enormities of religion to be examined." Determined that Doctors Peter, Tregonwell, Oliver, and Bellows should examine Cobbe and Sir William of Honny Lane, &c., and that the Bishops of Ely, Sarum, Rochester, and Westminster should examine Dr. Haynes.'[1] In 1546 the Council directed the Bishop of London 'and the rest of the Commissioners for the VI Articles' to 'dissolve their assembley tyll an other more comodious tyme to sitte aboute the same'.[2] This close control and supervision became even more marked when the adjustment of the most urgent difficulties left the Council free about 1564 or 1565 to turn its attention to the general administration of the Church.

The commissioners' competence and jurisdiction the Council regularly determined, and it decided in addition whether or not their power should be exercised in a particular case, and how they should proceed.[3] Usually it commanded expedition in execution, a prompt but full report of the proceedings, and an awaiting of further orders.[4] Often it directed the commissioners 'to examine the trothe of the matter and to procede according to equitie and justice, and in due course of the lawes in such cases provided'.[5] Not infrequently it submitted

[1] *Letters and Papers, Henry VIII*, XVIII, part i, no. 500.

[2] *Privy Council Register*, i, 418. This may not have been an ecclesiastical commission of the type we are investigating, for the Statute of Six Articles authorized the issue of commissions to enforce its provisions.

[3] The Council Register is full of evidence, but a complete discussion of all the incidents would be tedious and unnecessary.

[4] *Privy Council Register, New Series*, vii, 145. May 28, 1564.

[5] *Ibid.* ix, 59. 1575.

a case to them and then issued detailed orders regarding its settlement,[1] extending even to the penalty.[2] Many times it ordered the commissioners to imprison this man,[3] or fine that, or to take bonds for his appearance if sent for, or for his further good behaviour.[4] It ordered them to inquire into a case and try it,[5] directed a stay of proceedings already instituted,[6] the imprisonment of persons without any direct charge, and the liberation of persons held with or without charge.[7] It was not above appointing a messenger for the Ecclesiastical Commissioners in Lancashire and Chester.[8] If its orders were not carried out to its full satisfaction, sharp reproof was sure to follow. In 1580 the Council wrote to Grindal that the growth of nonconformity was 'to the greatt offense of her Highness, who doth not a little marvel by what means this relapse should happen ; having delivered sufficient authority unto your Lordship and others joined unto you, by virtue of her Commission Ecclesiastical, warranted by the laws of this realm, whereby you might at all times have repressed . . . the disobediency of such . . . if such care and vigilancy had been used within your charge as appertaineth'. The letter continued with explicit directions for a better execution of the commission and the laws, and ordered them to report all further proceedings.[9]

1 *Ibid.* xi, 149, 212, 322 (1579) ; also ix, 95 ; xi, 137, 175, 182, 362, 386, 445.

2 *Ibid.* vii, 127 ; xi, 322 ; xii, 324 ; xiii, 72, &c.

3 *Ibid.* vii, 345 ; viii, 108.

4 *Ibid.* xvii, 318.

5 *Ibid.* xi, 315, 415 ; xviii, 362 ; xxiv, 317 ; xxv, 113, 211, 505 ; and on recusancy, *passim.*

6 *Ibid.* vii, 330.

7 *Ibid.* viii, 235 ; x, 204 ; xi, 182.

8 *Ibid.* viii, 395.

9 Strype, *Grindal*, 377. June 18, 1580. Also *Privy Council Register*, xi, 456. The phrase, 'warranted by the laws of this realm,' is conclusive evidence that the Council believed the

During the first four decades, then, the commissioners were allowed little if any discretion, were very closely and immediately controlled by the Council, and executed, at the Council's commands, far more arbitrary acts than they ever performed in the later history of the institution. The Commission was at this time literally what it was accused of being in Laud's time—an engine of state arbitrarily turned this way and that. While in later days, as a court, they often heard cases referred to them by the Council, as in truth did all other courts in the realm, and while the wishes of that body were indirectly made known to the commissioners in regard to important cases, as they were in analogous instances made known to the common-law judges, yet never to our knowledge after 1600 was a decision directly dictated by the political powers.[1]

The administrative work performed by the commissioners after 1559 was extremely varied. The removal of 'popish' clergy, the watching of 'masterless men and vagabonds' in London to prevent the gathering of a crowd sufficiently large to make a religious riot possible, and the replacing of the Edwardian clergy under the guise of a general visitation,[2] was a species of work which, once done, did not have to be done again. Special work of great importance was, as before, entrusted to the commissioners, like the watching and warding of the chief Catholics in the critical years 1568–9, 1579–81, and 1587–8. So the attempt of Cartwright, Travers, and their followers to erect Presbyterianism under the guise of the

Letters Patent fully met every possible legal requirement of Statute or other law.

[1] The Council, however, continued to refer cases. See S. P. Dom., Docquet, June 19, 1604.

[2] These duties were explicitly enjoined by most of the general Letters Patent between 1549 and 1562.

Book of Discipline was discovered and frustrated by the commissioners, who furnished the evidence for the final trials in the Star Chamber. Yet this work was in the main visitatorial and a continuance of the earlier phase.[1] Duties far more ministerial and far more nearly part of an administrative routine soon appeared. In 1562 the Letters Patent directed them to visit all cathedral churches and grammar schools and to revise their statutes in conformity with the new religious policy. By that same Patent, the commissioners were empowered to administer the oath of supremacy to the clergy, and in 1576 to impose it on all who were required to take it. Offences against the Thirty-Nine Articles were placed in their care both by the Statute of 1572 and the Letters Patent of 1576. The same Letters Patent even ordered them to collect by distress the fines levied by the churchwardens under the Act of Uniformity. All offences committed by Papist or Puritan were the special province of the commissioners, and the examinations of the 'obstinate' and 'stiff necked' were numerous and time-consuming. In 1562 the commissioners ordered the second exhumation of the body of Katharine Vermiglia, who had been exhumed during Mary's reign as a heretic and buried in a dunghill at Oxford. She was now accorded an honourable burial in consecrated ground with all possible pomp

[1] All these cases are so well known and the voluminous material contains so very little information about the Commission, and that little of such minor importance—indicating, indeed, little more than that the commissioners were at the bottom of the proceedings—that it has seemed best to accord them here only a brief mention. After all, it must be recognized that a complete record of every case in which the commissioners were concerned would involve little less than a full history of the English Church during this period, and that even a list of their activities would be bulky and necessarily uninteresting and unreadable.

and ceremony.[1] On the whole, the Privy Council ordered the commissioners to do whatever needed to be done: in 1583, an examination into the condition of the ecclesiastical courts;[2] in 1581, a reform of the morals of the Inns of Court;[3] while the failure of the College of Physicians to attend church had roused sufficient comment to lead the Council to require the commissioners to investigate and reform.[4] Then, struck by the obstinacy of the men confined in the London jails, it ordered the commissioners to conduct a crusade among the prisoners in the interests of true religion.[5] All of this work, disciplinary in its nature, partook of the routine character of a disciplinary work intended for the correction of individual lapses from a given standard, rather than an attempt to create the standard itself.

A rather more exalted function had been intended in 1559 for the commissioners. They were to have been an advisory body, with whom the Queen might consult regarding ritual, doctrine, and the use of vestments. The Statute of Uniformity (s. xiii) said that the Ecclesiastical Commissioners would advise the Queen what further changes should be made in ornament and apparel. In January 1561 the Queen addressed a letter to certain commissioners, the Archbishop and Bishop of London, Dr. Bill, her almoner, and Dr. Haddon, the Master of Requests; and, after reciting the provisions of the Act, required two of them with any two other commissioners to peruse the order of the scripture lessons throughout the year, and make a new calendar; to consider the

[1] Strype, *Parker*, i, 199.

[2] Strype, *Aylmer*, 70.

[3] Strype, *Annals*, III, part i, 44.

[4] *Royal Historical MSS. Com. Report*, viii, 227. Feb. 1587.

[5] The commissioners' letter to the preachers has been printed by J. Waddington, *The Track of the Hidden Church*, 62–4. Feb. 25, 1589.

decay of churches, 'order of the Chancels, and *such like*;' to see that the Table of Ten Commandments in English were duly hung up in the parish churches; and to see that in all cathedral and parish churches 'one maner be used'. Then followed a remarkable command: the commissioners were especially to see that collegiate churches did not abuse the permission already given them of *translating* the Book of Common Prayer into Latin; 'so that our good purpose in the said translation be not frustrated, nor be corruptly abused, contrary to the effect of our meaning.' It might not improbably be a very delicate duty to see wherein the Book of Common Prayer translated into Latin with some freedom differed from the Mass. The chief taunt of the Puritans was that the Book was only the Mass 'done into English'. The commissioners were to put their own decision into execution, and certify the same to the Archbishop of York for observance in his province, but should do all 'quietly', 'without shew of any innovation in the church.' [1] The commissioners promptly met, and at their second session on April 12 commenced taking 'further order'.[2] 'Readers' were at once to be examined and the new 'declaration devised for unity of doctrine' was to be accepted, signed, and read publicly by all incumbents. All clergymen already in office were to be examined; all old service-books, ornaments, and the like defaced; a new catechism prepared; private chaplains were to take cures and be examined, or be at once excommunicated. To these measures they added a defence of the new church settlement, and entrusted its composition to Bishop Jewel. The famous *Apology* was thus 'recommended' by the Ecclesiastical Commissioners. In 1564/5 they completed the work of 'further order' by issuing over their signatures and seal

[1] Strype, *Parker*, iii, 46–8. [2] *Ibid.* i, 194.

the important Advertisements of 1564.[1] It is not now demonstrable that they had any share in drawing up the Thirty-Nine Articles.

In regard to the censorship of the press, the commissioners were early very active. The Star Chamber Orders, both in 1566 and in 1586, were issued at their request and were executed under their direction.[2] From the Wardens of the Company of Stationers and the Warden of the Cinque Ports and his aids, the commissioners received such constant assistance that it is possible that both were under their orders.[3] To obtain precise information of all books about to be published in London, of all there offered for sale, and of all entering the realm, was the object of these regulations as of the administrative orders [4] with which the commissioners supplemented them. A less desirable and reliable type of assistance came from the horde of private informers who made a business of supplying the State with 'recent valuable' information. In this, as in other matters, the commissioners and their reputation suffered severely from the unauthorized work of rascals.

How far the commissioners availed themselves of the unlimited discretion awarded them by their Letters Patent in questions of procedure is hard to say. Such indications as we have reveal more conservatism and more regard for justice and equity than we have been taught to expect. Before 1565 many heresy trials had probably been

[1] Cardwell, *Documentary Annals*, i, 321.

[2] Strype, *Parker*, i, 442 ; S. P. Dom. Eliz., 190, no. 48.

[3] The extraordinarily voluminous correspondence regarding books and censorship in the State Papers, Domestic, at the British Museum and at Hatfield House, contains nothing that throws more than a faint light on the Commission's procedure in such matters.

[4] None of these have survived.

conducted by the commissioners, especially during the reigns of Edward and Mary, with all possible secrecy and harshness, and some parts of the visitations which had inaugurated each attempt to settle religious matters had no doubt been performed with scant regard for mercy, charity, or justice. The tradition regarding this period is clear from the story Archbishop Bancroft later told of Gardiner, 'when he was before the Commissioners in King Edward's tyme, who prayed to speke without interruption.'[1] But after 1565 arbitrary and cruel conduct became unusual and even exceptional. While nothing very conclusive can be proved from a few cases scattered over so many years, it is clear that the commissioners did not invariably insist upon the mere letter of their Patent. Three commissioners, one of whom was of the quorum, possessed full legal authority; yet, out of thirty-two cases between 1565 and 1592, where we have enough details to speak confidently, six were heard by three commissioners and seven by four, while four cases were heard by five commissioners, three by six, two by seven, and three by more than seven. On the other hand, examinations of witnesses and minor inquiries were conducted by two or even by one commissioner.[2] The commissioners also took advantage of their privilege of sitting wherever they pleased, and met in churches, palaces, dining-rooms, corridors, gardens, and apparently nearly everywhere except the middle of the street. Most of the hearings previous to 1600 were no doubt private, though we have little reason to believe that any attempt was made to conceal the fact that a session was being held

[1] Lambeth MSS. 445, f. 424. May 1, 1606.

[2] Harl. MSS. 7042, ff. 13, 22, 195. See, however, other cases in this same volume where three or four commissioners sat for examinations.

nor what in the main was being done there. Certainly, when prominent Puritans were on trial, a goodly audience of lawyers, ecclesiastics, and perhaps the general public was at times, if not regularly, allowed easy access.[1] Witnesses, evidence, and the like, soon became common.

There are, however, very few traces of anything resembling a fixed procedure of any kind at the trials or hearings. The commissioners sat down before the culprit and questioned him as searchingly as their combined ingenuity could suggest. He replied as best he could, and the debate soon degenerated into a series of recriminations and insults in which the commissioners were not ordinarily victorious, if the Puritan version of these trials be correct. The first trial of which we have any detailed account is the examination or 'hearing' of the 'conventiclers', caught in June 1567, before the Lord Mayor of London, the Bishop of London, the Dean of Westminster, Master Watts, and others.[2] The culprits were brought in by the wardens of the jail and answered to their names. Then the bishop turned to the mayor and begged him to begin. The mayor declined the honour, and the bishop thereupon lectured the prisoners on the wickedness of their conduct in holding conventicles, and showed them a letter from the Queen and Privy Council ordering them personally

[1] e.g. Merburie's trial in Nov. 1578, 'many people standing by': *Parte of a Register*, 381. Also the Examination of Edward Gelybrand, Apr. 7, 1586, 'there standing by Dr. Percy with many Chaplains and servingmen to the number of 30 or more': Morrice MSS. C, p. 801. These must have been simply casual onlookers, and if they could attend, any one interested could probably have got in.

[2] 'A true report of our Examination and Conference (as neare as wee can call to remembrance) had the 20. day of Iune, Anno. 1567. Before the Lord Maior, the Bishop of London, the Dean of West., Maister Watts, and other Commissioners': *Parte of a Register*, 23–7.

to conform to the laws of the Church. After some little conversation as to the lawfulness of hiring a hall for a wedding and then holding a prayer-meeting, the bishop called on Smith (as the oldest) to be spokesman. White interrupted.

'I beseeche you let me answer.
Bishop. Nay, W. W., holde your peace, you shalbe heard anon.
Nixson. I beseeche you to let me answer a worde or two.
Bishop. Nixson, you are a busie fellowe, I knowe your wordes, you are full of talke, I knowe from whence you came.
Hawkins. I would be glad to answere.
Bishop. Smyth shall aunswere.'

Smith, thus commanded, replied that they met because they could no longer have service in church 'without the preferring of idolatrous geare aboue it', and that they followed Calvin's example at Geneva, and 'we will stande to it by the Grace of God'. 'This is no aunswere,' cried the Bishop; and the altercation continued over the meaning of Scripture with as complete a lack of judicial form as well could be. No oaths were tendered to the Puritans, no counsel appeared for them or for the commissioners, nor was anything remotely resembling a set argument or formal accusation or defence attempted. At the same time, even the Puritan account shows few traces of an attempt by the commissioners to crush these men by weight of authority. They argued the case with them at great length, fully convinced that the truth would prevail. Nor did the Puritans mince words.

'*Deane*. You speake unreuerentlie here of the Prince before the Magistrates: you were not bidden to speake, you might holde your peace.
Hawkins. You will suffer us to make our purgation, seeing that you persecute us. . . .
Smith. How can you proove that indifferent which is abominable?

Bishop. What: you meane of our cappes and typettes, which you saye came from Roome.

Ireland. It belongeth to the Papistes, therefore throwe it to them.

Bishop. I have saide Masse: I am sorie for it.

Irelande. But you goe like one of the masse-priests still.

Bishop. You see mee weare a coape or a surplesse in Pawles. I had rather minister without these things, but for orders sake and obedience to the Prince.

Roper. Maister Crowley sayeth, he could not bee perswaded to minister in those coniuring garments of poperie.

Nixson. Your garmentes are accursed as they are used.

Bishop. Where do you finde them forbidden in the scriptures?

Nixson. Where is the Masse forbidden in the scriptures? . . .

Nixson. This hath bin alwayes the doings of popish Bishops, when as they cannot mainteyne their doings by the scriptures, nor ouercome them, then they make the Maior and the Aldermen their seruauntes and butchers, to punishe them, that they can not ouercome by scripture: but I trust that you my Lorde, seeing you haue hearde and seene it, will take good aduisement.

L. Maior. Good Lord, howe unreuerentlie doe you speake here before my Lordes and us in comparing so. . . .

Bishop. All the learned are against you, will you be tried by them?

W. Wh. We wilbe tryed by the worde of God, which shall iudge us all at the last day.

Deane. But who will you haue to iudge of the word of God?

Hawkins. Why that was the sayinge of the Papistes in Queene Maries time. . . . Then they would saye, who shall iudge of the worde of God? The Catholike Church must be iudge.

W. W. We wilbe tried by the best reformed Churches.'

Six years later, William White was again before the commissioners, though apparently not for the second time.[1] The members present were the Lord Chief Justice,

[1] 'A note of my Examination and Answer as my weake memory could gather it, at my last being before the Worshipfull and

the Master of the Rolls, the Master of Requests, the Attorney-General, the Dean of Westminster, and the Sheriff of London. The Lord Chief Justice took the leading part.

'*Ch. J.* Who is this ?
W. White and please your honour.
L. C. J. White as black as the Devill.
W. Not so, my L., one of Gods children. . . .
L. C. J. Thou art a Contemptuous fellow, and will obey no Lawes.
W. Not so, my Lord, I do and will obey Lawes and therefore refusing but a Ceremony of Conscience, and not refusing the penalty for the same, I rest still a true subject.
Deane. Why so the Papists say. . . .
L. C. J. Thou art the wickedest, and the most contemptuous person that came before me since I sate in this Commission.[1]
W. Not so, my Lord, my conscience doth witnesse with me otherwise. . . .
Gerrard.[2] White you were released thinking you would be Conformable but you are worse then you were.
White. Not so, if it please you.
L. C. J. He would have no Lawes.
White. If there were no Law, I hope I would live like a Christian.
L. C. J. Would you have no Lawes ?
W. I say I would do no wrong, if I received wrong, so it weare.
L. C. J. Thou art a rebell.
White. Not so, my Lord, a true subject.
L. C. J. Yea, I swear by God thou art a very Rebell, for I see thou wouldst draw thy sword, and lift up thy hand and wouldst arise to rebell against thy Prince if time served.

honourable Commissioners, the 18th day of January, 1573': Morrice MSS. A, ff. 581–4. This, of course, is White's report, and very likely the commissioners' report would read differently.

[1] A notable bit of indirect evidence proving the frequent participation of the common-law judges in the work of the commissioners.

[2] The Attorney-General.

White. My Lord, I thank God my heart standeth right toward God and my Prince and God will not condemne though your Honour hath so judged.

L. C. J. Take him away.'

The tone of this trial is more distinctly arbitrary and overbearing than that of any trial whose details we at all know. It is noteworthy that only one of the six commissioners present was an ecclesiastic, who apparently took no part in the trial, and that the other five were leading common lawyers. Indeed, the insulting language here used by the Lord Chief Justice finds no parallel in the records of the Commission; it can be paralleled in the common-law records, especially by the words of Coke himself.

Another Puritan account tells of a trial before what was in all probability a diocesan commission at least ten years later.[1] The commissioners having taken their seats,

'then appeared Mr. Stevens with his Brother Minister. The matter being call'd, the Bp. did urge the Parties accused to take an othe to speake the truthe, and ye whole truthe concerning those matters which should be laid to their charges. The othes being taken, the Articles were read. Then said Knight, if they be sworn to those Articles, I will undergo the punishment of the Lawe. Then began Stevens to speake. Hold thy tongue, fool, said the Bishop, thou wilt condemn thy selfe. My Lord, said Stevens, I will not sweare myself, for I have witnesses. Where are they? said the Bishop. I have them not here, said Stevens. Let them be sent for, said ye Bishop. Then said Knight (the other minister) if that you send for Witnesses, I pray you let me except against two. For what cause? said the Bishop. Then the said Knight told him of the behaviour of them as aforesaid. You shall be tryed by others, said the Bishop. So there were sent for seventeen men by the means of the aforesaid

[1] Morrice MSS. C, p. 897. See also other examinations: of John Edwin (1584) in Morrice MSS. C, p. 576; of Udall (1586) in Morrice MSS. C, p. 778; certain Londoners (1576) in *Parte of a Register*, 29.

Stevens. In the mean time the said Knight, Prentis and Duck weare examined by the Bishop's man in a secreate chamber severally, which did write their examinations as pleased himself. Then thre or four daies after came there seventeen men with Stephens, those two men before *accepted* in the number and stoode before the Bishop.'

There is some reason to believe that the commissioners at this time abused their powers and committed injustice. We find the Privy Council blaming them for inflicting too heavy penalties, for imprisoning men without sufficient reason, or for detaining them unwarrantably long.[1] The Council ordered the mitigation of the lot of the prisoners in the Gatehouse in 1581, any order given by the Council itself 'or by the Lord Bishop of London and Commissioners Ecclesiastical to the contrary notwithstanding.'[2] In this case at any rate the commissioners did not stand alone. In 1579 the Council ordered them to release a man without bonds, and 'further, not [to] vex or molest the said Sharpe for unnecessary causes'.[3] In 1574 the Archbishop was commanded to recall a commission he had issued 'to persons unworthie', and to issue another to 'persons more fitte'.[4] Whether this blame of the commissioners proceeded from the righteous indignation of the Privy Council excited by extreme wrongdoing, it is not possible to say; but it is more than likely that the Council was in this convenient way disowning the responsibility for its own commands, which a turn of the political wheel had made inexpedient. Often, it wished a man detained for a time, and was quite unwilling or unable to assign any reason

[1] *Privy Council Register*, viii, 235; x, 204; xxi, 153.

[2] *Ibid.* xiii, 276; a similar order was issued concerning the Marshalsea, *ibid.* 327.

[3] *Ibid.* xi, 182. July 9, 1579.

[4] *Ibid.* viii, 271. July 20, 1574.

that could be made public. If the commissioners imprisoned him, he could, in due time, after petitioning the Council, be released with the full honours of an illegal detention. And no one but the commissioners was hurt. For just such business were the commissioners appointed.

We hear other complaints not so easily explained, of warrants issued by one commissioner instead of three; of warrants and, indeed, various processes, needing the co-operation of three commissioners, issued by one, and then carried around by his servant to other commissioners until the necessary three signatures could be obtained; of men arrested even by private letter.[1] All of this may very probably be explained by the comparative lack of judicial forms in the Commission and by the complete discretion vested in the commissioners by their Patent. A Puritan tract, published, to be sure, twenty years later, says of this period that a man wearing long hair was held down in court by force, while his hair was 'notted'. Then there were charges of men arrested by the commissioners' officers and offered their freedom for a sum of money; men cited to appear, and, when they came, charged with nothing, but threatened with a new summons if money was not paid the official. At least one such case was found true by the Council and the pursuivant in question was duly punished by the commissioners.[2] Other such complaints were unquestionably due to the rascals who went round with forged warrants and writs of summons purporting to be from the commissioners, and who required the payment of heavy costs for the serving of the paper, coupled with the usual offer to allow

[1] Charges of Allen and Carew against the Commission, Morrice MSS. C, p. 652 (Nov. 1584).

[2] *Privy Council Register*, xi, 456. Apr. 29, 1580.

the ' culprit ' to escape for a bribe.[1] There must have been a good many guilty men at large in those days to have made such a business really profitable. If we accept as valid the contemporary reasons for the commissioners' existence and the prevailing beliefs about heresy, we shall be forced to conclude that the commissioners' proceedings were far freer from even minor abuses than we should have expected from the traditional views so long promulgated regarding them.

[1] *Historical MSS. Com. Report,* X, part ii, 37. June 1593. Strype, *Annals,* iv, 396 ; S. P. Dom. Eliz., 240, no. 138 (1591).

CHAPTER III

THE ORIGIN OF THE HIGH COMMISSION

SECOND PHASE: THE GRADUAL EVOLUTION OF A COURT OF LAW, 1553(?)–80.

IT became apparent about 1580 that for a decade or more a great change had been transforming certain of the Ecclesiastical Commissioners for the Province of Canterbury into the judges of a permanent ecclesiastical court. An administrative committee without initiative or responsibility of its own, blindly executing the commands of the Privy Council, had gradually developed institutional permanence and vigour, and, instead of remaining a visitatorial body whose chief duty was the correction of offences sought out by its own machinery, it had become a law-court, finding its chief work in the hearing of causes between party and party, which it tried by a regular procedure and decided in accordance with precedent. A more striking and fundamental change in the character of an institution would be hard to imagine: the organization, once temporary, had become permanent; the procedure, once arbitrary, had become fixed; the jurisdiction, so long unlimited, had been defined and delimited.

The process of evolution by which a law-court emerged from a series of confessedly temporary commissions is difficult to describe without treating as precise what was far from definite and without incurring the danger of exaggerating some one aspect of a situation no one element of which is any too clear. Above all, we must never forget the peculiar and anomalous nature of this institution; we must bear carefully in mind that, to suppose the phrase 'the High Commission' connoted to contemporaries, or should connote to us anything altogether precise and definite at this time is to lose sight of undoubted facts of the utmost significance. The Commission had always before 1580 been something more than a commission, and it remained after 1580 something more than a court. The evolution with which we are concerned was not the sloughing off of visitatorial functions which were never to reappear, nor yet the assumption of judicial powers by a body of men who had never before exercised any such authority. It is clear that only a few of the members named as Ecclesiastical Commissioners for the Province of Canterbury by the various Letters Patent subsequent to 1580 ever became, in any proper sense of the words, judges of the Court of High Commission; we cannot be certain that the virtual right to sit as judge conferred additional dignities or privileges upon any individual or in any formal way distinguished him from other members; the Letters Patent were not altered in form or substance; the powers granted and procedure permitted remained practically the same; ostensibly the dependence of the commissioners upon the Privy Council was unchanged. The evolution resulted in a subtle but significant change in emphasis, rather than one in form. Despite the breadth of language employed in the Letters Patent, the actual work done by the commissioners shows that the Patent was an enabling document, not an actual grant of power and discretion, and gave the commissioners formal authorization for the performance of the orders issued by the Privy Council. In fact, the court was developed from the actual discharge of varied functions by commissioners, and not even from what was at first their most characteristic function.

This evolution promptly raises two questions which cannot be more than approximately settled: Had these commissions prior to 1580 (assuming that to be the true date) a continuous existence with what we have called 'the High Commission'? Were they the same or different? In any case, were they legal or illegal? Whether or not we say that these were 'high commissions', and that 'the High Commission' existed prior to 1580, will be wholly a matter of definition, and the conclusion will be as sound as, but no sounder than the premise. The common-law position in the later controversy assumed that the Statute of 1559 was passed to make 'the High Commission' legal; and therefore compels its supporters to date the existence of the rightful institution from the Statute and to relegate the earlier commissions to the place of precedents. Even if we do not regard the practical identity of the Letters Patent of Edward and Mary with those of Elizabeth as evidence of the existence of 'the High Commission' previous to 1580 or 1559, or even as proving a continuity of institutional life of some sort between them, surely we cannot deny the continuous exercise of the supreme ecclesiastical authority—probably from about 1543—by a body of men whose personnel changed so little that it may fairly be claimed to have been as permanent as that of most administrative bodies dependent upon the co-operation of many men. In our attempts at precision of judicial language, we must beware of denying this very real continuity of existence between the various commissions. Nor should we be so anxious to lay stress on the importance of the law-court as to refuse these earlier commissions a place in the history of the Commission as an institution, and insist that they were merely precedents for the creation or development of an institution. In some way, how we cannot say, an institutional tie existed.

From the very first, the commissioners had exercised judicial authority of a peculiar and 'supreme' nature, and had been intended by Henry to try cases according to a jurisdiction and a procedure which he clearly believed legal, and which, as clearly, depended upon the royal prerogative for its authority. An institution depends, however, for its permanence and stability on the necessity for the continuous performance of important duties, rather than on the regular association of certain men with each other for the execution of any orders they may receive. The permanence of membership in these commissions was partly concealed by the fact that their work was in its very essence temporary, and not by any means judicial in the ordinary sense of the word. The first vital step in the 'creation' of an institution which would appear to contemporaries like an institution, was taken when the Privy Council delegated to the commissioners the routine ecclesiastical work which the Council had hitherto performed itself. This was permanent, but not judicial, business; and before there could be a new court, regular judicial work for it would have to be found in suits between party and party clamouring for justice and unable to secure it in the regular tribunals.

The considerations underlying this new development were, then, precisely those which had actuated the formation of nearly all, if not quite all, the courts then in England—administrative convenience; and while not an offshoot of a royal council or of Parliament,[1] in the same

[1] Throughout this volume stress has been laid upon the judicial functions of the parliaments of the Middle Ages and the extent to which they survived in the sixteenth century, despite the rapid increase of legislative authority under the Tudors,

sense that the common-law courts were,[1] the commissioners' new jurisdiction was acquired in precisely a similar manner. The completion of the breach with Rome and the judicial tangle consequent upon the loss of the Pope's jurisdiction had entailed judicial and administrative consequences not less important than the visitatorial difficulties which had originally caused the appointment of Ecclesiastical Commissioners. Having solved the one, the commissioners were now put to work upon the other. The most insistent evidences of these administrative and judicial complications were large numbers of petitions to the Privy Council in which some party claimed a relief which the ordinary ecclesiastical or common-law courts did not afford him. The situation was created partly by the constant complaints from such exempt and peculiar jurisdictions as survived the Reformation, that to subject them to archbishop or bishop was in very fact to abolish their privilege; that, in fact, precisely to the regular hierarchical authority was their exemption meant to apply. To the justice of this claim was added Henry's belief, shared by his children, in the extreme undesirability of awakening what seemed to be unnecessary opposition to the new régime. Thus, while the reformation legislation subjugated such districts to the metropolitan's authority, in practice they were let pretty much alone by both Archbishop and Privy Council, and complaints and disputes between them and the hierarchy were ordinarily decided by the Council, by virtue of the residual authority which the King in Council had

which Professor McIlwain has demonstrated in *The High Court of Parliament*. The position of Parliament as the highest law-court in the realm, the fact that contemporaries thought of it as a court rather than as a legislature, the notion of the legal obligation of a statute, are all of the first importance in the history of the Commission.

exercised from time immemorial, now augmented by the resumption of the ecclesiastical powers to the Supreme Head appertaining.

The loss of the papal and legatine authority was felt keenly by English litigants. Stoutly as the English Church had always taken the side of the local clergy against the Pope, it had nevertheless 'received' the Canon Law and had bowed more or less submissively before numerous legates and commissions.[1] Nor had the extraordinary authority wielded by Wolsey weakened the conviction of the English clergy that their ordinary authority was small and on the whole despicable. Long accustomed to performing even comparatively ordinary ecclesiastical routine by virtue of some unusual authority, and, above all, accustomed to appeal from the archbishop or bishop to some higher authority, it was not to be expected that the clergy should at once accept without question the union of all such powers in the Archbishop of Canterbury.[2] York's traditional jealousy of Canterbury, and the smouldering remains of the hot controversies between each archbishop and his own bishops, blazed up once more. Above all, laity and clergy alike declined to accept the Archbishop's courts as final, and, finding the new Commissions of Review clumsy, expensive, and slow, appealed at once to the Privy Council by the time-honoured process of petition for the redress of those grievances which possessed normally no judicial remedy. The problems raised by such litigation, however, sank into insignificance beside the larger issues confronting Henry, Edward, and Mary, and temporarily King or Council

[1] F. W. Maitland, *Roman Canon Law in the Church of England*. London, 1898.

[2] This point is more fully discussed in Usher's *Reconstruction of the English Church*, i, 91–100.

settled the important cases in person and postponed the consideration of a permanent remedy until the moment should be propitious for codifying ' the Ecclesiastical Law of England ', lately restored in its pristine purity, and for the creation of a special court to try cases arising under it. About 1565 the Privy Council found time to give some attention to a method for handling the ever-increasing number of such petitions.

Gradually it began to refer simple cases to the Ecclesiastical Commissioners already in existence, as a part of the routine work of which the Council was anxious to get rid. Gradually, too, as it was discovered that the commissioners were quite capable of handling such business to everybody's satisfaction, the reference of such cases to them became a matter of course ; [1] the extremely close supervision hitherto exercised over them was relaxed except in visitatorial matters of moment ; and soon suitors discovered that they might themselves apply for relief directly to the commissioners. No sooner was this fact definitely established and noised abroad than the number of litigants increased by leaps and bounds, and soon included not merely those desperately injured and despairing of a remedy anywhere, but all those who for any reason thought the jurisdiction and procedure of the Commission was more advantageous for them than that of the many other courts already in existence. It would be difficult to exaggerate the fundamental importance of the share played by the English people themselves in the evolution of this court. Without their ready acceptance of its legality, without their belief in the useful function it performed, neither royal fiat nor Statute

[1] Lord North was told in 1574 that he should have sent his information about Anabaptists to the Commission instead of to the Council : *Privy Council Register*, viii, 220.

could have ' created ' such a court and compelled people to resort to it. To prove that the court grew into existence is to establish that the English people as a whole regarded it with distinct favour. Thus, in order to relieve the Privy Council of the burden of dealing with a new class of cases too numerous and petty for its personal attention, there came into being a new court—the Court of Her Majesty's Commissioners for Causes Ecclesiastical.

The numerous commissioners named in the Letters Patent did not, however, all become judges of the new court. Whitgift, the Archbishop, Aylmer, the Bishop of London, and a few civil lawyers (usually Cosin, Stanhope, and Bancroft) were really the only members who sat regularly for judicial business. To them, and especially to Richard Bancroft, was due the final shape the institution assumed. Other members attended ordinarily only when personally summoned by the Archbishop. No scruples or fears of illegality were entertained by Elizabeth or her counsellors in developing as rapidly as possible the competence and dignity of this new tribunal. No explicit changes in its Letters Patent were made : the latter contained no limitations of any sort upon procedure, and the broad and inclusive wording of the clauses concerned with jurisdiction made the task of judicial interpretation simple. The evidence now available is barely sufficient to indicate somewhat the manner of this growth, and enable us to approximate its date.

By 1570 the new phase had already begun, for in that year we find the Privy Council writing to one of the sheriffs that they did ' never thereby intend to prejudice or hinder justice or any *sentence* or order that was or sholde be taken by the commissioners for Causes Ecclesiastical *or any other Judge* in that behalf ', and they commended to him such ' orders, *decrees*, and *sentences* as shalbe *awarded* out from the said commissioners or *from any other Coourte* to be duely and effectually executed as he may, accordinge to thorder of lawe and justice '.[1] Three years later we find John Strowde pleading that the Archdeacon's Court could not hold plea of his case, because the Ecclesiastical Commissioners had jurisdiction of it.[2] It is rather peculiar, considering the reputation the Commission has acquired, to find a Puritan insisting upon being tried by it and finally accepting its decision. So imperfect, however, is our evidence that we do not find the Commission speaking of itself as a court in its own official papers until 1586;[3] nor is there open recognition of this fact in the Letters Patent until 1611, though the Letters Patent of 1576 spoke of 'decrees, orders, *judgments*', 'given or pronounced'. We get a few glimpses of the sort of cases between party and party the commissioners were trying at this early date. A case or two of adultery and divorce,[4] one of assault,[5] one of forgery,[6] are probably only instances of a sort of jurisdiction the commissioners drew very rapidly away from the regular channels. About 1580 we have note of two cases much more like genuine contentious jurisdiction. One vicar was sued by his parishioners for misconduct and was deprived;[7] another clergyman's living was

[1] *Privy Council Register*, vii, 361. June 5, 1570.

[2] Morrice MSS. C, pp. 191–7.

[3] Morrice MSS. B, ii, f. 103. This is the text of the Commission's decree in the case of John Walward, a Puritan, dated Apr. 7, 1586, which ordered him to attend 'till he be otherwise Licensed *by this Court* and in the meantime *this Court* hath suspended him from preaching and interpreting or reading in the Church till he have performed this Order'. Signed by six commissioners.

[4] *Privy Council Register*, viii, 108 (May 29, 1573); xi, 137, 175 (1579).

[5] *Ibid.* viii, 356.

[6] *Ibid.* xi, 322 (1580).

[7] *Ibid.* xiii, 335 (1581/2).

sequestrated by the commissioners to pay his debts.[1] The latter case looks like an encroachment upon the common-law jurisdiction, but seems to have provoked only the displeasure of the Privy Council, which 'thought yt a hard course his livings should be in sequestration and his body subject to be imprysoned'.

In attempting to trace the growth of a definite and regular procedure, we are on somewhat firmer ground. Of course we must bear in mind that the Letters Patent will help us but little, for we are not tracing the *right* to cite, or to use citation, or to issue a writ of attachment and the like, but the actual use of a regular formal process, which may have preceded its formal recognition in the Letters Patent, or may as probably have become habitual years after it was granted. For instance, the commissioners do not seem to have insisted upon the taking of the *ex officio* oath till two decades after 1556, when the power to administer that oath was granted; on the other hand, they probably took depositions before the Patent of 1572 accorded formal permission. The use of a seal directed by the Patent of 1576 was indeed formal and denoted official importance and permanence, but it did not necessarily presume the performance of judicial work. In fact, we are interested, not in the mere use of judicial forms, but in their regular use for judicial purposes, and the former by no means presumes the latter. We must beware of implying that the commissioners had 'a' procedure before 1570; it is hardly likely that they had employed the same methods or lack of method for even the same class of cases in the same year, much less in different reigns. It is probable that, till the reign of Mary, nothing approaching any judicial form then known was *regularly* employed by the commissioners: most of their work was done by a simple

[1] *Ibid.* xv, 196 (1587).

letter stating their wishes, signed by at least three members, and including perhaps the phrase, 'And this shall be your warrant.' Such seems to have been the form ordinarily used by the Privy Council throughout the Tudor and early Stuart periods, and the close connexion between the latter and the Commission would lead naturally to a similarity of procedure. The regular forms of the Commission in later years were for the most part epistolary, and are distinguished from correspondence simply by the stereotyped nature of the phraseology.[1]

Probably regularity of judicial form was first attained in those preliminary and final stages where the commissioners came frequently into contact with judicial officers and bodies, who would naturally demand in the warrants and writs they were expected to serve, or the decrees and sentences they were commanded to execute or recognize, something approximating a regularity of form. Such a demand was inevitable if only to authenticate positively the commissioners' orders and ensure their prompt execution. To this category belong writs of summons, citations, attachments, bonds for attendance, bonds for performance of the commissioners' orders, sentences, and decrees—all those formalities, in fact, connected with getting the culprit before the commissioners, or supervising his actions after he had been dismissed, for which the commissioners were at first dependent upon the ordinary local judicial hierarchy.[2] If not in Mary's reign,

[1] See the order of the Commission quoted in Stoughton's *An Assertion for True and Christian Church Policy*, 333–4. As late as 1584 the formal summons was simply a letter: Morrice MSS. C, p. 422. See the order quoted in Waddington's *Track of the Hidden Church*, 62–4 (1589); and in the *Royal Historical MSS. Commission Report*, viii, 227 (1587).

[2] The first formal documents of the Commission that we find are of this type, and by 1570 we find that all these processes

at least early in Elizabeth's, this stage was attained, though very few of these forms had at this time any close connexion with strictly judicial business. They formed the necessary paraphernalia of a visitatorial body whose work was beginning to fall into certain quasi-judicial ruts; they were, none the less, exactly the type of process needed by a court, and the use of these forms, once regularized for any purpose, only made the transition to a judicial tribunal simpler.

It is more difficult to trace anything like formality of procedure after the accused was before the commissioners, and it seems probable that the commissioners employed the full discretion awarded them by their Letters Patent till about 1570.[1] But no sooner did cases between party

have already crystallized in form. See the bond for personal appearance in S. P. Dom. Eliz., 35, no. 38, and the warrant for the apprehension of Cartwright, dated Dec. 11, 1573, in S. P. Dom. Eliz., 94, no. 4. The omission of all forms by the Edwardian Letters Patent must have originally had significance, and makes it reasonably certain that the regular use of most forms began with Mary. Hence it is clear that between 1553 and 1570 this process must have been completed. The inferences from the Letters Patent lead to the same conclusion. The Patent of 1559 (s. vii) mentions letters missive; and the provisions of 1572 regarding depositions, of 1576 regarding attachments and bonds, read more like the regularization of a process already found expedient or necessary than the inauguration of a new one. It is hard to see why any one of these Patents should mention these details unless the commissioners had begun to give up the full discretion in procedure accorded them by the earlier clauses of the Patent, and were beginning to desire a formality in practice which in theory was non-existent. The formal use of the seal mentioned in 1576 for 'your letters missive, processes, decrees, orders, judgments' could only be to authenticate them for the sheriffs and justices who were to execute them. Again, the clear recognition of the Commissioners' process by the Privy Council letter of 1570 (*Register*, vii, 361) presumes a certain definite formal process to be already in existence.

[1] The account of the Puritans examined in 1567 in *Parte of a Register*, 23, makes it clear that they were not examined upon

and party grow numerous than the necessity of some sort of preparation of the case for trial became apparent; evidence and witnesses were needed to discover which party told the truth; lawyers appeared to speak for one party or the other; and insensibly the commissioners drifted into the formalities of a court. Naturally, too, where judicial forms were evidently desirable, a body of ecclesiastics and civil lawyers would employ the forms most familiar to them. The procedure then customary in the ecclesiastical courts was soon introduced in its entirety. First came the insistence upon the taking of the oath *ex officio*, by which the accused swore to tell the whole truth concerning the questions *about to be* asked him, before he knew their tenor.[1] With the taking of this

any set 'Articles' already prepared; but the same tract at p. 73 gives in full the formal 'Articles Original' on which Deering was examined in 1573. Strowde's narrative in Morrice MSS. C, pp. 191–7, tells at length of his trial in November 1573, and certainly shows that some form was being followed, but with equal certainty proves that the form was not at all the procedure later employed. To be sure, all this evidence is only hearsay and consists probably of garbled accounts written by the accused, who was not attempting in the least to define procedure for future students; but the habitual quotation of all sorts of judicial documents of the following decade by these same Puritans raises at least a presumption in favour of the view that had any such forms been used at this time the writers would at least have alluded to them. Nor does it seem reasonable to suppose that the strenuous opposition to the Commission's procedure at the trial, which is so prominent after 1579, should not have been to some degree contemporaneous with the introduction of such forms, since the reasons for objecting to them would have been as urgent in 1573 as in 1583. When Cosin wrote his *Apologie* in 1591, the regularity of the procedure was assured, and he declared (part i, 113) that warrants of *Quorum Nomina*, upon which any one might be arrested [a sort of John Doe warrant], were little used, a statement that may imply that they had previously been common.

[1] The history of this oath is an exceedingly obscure subject; the ordinary notions of it are certainly wrong; but it is by no

oath the trial began. Articles, answers, depositions, examinations, proctors, advocates, and the like quickly followed. The commissioners long retained their discretion as to the exact procedure at the formal hearing itself, but certainly by 1592, if not some years earlier, the forms employed even at the final hearing had thoroughly crystallized.

Carew, the Puritan, who was before the Commission about 1583 or 1584, said that he was arrested by a pursuivant on suit of his parishioners; that he at once retained lawyers to defend him, who so handled the case

means easy to replace them with exact information. It was certainly used during the Middle Ages, though the existence of a Statute about it points to a certain amount of opposition. By the time of the Reformation it seems to have been regularly used by the ecclesiastical courts and was adopted by the commissioners with the rest of the ecclesiastical procedure. The date is uncertain, but the trials of 1567 and 1573 do not mention it (certainly make no point of it); those just before and after 1580 mention its tender to the accused, but also make clear that it was dispensed with if any objection was made; that is to say, the commissioners still claimed the right to use their discretion as to procedure, and still claimed that anything they chose to do would be legal. Apparently the commissioners doffed their judicial robes at slight provocation and resumed their earlier garb as visitors. But after 1583 we find the oath insisted upon as the cardinal point of procedure without which no trial could begin. The evidence (much of which is referred to in the notes of this and other chapters) is most unsatisfactory. We are continually dealing with hearsay, with prejudiced reports, written by opponents to blacken the Commission's reputation, and at best must attempt to deduce the regular procedure from confessedly unusual instances.

This bit of indirect evidence, however, which seems credible, indicates that the oath was not insisted upon in minor cases until about 1600. Fuller wrote in 1607: 'in other cases of lesse penaltie (to their knowledge) untill of late yeares, the Commissioners used not either to force any to accuse themselves or to imprison them for refusinge so to do': *The Argument of Nicholas Fuller . . .*, 31.

that the commissioners finally themselves undertook the promotion of his trial *ex officio mero*. They summoned him to appear at a certain date, or if the Commission was not then in session, at its next sitting. That the court days of the Commission were not yet regular appears from the fact that, when he came up to London on the date named, the commissioners were not in session. He therefore went home, but they called him back, and compelled him to give bond for his appearance whenever wanted. He and his witnesses took the oath *ex officio* and were examined on a set of articles they had not seen and of which they could not get a copy. He was suspended from preaching, but went home and preached as usual. Thereupon the Bishop of London asked the commissioners for an attachment to arrest him, which was not issued: 'it was said by my Proctor to be a thing unreasonable, seeing that I was not warned to appeare.' The commissioners, therefore, postponed action 'till the next Court', when Carew, having been duly warned by his proctor, was present. They offered him new articles, and, when he steadfastly refused to make a full answer to them, they committed him for contempt to the Fleet prison.[1] Here are certainly the clear outlines of the subsequent regular procedure of the Commission, and its well-settled character is attested by the fact that it was employed in a case of office,[2] and that a proctor was able to prevent the arrest of a well-known and disobedient Puritan on the ground that the Commission could use attachment only to apprehend a man who *refused* to appear, and that as Carew had not yet been asked to appear to answer to *this* charge he could not have refused to appear, so that

[1] Morrice MSS. C, pp. 653 ff.

[2] Even the cases begun by the commissioners themselves had apparently lost the visitatorial form and had become judicial.

the proper procedure was a citation or summons. It is inconceivable that the commissioners of 1538 or 1557 would have listened to any such plea for a moment. So long as the commissioners were ecclesiastical visitors, possessed of unlimited discretion, such an argument could only be an unwarrantable obstruction of justice.

The procedure in Cawdry's case is interesting both because we have such a full account of it, and because of the notoriety he later attained by delivering the first and best-planned attack on the Commission's jurisdiction. In November 1586 he was accused of various misdemeanours and was summoned by letters missive signed by three commissioners. The oath *ex officio* was administered to him by the Bishop of London and Doctors Stanhope and Walker in the bishop's dining-room. He asked to see a copy of the articles prepared against him before he was sworn, but was told that 'it was not the Order of that Court so to do'. A day was assigned for his examination, and in the meantime he was told to go to the registrar and answer such interrogatories as he might put to him, which he did apparently in December 1586. He then appeared on the day appointed, waited eleven days for his case to come up,[1] and then went home, getting permission (after some difficulty) for a friend to put in a bond of £40 for his appearance. On February 18 he appeared at Fulham, where the Bishop of London examined him informally in the forenoon (apparently alone) [2] and told him to attend the official hearing of the commissioners in the afternoon. The commissioners referred his case to the Archbishop of Canterbury and the Bishop of

[1] This might have been because the court was not in session, but also might have resulted from the necessity of waiting for his case to be reached on the court calendar.

[2] Is this not clearly the beginning of the later 'Informations'?

London,[1] with whom Cawdry had several long conversations. When with the latter 'in his Gallery', the climax came; Cawdry definitely refused to subscribe; the bishop 'called one unto him to make a note of it in a piece of paper, and so suspended me from exercising my Ministry'. Various gentlemen and lords, including Burghley, were now induced to intercede for him, and secured him another hearing on May 30, 1587, at which, however, he was still 'obstinate' and so was deprived.[2] It was this very procedure which Cawdry claimed was illegal in his famous suit against the bishop in the Queen's Bench.[3]

[1] Clearly we have here the beginning of the later habit of handing over a case to referees for decision.

[2] 'Articuli sive Interrogatoria Objecta et Ministrata ex officio mero Roberto Cawdry . . . per supremos Commissionarios Reginae ad Causas Ecclesiasticas rite et legitime fulcitos, &c.': Morrice MSS. C, pp. 790–5. Other documents illustrating this growth of procedure are: decree (1586) in Morrice MSS. B, ii, p. 103; numerous examinations in Harl. MSS. 7042, especially at ff. 12 b, 13, 22, 59, 60, 60 b, 62, 62 b, 64, 195, &c. (1588–95); orders, decrees, certificates of excommunication, search warrants, articles original (1575–90), in Stoughton, *An Assertion for True and Christian Church Policy* (1604), 334–46; declaration by the Mayor of Oxford, S. P. Dom. Eliz., 146, no. 84 (1580); decree in Morrice MSS. A, f. 136; hearings in Morrice MSS. C, p. 897; Morrice MSS. A, ff. 581–4; examinations and depositions *in partibus* (1584–6), Lambeth MSS. Carta Miscellanea, xii, f. 19 ff.; answers to articles original, Strype, *Whitgift*, iii, 153 (1585); examination in S. P. Dom. Eliz., 262, no. 25, i; and 273, no. 23, i; warrant for seizure of priests and 'massing stuff', Lansdowne MSS. 25, f. 167 (1577/8); Latin decree in Cawdry's case, Lansdowne MSS. 53, f. 72; discharge of a bond, Morrice MSS. M, no. viii.

[3] The very basis of the suit must have been an assumption that there was a definite procedure which the Commission ought to have followed. The Letters Patent, however, still said that the commissioners might proceed in any way they saw fit. Only a very well-established routine could have countenanced the suit as against this explicit clause of the Letters Patent.

About this time an incident occurred which throws an interesting sidelight upon the growth of procedure. A bishop prepared certain articles against a Puritan layman, of which the latter secured a copy by some means and took directly to Whitgift with a complaint of their injustice. The archbishop agreed with him, and wrote at once to the bishop: 'I cannot but greatly merveyle, that contrary to the orders of the Commission Court,[1] subscribed by yourselfe and the rest of the Commissioners, you would cause a Gentleman of such qualitie as Maister B is to be sent for by a Pursevant, before the ordinarie processe of a letter missive were served upon him, especially for matters of so small moment.' The whole matter would be discreditable to the Commission when the fact should appear that the Puritan in question was sued at common law by the bishop's kinsman. He therefore begged the bishop to proceed no further with the articles. Then followed, if we may believe the Puritan, the really remarkable part of the whole incident. The archbishop and another commissioner were then sitting on business of the court, and the former 'took pen and inke and crossed ye Articles all overthwart and so sent them backe with this letter'. It is extremely interesting to know that the commissioners were already issuing ordinances on procedure; it is also significant to find the commissioners treating each other's documents in public with contumely and disdain. The bishop, of course, gave way, and referred the whole matter to the archbishop.[2]

To facilitate the Commission's work and to ensure that stability and institutional strength so vital to a really powerful court, certain changes were made in its member-

[1] Note this early use of the phrase.

[2] Stoughton, *An Assertion for True and Christian Church Policy*, 338–46, gives the articles and correspondence in full.

ship.[1] Allusion has already been made to the excessively personal aspect of the earlier commissions, and to the fact that the vast discretionary powers conferred by the Letters Patent made the personnel of the men, to whom such powers were granted, of the very first consequence. The only formal trace of the change in the Privy Council's idea of the commissioners' activities is to be found, not in the powers granted by the Letters Patent, but in the members named. The Edwardian commissioners had been called upon to maintain an existing religious settlement, and had been essentially ecclesiastical, composed of bishops, deans, and doctors of divinity. The only lay members were ministers of state. The Marian and first Elizabethan commissioners, on the other hand, had been predominantly secular: eighty-six per cent. of the former and eighty-four per cent. of the latter being laymen. In truth, neither queen had dared to trust the clergy already in office with much responsibility. Elizabeth's policy—the State as a secular power imposing a religious settlement upon the clergy—was reflected in her first commission. But as the administrative and judicial work increased, the majority of the members named in the Letters Patent of 1572 and 1576 came to be clergy and civil lawyers; indeed, in those of 1584 they outnumbered the rest of the commissioners by more than three to one. The State was developing a court from an ecclesiastical commission by gradually appointing lawyers. Moreover, the attendance lists no longer show the Lord Mayor, the Lord Chief Justice, the Attorney-General, and Privy Councillors[2] playing a

[1] As complete a list as possible of the members of the Commissions for the Province of Canterbury has been printed in the Appendix, and the tabulations containing the results here given will be found at the end of this chapter.

[2] See the special warrant issued by the Bishop of London and

prominent part at the trials : the influential commissioners were now three or four bishops and half a dozen civil lawyers resident in London.[1] The new duties, however, meant many regular sessions and more work for the members, most of whom showed their appreciation of the fact by frequent absence from the sitting on slight pretexts,[2] and by requiring even down to 1604 a certain amount of pressure to secure their co-operation.[3] The amount of the work and the fact that no salary was attached or perquisites allowed in the shape of fees [4] soon reduced the long roster of members to a few diligent and energetic men.

The real power the commissioners could wield had been much increased by the enlargement of the total membership, and of the number of members who were ' of the quorum '. The membership had been about twenty till 1562, when it was made twenty-seven, only to be nearly doubled in 1572. At or about forty-five [5] the Canterbury Commission remained till 1605, when it became sixty-six. Then Elizabeth had in 1562 once more reduced to three the number needed for the transaction of business, and had at the same time in successive commissions greatly increased the number of those whose presence in conjunction with any other two members would make a valid quorum. The Edwardian quorums had been large,

six prominent councillors for the apprehending of priests, &c., in Lansdowne MSS. 25, f. 167. Feb. 6, 1577/8.

[1] Canterbury, London, Rochester, Winchester ; Bancroft, Lewis, Aubrey, Cosin, Stanhope.

[2] See Strype's *Aylmer*, 62 (1580).

[3] Barlow, *Summe and Substance of the Conference*, 1604. Third Day. Whitgift complained of the difficulty of keeping a quorum present.

[4] Cosin, *Apologie*, ii, 94.

[5] Twenty-eight members of the Commission of 1572 were to exercise authority only in the dioceses.

nearly half the total membership; the Marian commissions had contained no such limitations, and hence had had quorums of one hundred per cent.; cautious Elizabeth at first reduced the quorum to about one-third of the membership, but gradually increased the quorum until it contained in 1584 fifty-five per cent., and in 1601 sixty-two per cent. of the total membership. Such an increase simplified the subdivision of the Commission, and hence made several sessions at once easy; or made many successive sessions possible without too heavy a burden on any one individual. The importance of these simple changes in ensuring the flexibility and efficiency of the Commission was great.

Scarcely less important was the influence of the composition of the quorum. The quorum of 1549 contained nine ecclesiastics, seven of them bishops, and two lay ministers of state. That of 1559 was composed of two bishops, one lay minister of state, and four lawyers. Gradually the bishops and lawyers increased in number till at the end of Elizabeth's reign they formed the majority of the quorum and included most of the regular ecclesiastical judges. Regard was also had in appointing the quorum to the regular residence of the persons chosen. The earlier commissions had named men without fixed residence because, to be efficient, the commissioners must be constantly in motion. But, as time went on, the members of the Canterbury Commission were drawn from men officially resident in London, showing not only the tendency of the Commission to become stationary, but the opinion of the Privy Council that a permanent residence was expedient.

The flexibility of the Commission's organization and the vague wording of its patent, which had made possible so rapid and so thoroughgoing a transformation into a court, had allowed it to meet the judicial situation no less easily and surely than the early commissioners had met the political exigencies. Efficiency had been assured in many diverse duties by the large number of officials who belonged to it, making it representative of the best judicial and administrative experience in England. Yet, if it was to be successful as a law-court, if it was to develop an institutional strength and vigour of its own, the same men must associate together long enough to allow the formation of an *esprit de corps*, and for the establishment of that agreement as to forms, jurisdiction, and precedents which alone could commend it as a court to advocates and suitors. Its decisions ought to be based on so conservative an interpretation of the Canon and Statute law that they would naturally commend themselves to subsequent commissioners by that uniformity and harmony with each other and with the court's own previous decisions which alone can give the learned profession an abiding faith in the integrity and justice of acts of a tribunal.

This stability and opportunity, so essential for the growth of traditions and precedents, was ensured by the continuation of the comparatively permanent tenure of office of the most active members which had been characteristic of the early commissions. Many churchmen and civilians sat from ten to twenty years, and a few for thirty years; the high percentages of new members are explained by the rapid increase in the total membership plus the filling of vacancies caused by the death or promotion of men already advanced in age before their appointment as bishops and judges. But nearly a third of even Elizabeth's first commission had been members of her sister's commissions. The institutional weakness caused by the death of so important a member as the

Bishop of London or the Dean of the Arches was now avoided by naming the incumbent of such a position a member of the Commission *ex officio*. Other offices were sufficiently important to ensure their incumbent a place in the next commission issued after his appointment. About half the members belonged to one or the other of these classes from 1572 to 1601.

The Bishops of London, Winchester, Rochester, Chichester, Ely, and Worcester always sat, and less frequently the Bishops of Norwich, Salisbury, Lincoln, Peterborough, and St. Davids.[1] The selection of these bishops was due probably, not only to their relative rank and importance, but to the situation of their dioceses and their supposed need of unusual disciplinary authority. The dioceses of Rochester, Winchester, Chichester, and Ely lay along roads leading from London to the Continent, and were therefore likely to be troubled with priests and Jesuits. In the diocese of Worcester and in Wales the Roman Catholics were strong. Similarly in the dioceses of Lincoln, Norwich, and Peterborough, the nonconformists were sufficiently numerous to make wide powers seem essential to enforce the ecclesiastical policy undertaken in 1584 and 1605. Probably not a little weight is due to the fact that the personality of the men appointed to these important dioceses made them desirable members of such a body as the Commission was meant to be.

[1] Only sixteen bishoprics ever were represented on the Commission for the Province of Canterbury between 1559 and 1611. Canterbury, London, Worcester, Rochester, Chichester, Ely, and Winchester sat on all commissions between 1572 and 1611. Only Canterbury and London sat in 1559. In 1562 Ely and Rochester were added. Norwich was represented 1576, 1584, 1601, 1605; Peterborough, 1584, 1601, 1605; Lincoln, 1584, 1601, 1608; Hereford, 1601, 1605, 1608; St. Davids, 1572, 1576; Salisbury, 1584 and 1601; Exeter, 1601 and 1605; Gloucester, 1601 and 1608; Bath and Wells, 1608.

The secular State was represented by the Chancellor of the Exchequer, the Treasurer of the Household, one of the Secretaries of State, and sometimes by one or more of the Privy Council. The judicial branch usually included the Chancellor of the Duchy of Lancaster, the Attorney of the Court of Wards and Liveries, one of the common-law judges, the Attorney-General and Solicitor-General, the Recorder of London, the two Masters of Requests, two Masters of Chancery, and the Dean of the Court of Arches, with occasionally the Remembrancer of the Exchequer and the Judge of the Admiralty.[1] In the Commission of 1601 considerable additions were made to the *ex officio* list: the Lord Chancellor or the Keeper of the Great Seal, the Lord Treasurer, the Chief Justices and Chief Baron, the Learned Council, the Dean of the Royal Chapel, the Judge of the Prerogative Court, and the Provost of Eton. The 'occasional members' also came to include many of the other bishops, most of the common-law judges and barons, the clerks of the Privy Council, the Deans of Exeter, Rochester, Chester, and Christ Church (Oxford), the Archdeacons of Essex and Nottingham, and the Lieutenant of the Tower. Here was clearly a body of men representative of all parts of the State, calculated to give the Commission dignity as well as authority, experience as well as efficiency, and expert knowledge in all possible ecclesiastical, legal, and political fields.

The transformation of the Commissioners for the

1 Also at this early period we find Aldermen of London and the Governor of the Company of Merchant Adventurers. In all these early commissions there were a number of 'Esquires' who sat. These were at times the bulk of the new members. They disappear after 1576 and reappear in 1605: probably they were members meant to sit only *in partibus*, and hence were only on the diocesan commissions between 1576 and 1605, when a movement began to lessen the number of the small commissions.

Province of Canterbury into a court was further aided by relieving them of the burden of much of their earlier work. The watching of recusants, the warding of priests, and the banishing of Jesuits and priests was turned over first to the common-law members of the Commission and then to special commissions headed by the Lord Chancellor and common-law judges.[1] Similar commissions were issued to watch the ports, to prevent the 'going over seas', and to prevent the landing of Jesuits and priests.[2] Recusant fines were collected after 1590 by the Exchequer on certificate from the justices of the peace, or from the sheriff, or (during James's reign) by commissions issued for that purpose.[3] Gradually, too, the work of the Commissioners in dealing with nonconformity devolved upon the bishops under the Statute of 1572, the Articles of 1583, and the Canons of 1597 and 1604, which allowed the bishop to exact by his own authority the Oath of Supremacy, subscription to the Thirty-nine Articles, the wearing of the surplice, and the like. The Court of High Commission renounced none of the powers exercised by the early commissioners, but in practice tried very few cases of nonconformity after the failure to convict Cartwright and his friends : neither the Government nor the Commission could afford to fail in its purpose.

Other duties requiring a less extended authority were cared for by the issue of numerous diocesan commissions,[4]

[1] Rymer's *Foedera*, xvi, 597, 690 ; xvii, 367, 644 ; S. P. Dom. Car. I, 31, no. 56, &c.

[2] Most of these are in the Patent Roll. They are numerous between 1590 and 1610.

[3] The best single source of information is the voluminous record of pardons in the Patent Rolls of the first years of the reign of James, many of which describe at length all proceedings connected with the levying of the fine and the attempt to collect it.

[4] A list is in the Bibliography.

modelled upon the Patent of the Commissioners for the Province of Canterbury, but very inferior to it in power. In 1578 a special commission issued for Ireland; in 1579 one for Wales; while at about the same time commissioners were invested with broad powers in the Province of York and even in the individual counties of Lancaster and Cheshire and the Diocese of Durham. Until 1611 most dioceses probably had a special commission which was meant to relieve the Court of High Commission from visitatorial work altogether, and allow it (except in emergencies) to devote itself entirely to its new judicial duties.

A moment's thought will make clear the fact that a development of this nature could not have been the work of the commissioners themselves, though it may well have met their entire approval. The main impulse came no doubt from the Privy Council, anxious to rid itself of a troublesome and ever-increasing business of a quasi-ecclesiastical nature. But in the long run neither commissioners nor Council could create a law-court: a court must depend, as has been already said, upon the voluntary resort of suitors, and must in last analysis leave all initiative to them. The really powerful forces fostering the evolution of the Court of High Commission were those aspects of its jurisdiction and procedure which caused suitors to prefer it to the regular ecclesiastical or common-law courts. Unquestionably the general weakness of episcopal authority after the Reformation, the habit of appeal from the regular ecclesiastical courts, the clumsiness of the Court of Delegates, contributed many a case to the Commission's cause list. Nor should we for a moment forget the part inevitably played by the looseness of jurisdictional lines in the sixteenth century which made it by no means easy to know where remedy for a particular case could be found. Then the Reformation had made inevitable a great deal of ecclesiastical litigation, growing out of the disputes over monastic land, advowsons, impropriations, and tithes. From the economic changes—enclosures and the unprecedented rise of prices—sprang a new and troublesome type of cases concerned with the necessary readjustment of the old commutations and produce rents to the new scale of values. With so much to dispute, with so much doubt where a favourable decision could be obtained by either party, coupled to the sixteenth-century love of litigation for its own sake, suitors hailed the advent of a new court with joyful enthusiasm. Nevertheless, the chief attractions which drew them in crowds to the High Commission for more than half a century were its peculiar jurisdiction and procedure.

THE MEMBERSHIP OF THE COMMISSIONS FOR THE PROVINCE OF CANTERBURY, 1549–1608

	Total Membership.	*New Members.*	*Number in Quorum.*	*Clergy.*	*Bishops.*	*Ministers of State.*	*Civil Lawyers.*	*Laity.*	*Common Lawyers.*
1549	24	—	11	15	7	5	3	9	1
1551	32	12	12	17	6	6	8	15	1
1557	22	21	—	3	2	13	5	19	1
1559	19	13	7	3	2	9	5	16	2
1562	27	11	8	7	4	7	9	20	4
1572	71	47	25	20	9	6	15	51	8
1576	73	23	27	26	10	26	12	47	9
1584	44	8	24	24	12	5	10	20	5
1601	54	29	32	25	13	7	9	29	13
1605	66	24	17	27	11	2	15	39	13
1608	60	13	27	27	11	13	9	33	11

CHAPTER IV

JURISDICTION, 1580–1611

In studying the jurisdiction of the Court of High Commission, we are confronted with an anomalous situation which compels us to describe its powers in terms which are, from a strictly judicial view, paradoxical, if not wholly inaccurate. In writing of original, appellate, and concurrent jurisdiction, we are making for the sake of convenience a distinction which legally never obtained, for all the Commission's jurisdiction was original. It never formally held to any other court any definite judicial relation recognized by its Letters Patent to the extent of allowing appeals or assuming the existence of an equal power in the other court. Inherent jurisdiction by prescription or custom the Commission of course could not possess; from the Statute and more especially from its Letters Patent it derived all the judicial authority and position it had, and, until 1611, the language of the Letters Patent did not even by implication attempt to assign the Commission a definite place in the judicial hierarchy or even acknowledge that it possessed one. It seems to be, however, an impossible task to make clear the various aspects of the Commission's original jurisdiction without frequently employing familiar common-law phrases whose accepted meaning only partially corresponds with that aspect of the actual practice of the Commission to which, for want of anything better, we shall be compelled to apply them.

The Letters Patent, under which the Commission first

exercised jurisdiction as a court of law, were, until 1611, so far as jurisdiction was concerned, almost precisely the same as Elizabeth's first Patent of 1559,[1] whose wording was so broad and inclusive that it would sanction anything whatever. But there can be little doubt that the commissioners had never been allowed to exercise any such discretion, and the breadth of their Patent indicated rather the scope of the visitatorial and administrative work which the Privy Council intended to delegate to the commissioners from time to time, than its notion of the authority three commissioners could wield on their own initiative.[2] In reality the specific powers enumerated in the Letters Patent, plus the Reformation penal Statutes, had been the pretty definite measure of the commissioners' previous authority. It is extremely probable that the inclusive phraseology of the first Letters Patent was intended merely as a guarantee to the commissioners themselves that they should not later be tried for treason for exceeding their authority, when, at some future moment, the political situation might make it expedient for the State to disown them and their work.[3]

The formal recognition of the existence of the Court of High Commission absolutely altered its previous

[1] The earlier commissions are not here of consequence, for they were purely visitatorial and had their influence on the Commission's jurisdiction as a court simply through their influence on the form of the Patent of 1559.

[2] The Ecclesiastical Commissioners named in the Letters Patent of July 19, 1559 (with the addition of the Bishop of Ely), were empowered by a special Patent of Oct. 20, 1559, to exact the Oath of Supremacy from the clergy. If the language of the Patent of July 19 had been literally interpreted, it would have made additional authority superfluous. Rymer, *Foedera*, xv, 546. Dr. Dixon, *History of the Church of England*, v, 193, mistook this document for a reissue of the Patent of July 19 and calls it the first formal institution of the Court of High Commission.

[3] See Clause xvii of the Letters Patent of 1559.

relation to both State and Church. It was obviously desirable to free a law-court from the dictation of the Privy Council and to allow its judges considerable discretion in the interpretation of their own Patent and in its application to particular cases. As the grant of jurisdiction to a law-court, the Letters Patent were at once invested with new significance, nor could the commissioners consistently adopt any other view than 'that the acte and commission thereupon doe giue full power and authoritie for any course soeuer, for the gouernment in causes Ecclesiastical, that shall be mentioned in the letters Patents'.[1] Legally this was a mere truism. When, however, the language of the Letters Patent is examined, it becomes clear that even a strict and conservative judicial construction of its wording invested the commissioners with an almost unlimited jurisdiction.

[1] Cosin, *An Apologie for Sundrie Proceedings by Iurisdiction Ecclesiasticall* (London, 1593), part i, 112. This tract, written by one of the most active and able commissioners, is practically an official statement of its jurisdiction and procedure in 1592, and without it we should be embarked upon a sea of conjectures, not only in regard to those two most important topics, but upon the whole history of the Commission after 1565. From this tract, from the various cases already cited, from the prohibitions and cases in the common-law courts, and from the attacks made upon the Commission (which will be duly referred to in later chapters), this account has been drawn up. It seemed best to make a statement which would describe the jurisdiction and procedure (treated in the following chapter) as finally crystallized, rather than to attempt a series of conjectures as to its development which could be at best inconclusive. To attempt more than to make clear the broad fundamental jurisdictional lines seemed also to be out of place in a monograph intended for historians rather than for legal antiquarians. It is, furthermore, by no means clear that Cosin, in his attempt to defend the Commission, did not draw the jurisdictional lines with a good deal more precision than ever was applied in practice, at least before 1620, and in consequence minimize the discretionary and indefinite aspect which its jurisdiction never quite lost.

Clause iii gave cognizance of all 'heretical opinions, seditious books, contempts, conspiracies, false rumours, tales, seditions, misbehaviours, slanderous words', 'published, *invented*, or set forth', 'by any person or persons, against us, or against any the laws or statutes of this realm, or against the quiet governance and rule of our people and subjects'.[1] It could hardly be maintained that any criminal act, however slight, could not correctly and judicially be held a 'misbehaviour', while the Commission's discretion was absolute in the decision of what was against the 'quiet governance and rule of our people'.

Clause v was even more sweeping. 'And also we do give and grant full power and authority unto you and six of you [quorum as before] from time to time and at all times during our pleasure, to visit, reform, redress, order, correct and amend, in all places within this our realm of England all such errors, heresies, crimes, abuses, offences, contempts, and enormities spiritual and ecclesiastical whatsoever which by any spiritual or ecclesiastical power, authority or jurisdiction can or may lawfully be reformed, ordered, redressed, corrected, restrained or amended, to the pleasure of Almighty God, the increase of virtue, and the conservation of the peace and unity of this our realm, and according to the authority and power limited, given and appointed by any laws or statutes of this realm.' Here the opportunity for judicial construction was even greater and its necessity even more imperative. If 'visit, reform, redress' were capable of only one interpretation, it was by no means so easy judicially to define 'order, correct, and amend'. In the broadest

[1] All the quotations in this and the succeeding paragraphs are from the Patent of 1559 as printed by Prothero, *Select Statutes*, 227.

sense of the words, they sanctioned any judicial proceeding whatever. Moreover, few phrases could have been found embracing more completely all possibilities than *all* 'crimes, abuses, offences, contempts and enormities, spiritual and ecclesiastical *whatsoever*', which any ecclesiastical authority in England ever had tried or could then legally try. The Crown, moreover, claimed an absolutely inclusive ecclesiastical jurisdiction, and it could therefore be plausibly argued that these phrases were descriptive of the Commission's jurisdiction rather than limitations upon it. In the application to actual suits between party and party, 'abuses' and 'offences' were capable of almost unlimited judicial expansion. Nor did the Letters Patent fail to make it clear that the discretion of the commissioners in construing the meaning of this language was absolute. A sweeping *non obstante* clause, covering any laws, Statutes, proclamations or other grants, privileges, or ordinances, ended all doubts as to the conclusive nature of this grant and the authority the commissioners were to derive from it. Their discretion was to supersede everything else.

Strictly speaking, all this was original jurisdiction: any one might begin any suit in the Commission which its jurisdiction permitted, and the Commission's decision would be final. The importance of this fact cannot be overestimated, and it alone explains much of the popularity of the Commission with suitors. Of course proceedings initiated *ex officio* by the Commission itself were not in the common-law sense of the words original jurisdiction, but the civil law did and still does recognize such a power in the judge to prosecute the criminal. In the civil-law sense, cases of office were the purest type of original jurisdiction. We may, however, for convenience limit the Commission's 'original jurisdiction' to those cases which in practice the Commission alone might try. These were few—heresy, schism, and in the main, aggravated or extreme cases, where the station of the defendant or the 'enormity' of the offence demanded either summary procedure or an unusual penalty. It is difficult to separate such suits from the use of the Commission's visitatorial authority in which this 'original jurisdiction' was at times merged. This aspect can perhaps be best described by calling the Commission the Star Chamber for ecclesiastical cases.

A phase of the Commission's jurisdiction of far more consequence was its 'appellate' jurisdiction. The use of the word 'appeal' and its derivatives in connexion with the Commission's jurisdiction and procedure requires some defence, even though we mean by it no more than that the Commission tried a case already impleaded or decided elsewhere Technically and strictly, the commissioners never admitted the existence of anything remotely resembling a formal right of appeal to their jurisdiction from the ecclesiastical courts; still less did they formally recognize a regular and normal progression from the bishop's to the archbishop's courts and from the Court of Arches to the Commission. They tried every case on its merits, heard all possible evidence of fact, examined any and every suggestion about substantive law raised by any advocate or proctor, on the assumption that the case had never been adequately heard before. Nor had they any idea that the Commission was restricted in matter of 'appeal' to serious offences or merely to the adjustment of important differences of judicial opinion as to substantive law. Any case, however small, would be retried by the commissioners if the plaintiff raised a valid judicial presumption that he had been wronged. While in this retrial the commissioners were not in the least bound to recognize the earlier proceedings, and while it is clear that before 1600 they paid little or no attention to them, there can be no doubt that after 1611 they did as a matter of expediency take cognizance of the history of the case. At an even earlier period depositions and formal papers, already accepted by one of the ecclesiastical courts in judicial investigations, were readily given full credence and judicial effect by the commissioners, but it is very doubtful whether the proceedings in the lower court were ever thought to have assigned limits to the commissioners' power of inquiry or were ever permitted to confine their attention to some few points of the case. The whole matter in dispute, not some point in it, however crucial or important, became the subject for trial. No practice of remanding a case for action to the court of first instance obtained ;[1] the commissioners either gave final sentence or refused to interfere at all. It is not even positive that the ecclesiastical courts officially recognized decisions of the Commission which reversed or maintained their own—in other words, that the lower courts themselves conceded any right of 'appeal'.

Certainly this re-examination of cases by the Commission finds no exact parallel in English judicial history. The term 'writ of error' has been generally used by common lawyers to denote resort to a higher court for the decision of alleged mistaken rulings of the lower court in matters of substantive law. The term 'appeal' has referred chiefly to interlocutory

[1] The commissioners at Durham had such a practice after 1630 ; see *infra*, p. 300. It seems a little dangerous to argue the existence of a similar practice at London solely on the score of analogy and probability, without some positive evidence proving the existence of at least one case.

matters and to errors of form. Indeed, the practice of deciding most issues of fact by means of a jury, whose decision was judicially final, necessarily made resort to a higher tribunal possible only where errors of law or form could be alleged. The word 'retrial' has come to mean the examination of the question of fact by another jury on the ground that the first was unduly influenced or wrongly informed. In the Commission, none of these distinctions applied: it was as easy to 'appeal' a question of fact, in the common-law sense, as one of law. After the commissioners became judges in a law-court, no jury was used and there seems to have been no 'appeal' permitted on purely formal errors. In the nature of things, the redress of technical or formal errors, committed by one of the ecclesiastical courts, belonged to the Court of Arches, the finality of whose decisions in such questions was early recognized by the commissioners. As the latter would have phrased it, their own court was 'of too high and eminent a nature' to interfere in a case already impleaded elsewhere unless a substantive wrong of real magnitude had been or was being committed. Probably actual proof of the reality of the injury committed by the lower court was not required as essential to the beginning of an action; perhaps the sentence or the pleadings were accepted as *prima facie* evidence justifying the commissioners in instituting a further inquiry; but proof of a very real injury was indispensable to a judgement in the plaintiff's favour. What the commissioners wished, too, was not evidence that the lower court had exceeded its jurisdiction or had not observed the technicalities of Canon or Statute law, but a clear presumption with subsequent proof that it had failed adequately to settle the dispute out of which the action arose. Lack of jurisdiction, inability to enforce the sentence in the lower court because of the defeated suitor's failure to obey, or the failure of the ecclesiastical judge to investigate the facts thoroughly, were considered excellent and valid reasons for ' appeal '.

This right of appeal was, however, less important in its judicial than in its administrative consequences. The episcopal power had never been judicially strong in England, and the Reformation had sapped what little strength had been inherent in its judicial decrees, by sanctioning on theological grounds the tendency of the laity to value lightly excommunication and all other ecclesiastical pains and penalties. The mediaeval churchman had expected to terrorize the laity into obedience by the fear of punishment hereafter, and, when laymen cheerfully remained excommunicated for years, as was not uncommon in Elizabeth's reign, it became clear to all that the validity of the old ecclesiastical process had disappeared. The Church no longer possessed a method of coercing the disobedient suitor at ecclesiastical law. If the penalties of fine and imprisonment, as wielded by the High Commission, could alone compel obedience to the Oath of Supremacy and the Act of Uniformity, and if each bishop was by 1590 clamouring for a diocesan commission to enable him to perform the ordinary visitatorial and disciplinary work of his see, it was no less clear that the process of the Commission and the possibility of appeal to it by bishop or suitor was the only sanction behind the sentences and decrees of archdeacon and bishop in cases between party and party. As Whitgift said, ' Yt ys the onlie meanes we have to punish and restraine sectaries and contentious persons which refuse to observe Lawes and to keep order.'[1] ' The whole ecclesiasticall

[1] Additional MSS. 28571, f. 172. 1592–3. Whitgift to the Queen.

law is a carcasse without a soul, yf it be not in the wantes, supplied by the Commission.'[1] For this reason, cases were regularly transferred by the bishop himself from his own courts when it was clear they could not be successfully prosecuted there. Sentences, decrees, and processes of any kind which the episcopal authority had failed to execute were 'appealed' to the Commission for execution or specific performance. Thus, the latter became practically the mainstay of the regular ecclesiastical courts and was by 1600 admittedly the only power capable of enforcing the ecclesiastical law. Usually, after that date, the mere knowledge of the existence of the Commission was sufficient to frighten into obedience most recalcitrant culprits. In this way, by the use of a process which can only by courtesy be called an appeal, a sort of administrative law grew up in the Commission.

As time elapsed, however, this fact was borne in upon the minds of lawyers and litigants, that if the Commission could hear such cases 'on appeal', it could hear them in first instance, and parties soon began to bring their cases directly to the Commission. Thus was developed a concurrent jurisdiction with the ordinary ecclesiastical courts which soon formed the bulk of its business. To such an extent did the Commission absorb all important cases that Coke later sarcastically expressed his sympathy for the deserted courts of the bishops. One fact prevented their total desertion. The largest item in the expense of prosecuting a suit before the Commission was the journey to London and residence there pending examinations and hearings. It was not worth either party's while to carry a small case so far, unless one of them became imbued with that determination to defeat his adversary at any cost which was so common in the sixteenth century.

[1] Strype, *Whitgift*, i, 267.

In addition to this appellate and concurrent jurisdiction, the Commission exercised an equitable jurisdiction in ecclesiastical cases and performed the functions of the Court of Requests for ecclesiastical suits *in forma pauperis*. In all probability, this was the oldest branch of the Commission's jurisdiction, and formed the most numerous portion of the suits between party and party impleaded as late as 1590, for it was precisely this class of cases which was least likely to find remedy in the regular tribunals, and in which, therefore, suitors most often petitioned the Council to exercise the residual power of the Crown in their behalf. These the Council, at an early date (perhaps as early as 1565), began to refer to the Commission, where the general informality of procedure and unsettled jurisdiction were a positive aid to the litigant and increased his chances of securing a remedy. What limits, if any, existed at this time to the Commission's readiness to relieve cases otherwise without remedy and to prosecute suits for men too poor to be able to afford justice, is hard to say; but the general tenor of the Council's letters makes it likely that the Commission was commanded to give relief wherever the plaintiff could prove his injury to have been substantial; or could satisfactorily demonstrate his poverty plus the excellence of his case. On the whole, this aspect of the Commission's jurisdiction was that most widely approved by civil and common lawyers, and to it little if any objection was ever made. Probably for many years no question of jurisdiction was raised in these cases; proof of the reality of a substantial grievance would ensure a remedy.

Like the present courts of equity, the Commission possessed the power of compelling the specific performance of its orders, and of securing their observance by bond, or by fine and imprisonment. This power greatly increased the Commission's jurisdiction, for it was considered to confer the right to compel the affirmative performance of a duty, a promise, an oath, or whatever the ecclesiastical or Statute law might require. The negative decree and injunction or inhibition so much used in modern equity practice was of comparatively little importance in the Commission. Modern equity hesitates to do more than insist upon the performance of contracts and promises which the defendant has expressly undertaken. No modern ecclesiastical court would think of compelling a clergyman to preach certain doctrine : it will punish him for breach of his duty, but it must to-day rely upon the visitatorial authority for the specific performance of such matters. Nor is it now usual to compel laymen (unless corporations) to perform a specific duty laid upon the individual only by the general law. All these things and more the commissioners had done from the first, and the fact that the only remedy in the case was a decree of specific performance was, to the commissioners, good reason for accepting jurisdiction. The great bulk of such decrees issued in matrimonial and testamentary cases. Where the payment of money or the conveyance of land was necessary, the Commission still compelled specific performance. One of the earliest cases recorded shows the Commission sequestrating a rector's income to pay his debts.

It is abundantly clear, then, that, in addition to cases which would now be recognized as ecclesiastical, the Commission regularly held plea of a vast jurisdiction now absorbed by the common-law courts—probate and divorce, slander, perjury, blasphemy, drunkenness, adultery, fornication, and all lesser moral offences—together with a good deal now heard in equity, and a great deal against which there is to-day no remedy at all. The Commission was thus something not unlike a combination of the Judicial Committee of the Privy Council, the Lord Chancellor, the Division of Probate and Divorce, the Court of Arches, the Archdeacon's courts, and the police-courts.

Nevertheless, it would be a gross error to assume that because the Commission's jurisdiction was varied and broad, it was unlimited. Its limitations were distinct and, while not always clearly seen nor always closely observed in its early years, they were none the less practically followed. It could assume jurisdiction only *in personam*, only over actions to enforce rights or obligations either of contract or tort held by some individual against some particular person, without reference to the nature of the property involved, if there was any. Of necessity, too, these must be actions upon a recognized ecclesiastical right or obligation, or against an ecclesiastic. Actions regarding real property, title to the glebe, tithes, church lands, boundaries of parishes, advowsons, impropriations, and the like properly belonged to the regular ecclesiastical courts or to the common-law courts, and such matters could not come before the Commission as the principal issue in the case, though, when they appeared incidentally, it is by no means clear that the Commission referred them to the regular tribunals for decision. We know that such cases were constantly before it, and we have nowhere a hint that the Commission did not itself decide all the subordinate issues. Probably the presence of the chief ecclesiastical judges at such hearings resulted in a following of their precedents in such matters.

Another limitation not usually believed to be true of the Commission was, that, like other courts, cases of party and party could not be initiated by the commissioners;

and that of most, if not all, the matters referred to in this chapter the Commission accepted jurisdiction only when they were brought before it in an actual suit.[1] A third limitation of great consequence lay in the fact that the wording of the Statute and of the Letters Patent, not only restricted its jurisdiction to cases *in personam*, but to criminal matters as well. Despite the many indirect ways which in time were suggested by the importunity of suitors, the ingenuity of advocates, the looseness of jurisdictional lines, and the natural desire of the commissioners themselves to increase their jurisdiction, it was not easy to implead a purely civil suit in the Commission. The Letters Patent, in addition, limited the Commission territorially, at first to England, at times to England and Ireland, and only occasionally ran to the whole of the Crown's dominions. It was intended, however, that within the limits assigned, the Commission, general or special, should override all diocesan and peculiar jurisdictions. Probably, too, the Court at London superseded at all times all other commissions, including those for York, and after 1603 for Scotland.

A final limitation appeared where men least looked for one. As one Letters Patent after another had been issued, the tendency in drafting them had been towards greater precision and explicitness of language, towards the use of long legal phrases, and towards a more logical and formal arrangement. Accordingly, the length of the Commission of 1608 was much greater than that of 1559 without really conferring much more power. In many instances,

[1] The frequency of suits *ex officio mero* in any court seems to have been much exaggerated. 'As for the Courts of Ordinaries, I know some of the greatest of them in England, that have not two matters *ex officio mero* prosecuted in them, in three yeeres space': Cosin, *Apologie*, ii, 94 (1593).

no doubt, the extension of wording was felt at the time to be an increase of power; yet definition, precision of language, the use of customary phraseology, were certainly quite as likely to create the impression that other powers were excluded and that the customary meaning must be placed upon certain phrases, as to support the contention that they extended the powers previously possessed. The broad clauses of Elizabeth's first Patent might have sanctioned many a proceeding, however irregular, and many a case, however dubious, which, under the voluminous Patents of James, many were inclined to question.

It was, nevertheless, the breadth of the Commission's jurisdiction which attracted suitors. It would reach crimes that no other ecclesiastical court could, and would render a final decision. In addition, the diocesan and county boundaries, which had hitherto so assisted rascals, were of no avail against it. Quite as important, however, in the eyes of suitors was the Commission's procedure, the writ of attachment, the bond for specific performance, the fine and imprisonment at discretion, as well as the rapidity of the court's work and the equity of its decisions.

CHAPTER V

PROCEDURE, 1580–1611

THE secret of the Commission's influence and popularity lay, in fact, in its procedure rather than in its jurisdiction. The differences between its procedure and that of the regular ecclesiastical courts caused the resort of many suitors to it, while the differences between its procedure and that of the common-law courts were responsible for the presence of another class of suitors. If the battle waged so stormily in later years was chiefly directed at the Commission's jurisdiction, no small part of it was aimed at its procedure, and the whole controversy would perhaps never have attained such proportions and excited such bitter feelings had the latter been less effective and efficient.

The Statute and Letters Patent left procedure largely to the commissioners' discretion.[1] They might 'enquire as well by the oaths of twelve good and lawful men as also by witnesses, and all other ways and means ye can devise' (sect. iii); or might 'use and devise all such politic ways and means for the trial and searching out of all the premises as by you . . . shall be thought most expedient and necessary' (s. ix). They should punish offences 'sufficiently proved against any person or persons by confession of the party or by lawful witnesses or by any

[1] The wording of the Patent of 1559 was not essentially changed till 1611. Later Patents added at times more specific details covering a power already delegated, such as the collection of fines or the examination of witnesses. Compare § xi of 1559 with § xi of 1576 in Prothero, *Select Statutes*, 230, 238.

due means' (s. ix) including examination 'upon their corporal oath' (s. x). Nor was 'proof' defined. By a tacit consent, however, torture was understood not to be included, and to our knowledge was never inflicted by the commissioners. As with jurisdiction, these clauses were not at first utilized to construct or authorize the regular organization of a court; but as the character of the Commission changed from a body of high officials called together for a short time for some special investigation to a permanent court of law, the regular ecclesiastical procedure was with some modifications adopted.

Procedure was either plenary or summary, plenary in ordinary criminal and all civil cases, summary in important criminal cases.[1] The great majority of suits before the Court were those instituted by one party against another, called *ex officio promoto*. The rest—*ex officio mero*—were prosecutions of some criminal by the Court itself, upon presentation or information regarding the crime by some party, who himself refused to prosecute, or, in rarer cases, upon information gathered by the commissioners themselves.[2] The procedure in the latter differed from suits

[1] This account of the Commission's procedure is based on Trinity Coll. (Camb.) MSS. O. 5, 21, supplemented by the brief but trustworthy account in Cosin's *Apologie*, ii, 48–50. A brief statement by Sir John Lamb, a very prominent commissioner during the decades 1620–40, is in S. P. Dom. Car. I, 450, no. 82; and has been printed in *Parl. Doc.* 1867/8, lvii, Appendix, and *Parl. Doc.* 1883, xxiv, Appendix. Considerable additional light is shed by the scattered original documents preserved in the State Papers Domestic, in the Exchequer Documents, Q. R. Eccles., among the muniments at Durham, and elsewhere. A select bibliography of these will be found in the Appendix. In the Bodleian Library, Rawlinson D 363, ff. 270–322, is a complete record of the case of John Vernon. There are other complete sets of papers in S. P. Dom. Car. I, 268, no. 63; 290, no. 73; 383, no. 47; 432, no. 27.

[2] Cosin declared (*Apologie*, ii, Preface A 3) that the court

ex officio promoto only in the preliminary stages: the Court took the place of a party in furnishing to a proctor the materials for the preliminary accusation, and then appointed an advocate to conduct its case against the accused.[1] Once begun, cases *ex officio mero* were called *ex officio mixto*, because, though instituted by the Court, they followed the regular routine procedure, and thus possessed characteristics of both methods. In suits either *ex officio mero* or *promoto*, the plenary procedure might be changed for a summary procedure, more rapid and secret, and less controlled by precedent.

The regular (plenary) procedure ran ordinarily thus. First, articles, containing the grounds of the case, called the articles original, were framed by the plaintiff's proctor or by the proctor for the Court, and had to be accepted and signed as sufficient basis for an action by the advocate of the plaintiff and by some commissioner. Then, by a writ called Letters Missive, the defendant was commanded to answer the charge, or, if he were a fugitive, he was forcibly brought before the court by a writ of attachment. The pursuivant, who served the first of these writs, was required to make an affidavit on returning that the writ had been served on the defendant's person,

proceeded *ex officio* only in criminal cases. The difficulty, however, of impleading a civil case in the Commission made this limitation less important than it at first appears.

[1] 'If a delinquent be proceeded against *ex officio mero*, the Commissioners by a publique Acte sette downe in Courte doe assigne one or more Advocates or Proctors in necessarios promotores officii.' The party proceeded against *ex officio* was protected by the court in a way later sanctioned by Patent (1611, s. xv). 'When any person shall be convented . . . at the instance . . . of any person promoting the office in that behalf, that then you shall have full power to award such costs and expenses of the suit as well to and against the party that shall prefer or present the same offence as to and against the party that shall be convented.'

left at his house, or posted on the door of his parish church. The defendant, on appearing, took an oath (the oath *ex officio*, because imposed by the judge himself by virtue of his office) to tell the truth about this matter of which he was charged 'to the best of his knowledge and belief and as far as the law would allow him'. Meanwhile he had not seen the charges against him in detail, nor had he had any legal advice if the court could hinder it. After the defendant had taken the oath, the plaintiff's proctor or the proctor for the Court might file articles additional to the articles original first presented. The defendant answered both sets of articles on oath, and his answers were written down. Then a proctor and an advocate were appointed him, if he had not already employed them, and his personal share in the case was over. The case might now be continued in one of two ways. The plaintiff might decide that the defendant's answers were such as to prove the case against him, and, in that event, the plaintiff might move for a hearing at once. In this case, however, he accepted as true the whole of the defendant's answers, and could not traverse allegations or denials; on the other hand, his own allegations, which the defendant had not already challenged or denied, were considered proved. Practically the plaintiff claimed that, even if the most favourable construction were put upon the defendant's answers, they could not clear him of the charges advanced. The advocate for the defendant might, however, demand proof from the plaintiff of some of his allegations already denied by the defendant, or might demand time to prove by witnesses his own contentions not already accepted as true. In most important cases prosecuted by the commissioners themselves the only evidence used was the defendant's answers. At the hearing before at least three commissioners, the articles original and additional and the answers to them were read in open court. The advocate for the plaintiff pointed out what made against the defendant and the advocate for the defendant replied. The commissioners gave their opinions *seriatim*, and the registrar drew up the decree according to the decision of the majority.

Usually, however, the plaintiff found he must prove his case to the Court by other means than the defendant's answers. In this case, 'terms probationary' were assigned, within which each side should present its evidence in writing, every document signed and approved by its advocate, who became responsible to the Court for any wrong-dealing or any unnecessary delay or trouble to his opponent. Each might present any number of interrogatories for the other to answer. When the evidence was all taken, the plaintiff's advocate moved that the case be heard, technically, moved 'to go to report', and the Court issued to the defendant a 'monition' of the date appointed. The Court now commanded both advocates to file with the judges a complete brief of their case and to do it a sufficient number of days before the hearing for each advocate to peruse carefully the other's brief. On the morning of the day of the hearing, in some public place, at least three of the commissioners met for 'informations', where the admissibility of evidence, the fullness of an answer, the force of an objection, the exact value of some deposition, and the like, were finally decided. The purpose of this preliminary hearing was to dispose of all that could 'hinder the dispatch of the court in the afternoon'. Either advocate might now require the other to prove any statement, but the briefs, thus amended, if approved and signed by the commissioners present, could not afterwards be questioned for matters of evidence. Either party might raise and argue a point of pleading or any other technical objection, but he must accept the ruling of the commissioners as final, and could not afterwards question the technical correctness of his opponent's case.

In the afternoon followed the actual hearing or formal trial. The procedure was in this order: the reading of the brief (approved that morning) of the plaintiff, followed by the reading of the brief for the defendant; the speech of the advocate for the plaintiff; the speech of the advocate for the defendant, neither being allowed to interrupt the other; the opinions of the judges individually; and the decree made out by the registrar.

Such was the course of proceedings provided all worked smoothly. It was more difficult to deal with an obstinate party. The fact that the Commission possessed jurisdiction only *in personam* undoubtedly had here a strong influence upon its procedure. It was absolutely necessary that the person of the defendant should be in the jurisdiction of the Court, and, if possible, in its custody. Personal service upon him of the Letters Missive was requisite to give the Court jurisdiction. If he attempted to evade service, or could not be found, constructive service was allowed by leaving the writ at his house, or by affixing it to the door of his parish church. Till this service was complete and certified to the Court, no process of contempt could issue. If, being served, he refused to appear, an 'attachment could be issued to apprehend him or an 'intimation' could be served upon him, summoning him to appear before a certain day under penalty of a fine named. These could be repeated and the fine increased until he appeared; but if he still 'stood out', nothing more could be done than to certify the fine into the Exchequer for collection. If, however, he was apprehended under an attachment and brought into court, he might then completely block proceedings by refusing the oath *ex officio*, or by answering only part of the articles proffered him. The oath *ex officio* called upon a man to 'answer the Articles or Interrogatories truely (being matters of his owne facte and knowledge so farre foorth as by lawe he is bound), before euerie particular thereof be made knowen unto him '.[1] It was of cardinal importance in the procedure. Until the defendant had been sworn he could not be examined, and until his examination was complete he could not be tried, for it was considered that until then there was nothing before the Court to justify a trial. If he did refuse to answer, he could not be pressed with lead weights until he pleaded or died, as at the common law; or tortured, as on the Continent; he could, however, be imprisoned or fined until he fulfilled the requirements of the Court. The Commission throughout had jurisdiction only of his person, and could penalize only his person or personal estate (by fines), and enforce only such decrees as they could compel him personally to execute.

If the procedure was personal and by examination upon oath, it was further entirely written. Every answer of either party or of his witnesses was taken down by 'examiners' appointed by the Court, and copies furnished his opponent as of right. All arguments and pleadings, which it became necessary to submit to the Court itself, were in writing. When the Libel had been filed by the plaintiff, the defendant filed in answer his Objection or *Exceptio*, to which the plaintiff might reply with the *Replicatio*, the defendant answer in turn with the *Dupli-*

[1] Trinity Coll. MSS.; Cosin's *Apologie*, ii, 49; Morice, Defence of a treatise of Oathes: Lambeth MSS. 234. 'In the Common Law Courts this oath is still in constant use without objection in interlocutory proceedings': Stephens, *Criminal Law*, i, 342 (London, 1883).

catio, and so on till both had exhausted their ingenuity. Each might, and indeed usually must, prove his statements by examinations and depositions of witnesses or other written evidence. Each might have the other examined on any set of questions he might prepare. A procedure so largely in writing was necessarily one which took place mainly outside the Court and in private, but rarely (if ever) in secret, in the sense that neither the accused nor his friends could find out what was going on. Even in the trials of the most obstinate Puritans, the accused was seldom really in the dark as to the nature or object of the trial, nor did he often experience much difficulty in communicating with his friends. Usually the only point in doubt was how much of his 'wrong-doing' the Commission could judicially prove. We have no evidence to show that the commissioners arrested men silently, condemned them secretly, and immured them in some dungeon, so that their friends only knew that they had disappeared. In ordinary cases, the privacy of the trial was not considered objectionable. Each party receiving from the Court examiner a sworn statement of what each witness said, neither felt it necessary to be present in person. Each party's pleading being of necessity read and answered by his opponent long before any hearing in court, it would have been superfluous to require either to plead orally. The ordinary trial seems to have been not so much in secret as outside the court-room. The safety of the accused seems to consist not in the presence of an audience, but in the right to have counsel, to know beforehand all that is to be submitted to the court at the final hearing, and to be able to make arguments and produce evidence in his own favour.

A procedure, outwardly at least, very similar to this then obtained in the common-law courts in criminal cases.

Sir Fitzjames Stephens thus characterizes criminal trials at common law between 1550 and 1637:[1]

'(1) The prisoner was kept in confinement more or less secret till his trial and could not prepare for his defence. He was examined and his examination was taken down.

'(2) He had no notice beforehand of the evidence against him, and was compelled to defend himself as well as he could, when the evidence, written or oral, was produced on his trial. He had no counsel either before or at the trial.

'(3) At the trial there were no rules of evidence as we understand the expression. The witnesses were not necessarily (to say the very least) confronted with the prisoner, nor were the originals of documents required to be produced.

'(4) The confessions of accomplices were not only admitted against each other, but were regarded as specially cogent evidence.

'(5) It does not appear that the prisoner was allowed to call witnesses in his own behalf; but it matters little whether he was or not; as he had no means of ascertaining what evidence they would give or of procuring their attendance. In later times they were not examined on oath, if they were called.'

The jury decided the questions of fact upon the 'evidence' produced in court, or upon their own personal knowledge of the case. The judge gave the decision.

Here, as in the Commission, the examination of the prisoner was the essence of the trial.[2]

Yet, despite this outward similarity in procedure and in their common attitude of hostility to the prisoner, there existed, nevertheless, between the procedure in the Commission and that at common law certain deep-rooted dissimilarities. A trial before the Commission was written

[1] *History of Criminal Law*, i, 350.

[2] 'The examination of the prisoner . . . was the very essence of the trial, and his answers regulated the production of the evidence; the whole trial, in fact, was a long argument between the prisoner and the counsel for the Crown': Stephens, i, 325.

and in private, or at least outside of the court-room, for most of its course. The common-law trial was entirely oral, public, and transacted in presence of the judges and of an audience. Further, in the Commission the trial was 'by witnesses', as the parlance of the time had it, and at common law was 'by a jury'. To the jury, however, still clung many of its early attributes.[1] They were still the chief witnesses in the case, men summoned not only because of their integrity and honesty, but for their special knowledge of the facts or of the parties.[2] It was, in truth, beginning to be necessary that they should be 'informed' by counsel and witnesses of the facts of the case, but they were nevertheless to follow their own knowledge even if it contradicted all that counsel had apparently proved. If they gave a wrong verdict, they might be punished for it.[3] This character of the jury naturally influenced and retarded the development of the law of evidence at common law,[4] for its essential principle has been the exclusion from the jury's knowledge of all the matter of fact or of opinion which was not relevant or admissible in that particular case. Yet, so long as the jury might upon their own knowledge give a verdict

[1] On this general subject see J. B. Thayer, *Trial by Jury*.

[2] Nicholas Fuller, *Argument in the case of Ladd and Mansell*, 12 (1607). 'The Jurors being all sworn to trie the particular matter in fact . . . being 12 persons different without any affinitie to either partie, who better knowe the witnesses than the Judge and may perhaps know the cause in question as well as the witness.' 'The evidence of witnesses to the jury is no part of the trial, for by law the trial in that case is not by witnesses, but by the verdict of twelve men': Coke, *Third Institute*, 26. Cf. *id.* 79, 110, 163.

[3] 'A jury's verdict then meant the solemn sworn statement on their own knowledge given under the penalty of an attaint': Thayer, *Cases on Evidence*, 419, note (2nd ed.).

[4] 'The English Law of Evidence had hardly begun to come into existence,' in the year 1609: *id.* 508, note.

contrary to the evidence produced by witnesses and parties,[1] the jury's knowledge far outweighed in importance the evidence submitted to them, and made consequently of little value rules of admission and exclusion which applied to the latter only. Until all evidence, except what was admitted in court, could be kept from the jury, there was little value in building up a system of rules regarding its admission or rejection. So long, too, as this wide discretion of accepting or rejecting what was told them remained to the jury, and so long as they might keep to themselves what they knew and not state the evidence which guided their decision,[2] it was immensely difficult to know how a point could be proved or disproved to their satisfaction. In truth, almost any kind of evidence was admitted, direct, circumstantial or hearsay, without any attempt at distinction, except between the testimony of an eyewitness and all other evidence whatever.[3] One witness was amply sufficient to prove any charge except treason,[4] and even in treason trials the statutory requirement of two witnesses was by no means literally interpreted.[5]

[1] 'The evidence in Court is not binding evidence to a jury': Bushell's Case, Vaughan's *Report*, 152 (1670).

[2] *Bennet* v. *Hundred of Hartford*, Styles, 233 (1650).

[3] 'The (common law) Judges of that day recognized no distinction between different kinds of evidence, except the distinction of an eye witness to the actual crime and every thing else.' If this was abandoned, 'no other line could be drawn. There was no reason why the most remote and insignificant hearsay should not be admitted': Stephens, *Criminal Law*, i, 336.

[4] 'In almost every other accusation (except treason) one positive witness is sufficient': 4 Blackstone, 357. 'Those laws which condemn a man to death in any case on the deposition of a single witness are fatal to Liberty' (Montesquieu), of which Blackstone disapproved. 'They must here proceed according to the rules of the common law and therefore cannot require two witnesses': Burn, *Ecclesiastical Law* (Phillimore's ed.), ii, 48.

[5] Stephens, *Criminal Law*, i, 336.

The trial in the Commission, on the other hand, was in essence a trial by witnesses and by strict rules of evidence. At common law all evidence was admitted, but the question of its weight was left solely to the jury, who might give it any weight they saw fit or leave it altogether out of consideration. In the Commission, all evidence was likewise admitted, but its weight was determined by the civil-law rules and precedents,[1] which weighed each bit of evidence and assigned it a definite place in the scheme of proof. The proof must of necessity be conclusive ‘ beyond possibility of doubt ’, but it need not be composed wholly of evidence of the first calibre. Proof was of three grades of pertinency: complete proof,[2] other evidence directly in point (indices prochains), and other evidence indirectly in point (indices éloignés).[3] These might be made up from four sorts of evidence, witnesses, confessions, documents, and circumstantial evidence.[4] From any one of these might be created a ‘ complete proof ’ which alone could convict. The strongest complete proof was that of two eyewitnesses to the fact, concurring in their testimony. This being but rarely available, complete proof was usually deduced from a combination of other evidence,

[1] Menochius, *De Praesumptionibus, Conjecturis, Signis et Indiciis*; Esmein, *Procédure Criminelle en France*; Practica Juris Civilis in Curiis Ecclesiasticis, Harl. MSS. 1749; Cosin, *Apologie*; Fulbecke, *A Parallele or Conference of the Civil Law, the Canon Law, and the Common Law of this Realme of England.*

[2] See Cosin, *Apologie*, ii, 104. ‘ Perfect proof ’ at civil law applied only to capital crimes. These were beyond the Commission's competency, so it possessed only the jurisdiction recognized at civil law as non-capital. ‘ Dans les accusations qui ne sont pas capitales, il est évident qu'il ne faut pas de preuves aussi fortes, . . . mais lorsqu'il n'y a que de forts indices, leur force ne peut déterminer que des peines pécuniaires ’: Poullain du Parc, tom. xi, 116. Esmein, 266.

[3] Esmein, *Procédure Criminelle*, 269.

[4] *Ibid.* 266.

which, even though specific and exactly in point, must be valued (because less than complete proof) in a fashion which approached a rough mathematical scale,[1] so as to show its value relative to the testimony of two eye-witnesses. In determining the relative value of this indirect evidence, and in deciding whether it was half-proof, or only one-sixteenth proof and the like, the presumption raised by a particular fact for or against one party was felt to be of great importance, and was held to create a burden of proof which told heavily for or against him until removed.

These presumptions were exceedingly numerous and of all possible degrees and values.[2] In the Commission, where there was no torture and confessions were few, these came to occupy a position of utmost importance. So great was the difficulty of convicting the accused under this system, that the initial presumption was held to be against him. In fact, this meant little more than that his accusation had thrown a suspicion upon his innocence which must lie there till removed, nor could it in theory possibly be detrimental, for, unless the proof of his guilt were perfect beyond possibility of doubt, he could not be convicted.[3] The articles of the plaintiff thus raised a presumption against the defendant, which the latter's answer ought to refute and, by raising a similar presumption in his own favour, shift the burden of proof to his adversary.

[1] 'Indices prochains' were sometimes called 'semi-preuves'; English writers say that the valuation was carried out to the point of giving every variety a fraction of one. The civilians, however, protested against any such statement of 'semi-preuves'. 'C'est un nom barbare et imaginaire . . . il n'y a point de demi-vérité': Esmein, 275.

[2] See Menochius, *De praesumptionibus*. Also Bonnier, *Traité des Preuves*.

[3] 'Without the parties confession, or two witnesses, none may be absolutely conuicted': Cosin, *Apologie*, ii, 104.

Attention was chiefly directed toward these points in a trial before the Commission, for by them alone was there much chance of breaking down a strong case. So, while at common law forms of action and oral pleadings were most important, in the Commission's practice most attention was devoted to shifting the presumption and the burden of proof by written pleadings.

A further characteristic of trials in the Commission was the attempt to elucidate all the facts possible, and to prove or disprove every fact, because, theoretically, the case must be completely proved, and each fact, however small, might be of value. Hence nothing was admitted at the beginning of the case. At common law, on the other hand, the lawyers endeavoured to separate the law and the facts. The whole case was narrowed down to a single point, the point at issue, whose decision would settle the case and which was to be, moreover, one suitable for a jury to pass upon. Hence all facts not material to the issue were often admitted by the parties.[1] A judge, trained in the law, might well be trusted to separate the issue, weigh all the facts, and pronounce a just decision upon the whole of the evidence. On the other hand, a jury was not trained in the law and its subtleties, and its members were ill fitted to select the point at issue, although their qualifications might be clear, as witnesses and as men knowing the case, to decide it correctly, once it was developed. This single issue could further be discussed in court, and indeed must be elucidated orally in order that the twelve men might all hear it at the same

[1] 'Contrarie to the maner of the Ciuill Lawe where first the fact is examined by witnesses indices . . . to finde out the trueth thereof, . . . here the sergeants . . . doe in passing forward with their pleading . . . come to the issue and state of some fact which is denied of the one partie, and auerred of the other': Sir Thomas Smith, *Commonwealth of England*, 78.

time. Where, however, the judge was required to examine all the evidence and weigh presumptions, great and small, it was expedient that the greater part of the pleadings should be written and should be perused outside the court-room. By both procedures, the judges in practice controlled the trial. In the Commission, it was doubtful whether their associates could legally hamper the discretion of three commissioners. At common law, the jury was in the judge's hands. Unless the civil-law rules were followed for the production of evidence, 'the jury were practically absolute and might decide upon anything which they thought fit to consider evidence. On the other hand, as the prisoner had no counsel, no books, no means of procuring evidence, no right to give it if he did procure it, the jury were practically in the hands of the court.'[1] The judge had full discretion to punish them if they did not decide as he thought they should, and the possibility of attaint was very much alive to a sixteenth-century juryman.

[1] Stephens, *Criminal Law*, i, 337.

CHAPTER VI

THE GROWTH OF SYSTEMATIC OPPOSITION TO THE COMMISSION

THE very existence of an ecclesiastical commission for the maintenance of the royal supremacy is proof that an opposition also existed : the commissioners were appointed solely to overcome opposition, and the broad powers and unlimited discretion vested in them testify eloquently to the contemporary belief in its strength and tenacity. The early commissioners, in fact, had been allotted the difficult task of coping with those who opposed the new religious settlements from conscientious reasons, and could hardly have expected their victims, whether Roman Catholics or Puritans, to kiss the rod that smote them. Neither could fail to consider any instrument tyrannical which attempted in even the gentlest way to secure their observance to ceremonies which they believed were not approved by God.[1] Not less harsh was the language of the brutal husband or simoniacal curate, who knew that

[1] 'Or let them signifie unto us what a good manner of discipline and moderation it was for a Bp. and his associates, to make an act, in the High Commission Court, repugnant to the institution of our Saviour Christ and contrarie to the order appoynted by the booke of common prayer, that the minister should put the sacramentall bread into the mouth of a superstitious communicant' : Stoughton, *An Assertion for True and Christian Church Policy* (1604), 333. There is no other evidence of the exercise of so important a function by the commissioners after 1565. This shows how far we are from possessing enough information to write a really detailed account of the commissioners' doings which would even *prima facie* appear complete.

but for the commissioners he would not have been punished at all. Again, the acquiescence of the laity in the moral jurisdiction of the clergy had been accorded with less and less readiness for nearly two centuries, and when the commissioners undertook the task of enforcing it, the very notion of such an authority had become abhorrent to a considerable proportion of the population. In enforcing the censorship of the press, too, the commissioners were running counter to the ideas of that increasingly large number of people who were claiming liberty of thought and expression. Nor has it been difficult on all these grounds for the commissioners' opponents to gain the ear of posterity and 'prove' 'the High Commission' tyrannical, brutal, and oppressive, an enemy of liberty and freedom and of the truth itself.

Yet the commissioners were obviously not responsible for any one of these notions they were enforcing. Such ideas were the legacies of the past. Nor did the commissioners take the initiative and choose them as their especial duties. While no doubt they believed honestly in the justice and rightness of their course, State and Church, which controlled them, and which decided that Puritan and Roman Catholic should conform, that the moral jurisdiction over the laity should be upheld, and that the press should be censored, must bear the ultimate responsibility. In last analysis, both State and Church expressed simply the general consensus of opinion in the western world at that time ; both naturally sought some method for executing the conception of law and justice then prevalent. That ecclesiastical commissioners, expressly appointed for the performance of work certain to meet with vigorous resistance, should have acted in a way which their victims would be certain to consider oppressive, proves, therefore, not that the commissioners were really brutal and unnecessarily severe, but that a sharp clash of opinion existed in England at this time as to which was the true religion necessary for salvation. The State had chosen one side, and was employing the commissioners to secure conformity to its creed by such forcible means as they might find necessary.

We must be careful, however, not to confuse the active opposition to the commissioners' visitatorial authority, on the part of the 'culprits' they were ordered to punish, with a systematic opposition on legal grounds to the jurisdiction or procedure of the Court of High Commission. A court of law, slowly evolved by circumstances to meet an actual need, meets no 'inevitable' opposition, and, in sooth, the mere recognition of its existence predicates with certainty the approval of the great majority of the community. We can be perfectly sure that every man examined or tried by the early commissioners was present against his will; we can be no less positive that every man who sued another individual before the Court of High Commission was present at its bar because he expected to derive some positive advantage from bringing suit there. In the one case opposition was the normal state of affairs; in the other it was, and always would be, exceptional. If in the one case its existence was the efficient cause for the commissioners' own existence, in the other an equally widespread opposition would have made the growth of a law-court impossible. Nor could a systematic legal opposition begin until the Court had become definitely established. An attempt to insist that a certain case could not be heard or a certain procedure could not be used, could not hope for success as long as the commissioners' jurisdiction and procedure were limited only by their own discretion. A claim that the oath *ex officio* was illegal, and that a copy of the libel should be given to the accused before, and not after the oath was taken, could only arise after the Commission's procedure had assumed a definite judicial form officially recognized. Nor could the commissioners be in the least concerned about opposition to this or that procedure so long as they could in practice proceed with equal legality in any way they saw fit. The whole force of any legal opposition depended entirely upon the assumption by the Commission itself of the position of a law-court for the trial of suits between party and party by a definite regular procedure in consonance with a jurisdiction which must have had some recognized limits, however broad a competence they may have assigned to the Court. Nor can anything testify more convincingly to the extent to which the Commission had assumed such a position than the rise of such an opposition. The arbitrary power and summary procedure of the early days must have absolutely vanished.

In 1584 the Puritans delivered the first[1] quasi-legal assault. To be sure, a few of them had already defied the commissioners; from time to time a prisoner had escaped or been rescued from the commissioners' pursuivants; a good deal of contempt of the Commission's process and sentences had appeared;[2] yet much of this trouble was

[1] 'As for the Ecclesiastical Commission, I see it foully abused and if it be not reformed by a new [Patent ?] it will work inconvenience': Parker to Burghley, Nov. 15, 1573; *Parker Correspondence*, 450. Does this mean that the Commission was opposed or that the Commissioners themselves were abusing their powers? Cosin (*Apologie*, i, 109) says, in 1593, that the opposition was recent, and this would support the contention that systematic opposition must have dated from about 1584. The fact that the Court did not probably take definite shape much before 1580 also makes it unlikely that the opposition began earlier.

[2] Cases have already been cited in the previous chapters. The Duchess of Suffolk attempted to save Robert Browne from the

incidental to the establishment of a new court, whose judges had in the past exercised chiefly visitatorial functions and whose judicial status was not yet clear. The cause of the assault, delivered in the autumn of the year 1584, was Whitgift's Twenty-four Articles, upon which the commissioners proposed to examine Puritans and (perhaps) others after they had taken the oath *ex officio*. Unquestionably, this work was visitatorial in character, and in it we see the confusion of functions entailed by the transformation of the old session of the commissioners into a judicial hearing. The attempt to conduct these visitatorial investigations under the new judicial forms gave the Puritans opportunity for a new type of obstruction which may fairly be called legal.

From their friends among the courtiers and ministers of state, as well as from the first culprits examined, the Puritans soon learned that truthful answers to these Articles would undoubtedly convict them of individual nonconformity, and, what was infinitely worse, furnish the State with proof of the deep-laid plans for creating a presbyterian system within the English Church. They had just been assured by certain common lawyers that their scheme was not contrary to Statute law; they had already instituted presbyterian classes and were planning to hold provincial, and even national, assemblies as soon

commissioners by claiming that he was privileged as the chaplain of a peeress. Parker promptly wrote her: 'Our commission extendeth to all places as well exempt as not exempt within her Majesty's dominions, and before this time never by any called into question. . . . We would be loth to use other means to bring him to his answer, as we must be forced to do if your Grace will not like hereof': *Parker Correspondence*, 390, Jan. 13, 1571/2, from the original in the Petyt MSS. Strype (*Parker*, ii, 68) says the letter was written to the Duke of Norfolk and gives the date as June 13. See also *Parte of a Register*, 393; *Privy Council Register*, xi, 137; xiii, 30; Strype, *Annals*, III, part i, 177–9.

as a sufficient number of districts could be organized. To take the oath and then not tell the truth was to commit perjury and was manifestly out of the question; but, as the Commission's procedure, like all civil-law procedure, required for the proof of the guilt of the accused no further evidence than the admissions in his own sworn testimony, it was evident that the Puritan who took the oath and told the simple truth would instantly provide legally perfect proof of his nonconformity. This was the more galling because the Puritans were almost positive that the commissioners possessed no direct evidence sufficiently conclusive to prove their guilt according to any judicial forms then in use, and they therefore believed that, if they could avoid the oath and hence not testify, they could not possibly be convicted at all. After long and anxious debates in the classes and earnest discussions with the 'godly' lawyers, they finally determined to refuse to take the oath and alleged in defence a great variety of reasons regarding its injustice and cruelty in compelling a man to convict himself, its moral turpitude, and its lack of consonance with the Scriptures.[1]

The whole situation was, of course, understood by the commissioners, who promptly declared that the reasons assigned by the Puritans for declining the oath were mere subterfuges to thwart the execution of justice. The oath itself, they protested, contained no trap, nor was it in any sense an engine of unfairness or oppression. The accused,

[1] The most important original documents for this subject are in Usher, *Presbyterian Movement in the Reign of Queen Elizabeth*, Camden Society, 1905; Bancroft's *Survay of the Pretended Holy Discipline*. Fuller in his *Church History*, a Brewer's edition, v, 105, gives certain arguments *pro* and *con* the oath *ex officio*, dated 1587. Fuller does not state clearly how they appeared, nor who made them. Probably the date should be twenty or more years later, for they seem to belong to a more advanced stage of the controversy than had been reached in 1587.

if he took it in the fullest manner, only swore to answer truly the questions asked him. The mere fact that he had not seen the questions to be asked was of no consequence; surely, an innocent man could not possibly be injured by answering truthfully any number of questions he had never seen about crimes he had not committed. Nor could he be legally convicted by sworn answers which denied all knowledge or participation in the crimes charged. The only possible adequate reason for refusing the oath was the man's own knowledge that he was guilty and would legally convict himself. Distrust of the commissioners' probity was no valid reason, they declared; for, if the commissioners were so determined to punish him, whether he was guilty or not, that they would distort the testimony of an innocent man into a confession of guilt, he was at their mercy already, and the refusal of a dozen oaths could not save him from conviction; their Letters Patent explicitly authorized them to proceed by any means they might see fit to employ. The very tender of the oath, insisted the commissioners, was an evidence of their good faith and intention to convict only those whom they could prove guilty by ordinary judicial methods. When the Puritan offered to testify unsworn, the commissioners ill concealed their scorn. Did he suppose, they demanded, that God listened any the less when he perjured himself unsworn than when he had taken the oath? Did he perjure himself any less truly by intention than by words? There was much searching of consciences among the Puritans, but they finally concluded that they were warranted in misleading the examiners if they could; without swearing, if possible; even when sworn, if they must.[1] They were doing the

[1] 'Formes for Answering Interrogatories': Queen's College MSS. (Oxford) 121, f. 380. '(1) What termes to denie the whole

Lord's will; should they, then, deliver themselves into the hands of the Spoiler merely because he requested them to tell him the truth? These 'Baal's Minions' meant to convict them thus of the crime of believing in the true doctrine of Christ Jesus and of worshipping Him in the exact way He had commanded. Should they, then, allow themselves to be ejected simply because they refused to countenance mummery and lip-service and declined to bow down in the House of Rimmon? Should they deny their Master and serve Mammon? They were, however, more than anxious to save themselves from the dilemma by preventing the tender of the oath at all, and to this end attempted to secure an order from the Privy Council or from the Queen to the commissioners forbidding the latter to employ the oath. This, they seem to have felt, would have solved the difficulty, and they would have answered unsworn whatever was asked. Petitions in a flood were sent to the influential lords and to Elizabeth herself,[1] and the correspondence between Whitgift and Burghley on the subject is too well known to require more

interrogatory. To a fact of his owne or owne knowledge, responsum. I did not doe as in the Interrogatory; I did not to my memory doe, etc., I doe not know that I did or said any such thing. (2) How to answer some facts and deny the rest. He did doe or say such a thing and the rest he answers negatively as he denies the Interrogatory. . . . . (6) What to say to a Commissioner that shall presse him to sweare and to remember himselfe. I am upon oathe and not you and I pray you to forbeare. I am upon oath leave me to my conscience. You are to take my answer not directe itt. (7) What to an Interrogatory if he hath been instructed or taught what to say . . .'

[1] Copies of many of these petitions are in Morrice MSS. A, B, C. Harl. MSS. 360, ff. 85 and 86 contain a contemporary list of the Puritans hardly dealt with and a list of 43 petitions made between 1580 and 1586. For the general ecclesiastical situation see Usher's *Reconstruction of the English Church*, Book I, chap. iii. See also Morrice MSS. L, V, f. 9.

than an allusion.[1] It failed, however, to avert the dilemma. The leaders then began a consistent attempt at legal obstruction.

Allen and Carew complained to the Privy Council in November 1584 [2] that the proceedings of the commissioners were illegal, for they refused bail, 'whereas the Law of England permitteth Bayle'; and 'whereas the Commission Ecclesiasticall requireth their warrants to be made under the hands of three which is to be intended ioyntly, upon Information in the cause, the warrants are made by the B[ishop], and sent hither and thither for the subscription of hands, and many times men Arrested and haled up by private letters of one out of the Dioces'. In other words, they declared that the commissioners did not observe the technicalities of their own procedure, and hence could not be proceeding legally. Carew even told the commissioners that he was not obliged to make a full answer to the Articles because that 'maner of proceeding [by oath *ex officio*] is meere contrary to the Lawe of England and to the said Commission'. The Court then committed him for contempt, which he also declared was illegal. 'The Commission Ecclesiastical giveth him (*sic*) no authority to committ to prison but in cases of the Commission and after a fact duely proved, and therefore this Commitment is contrary to the Lawes of England.' [3] Paget also assured the commissioners that they could not deprive him, 'for the ground is refusall to Subscribe to Articles tendred by the Ecclesiasticall Commissioners, who had no warrant to offer any such Articles at all. For their authority reacheth no further than to reforme and

[1] An accurate reprint from the originals of these famous letters is in *Historical MSS. Com. Report, MSS. of the Marquis of Bath*, ii. Copies from Whitgift's Letter-book (now lost) are in Morrice MSS. L, V, f. 13.

[2] Morrice MSS. C, p. 652.

[3] Morrice MSS. C, p. 651.

correct facts done, contrary to certaine Statutes expressed in their Commission, and contrary to other Ecclesiastical Lawes, but there was never yett any Clause in their Commission to offer subscription to Articles other then to Mass Priests in the Case of the Statutes made the 13th of her Majesties Reigne.' [1] Here we certainly have objections based ostensibly on something more than theological disagreement. These are appeals to law to settle definite questions of jurisdiction and procedure. The only answer, however, vouchsafed by the Commission to this denial of the legality of its acts was to commit the offenders to jail for contempt.

The Puritans straightway petitioned Parliament to abolish the oath, and amongst other things, prayed that there should be only two Commissions, one at London and the other at York, ' seeing the manner of proceedinge in the Commission is fownde to be greevous to the subjects and not ordinarie in itself,' and declared that in 1559 only one commission was issued at a time when the need was much greater than at this time. They also asked for the reform of citations by including ' the matter of accusation and name of the accuser '. An answer to this petition accepted the first point, but demurred to the second, on the ground, first, that churchwardens would not present crimes if compelled to go on record individually as accusers, and second, that the common-law process did not give such information and yet had roused no opposition.[2] The bishops also answered the petition,[3] and claimed that the oath *ex officio* could not be abolished without practically making impossible the use of excom-

[1] Morrice MSS. B, II, f. 68.

[2] Harl. MSS. 358, f. 224 (1584 ?). The petition is lost, and we learn of it only from the answer.

[3] Strype, *Whitgift*, iii, 124–30.

munication altogether, 'saving when the partie confesseth his impenitence; which very seldom or neuer will happen.' Again, they urged, 'eyther the Bishop must dismisse the preacher upon his single deniall of the fact, or ells, *ex officio*, putt him to his oath.'

Thus prompted, the House of Commons actually passed a Bill reforming the ecclesiastical procedure against ministers and containing certain provisions hostile to the commissioners, whose details we do not know, but which greatly excited the Archbishop.[1] The Commons then respectfully requested a conference with the Lords. They explained that, after all, they did not ask much: 'it is only required that the abuses of the Bb. and Commissioners Ecclesiasticall against the word of God, the prerogatiue of the Crowne, the Lawes, liberties, and Customes of this free realm of England, against the auntient Canons and Councills and *against her Majesties Comission Ecclesiasticall* should be reformed and redressed.'[2] The Commission ought to be expounded, 'stricti juris according to the letter,' which showed no warrant whatever for the oath *ex officio*, 'the swearing of them to answere to they know not what,' for citing ministers from remote places to London, for refusal to show the articles to the accused before he was sworn, for refusing bail, and the like. An even more precise statement appeared in a Puritan offer to the bishops, called 'Meanes of Unitye', which asked that the jurisdiction of the Commission be limited to 'heresy, schisme, abuses,

[1] 'There is likewise now in hand in the same house, a Bill concerning Ecclesiasticall courts, and Visitations of Bps. which may reach to the overthrow of Ecclesiasticall Iurisdiction, and Study of the Civill Lawes': Whitgift to the Queen, Mar. 24, 1584/5; Morrice MSS. L, V, p. 15 (from Whitgift's Letter-book).

[2] Petyt MSS. 538. 36, f. 319. The italics are the author's.

offences, enormities, according to lawe and the Comission Ecclesiasticall and the true meaning of the same '.[1] In reality these demands, which apparently contained nothing more than the very reasonable request that the commissioners should observe the law and their own Letters Patent, attacked vital points of the new law-court's institution ; the right to obtain the defendant's sworn testimony before he had had a chance to find out just how much was known of his doings, the right to imprison for contempt, the right to extend its jurisdiction over all England without respect to persons and without regard to other jurisdictional lines. The intervention of the Queen, and the support of the common-law courts defeated for the time this scheme to limit the Commission's authority. The next year a Puritan named Black took the oath with the important reservation that he did not consider himself bound ' to answere to matters criminall or captious '. He seems also to have claimed the right to object to the testimony of certain men who, he said, were his enemies.[2]

It was in the year following, however, that the Commission found its procedure for dealing with the refractory severely tested by Barrow's use of these objections.[3] After a long attempt to get him to swear in any fashion or form, the commissioners found they must either go on without any oath or stop proceedings. They got no satisfaction

[1] Petyt MSS. 538. 36, f. 324.

[2] Lambeth MSS., Carta Miscellanea, xii, f. 19.

[3] *The Examinations of Henry Barrowe, John Greenwood, and John Penrie, before the high commissioners and Lordes of the Counsell, Penned by the prisoners themselves before their deathes.* No doubt the account is exaggerated and was meant to prove the cruelty and tyranny of the commissioners. C. Burrage, in *Early English Dissenters* (Camb. 1912), i, 128–9, believes the date in the tract, 1586, to be an error for 1587.

out of him. Whitgift asked him when he was at church last. 'That is nothing to you,' returned Barrow. To the question, 'Haue you spoken these wordes of the church of England,' he replied, 'When you produce your witnesses I wil answer.' 'Of what occupation are you?' 'A Christian,' he said. 'So are we al,' interposed Whitgift. 'I denye that,' challenged Barrow. In the end, as he refused to take any oath, to give bond, or to answer properly any questions at all, he was sent to the Gatehouse. Eight days later he was again before the Court, and this time offered to swear, if he could first see the articles prepared against him. When, however, Whitgift had them read to him, he promptly declined to take an oath to answer truthfully any such questions. He was remanded to the Gatehouse, where they left him five months to think it over, and then, on March 24, 1586/7, called a special session to deal with him, at which were present both Chief Justices, the Lord Chief Baron and another Baron of the Exchequer, the Master of the Rolls, the Archbishop of Canterbury, the Bishops of London and Winchester, with their Chancellors, and several civil lawyers and notaries. But this imposing array of judicial authority did not in the least shake Barrow's determination not to swear. Whitgift then dispensed with the oath and even allowed Barrow to write out his own answers to the interrogatories. But all to no purpose; the Commission was as far from having any judicial basis on which to proceed as before. This insistent attempt to conduct his trial according to set form and precedent is the more remarkable in view of the unlimited discretion still vested in the commissioners for dealing with obstinate men by any procedure or lack of procedure. After six months of effort, the Commission as a court gave up a case which the earlier commissioners would have disposed of with ease and rapidity, and appealed to the Privy Council to sustain its jurisdiction.

Accordingly, on May 18, 1587, Barrow was brought before the Council and showed that august body no greater respect than he had the Commission. In describing the case, Whitgift declared that the culprit was not a learned man; whereupon Barrow promptly interjected this soothing remark: 'The Lord knoweth I am ignorant. I haue no learning to boast of: but this I know that you are voide of al true learning and godliness.' 'See the spirit of this man,' exclaimed Lord Buckhurst. Finally, according to Barrow, the Lord Chancellor pointed to the Archbishop, and asked, 'What is that man?' 'The Lord gave me', says Barrow, 'the spirit of boldness so that I answered: He is a monster, a miserable Compound, I know not what to make him: he is neither Ecclesiasticall nor ciuill, euen that second Beast spoken of in the Reuelation.' And being asked to explain himself, he turned to the thirteenth chapter of Revelation and 'read a little', comparing Whitgift to the Beast with horns like a lamb that spoke like a dragon, which 'deceiveth them that dwell on the earth by the means of those miracles', and compelled people on earth to worship the image of the first Beast or be killed, and which marked all men with the sign of the Beast. 'Then I turned to 2 Thess. 2.' and read: 'Let no man deceive you by any means: for that day shall not come, except there come a falling away first, and that man of sin be revealed, the son of perdition; Who opposeth and exalteth himself above all that is called God, or that is worshipped; so that he as God sitteth in the temple of God, shewing himself that he is God.' 'But the Beast arose for anger gnashing his teeth and said wil you suffer him, my Lords? So I was pluckt up by the warden's man from my knees and carried away.' Greenwood made a somewhat similar scene and was similarly incarcerated.

An even more notable and much better known case occurred in 1591 and 1592 at the trial of the Puritans arrested for attempting to practise the Book of Discipline.[1] Cartwright, their leader, imitated Barrow's tactics, declined the oath *ex officio*, and demanded the right to give his testimony informally. He objected, in fact, to every step that looked like judicial procedure. His friends followed his example, and the Commission, after a long attempt to break down their firmness, was at last constrained to call in the aid of the Star Chamber, whose authority would at least frighten the Puritans into pleading to the jurisdiction of the court. For this trial the commissioners furnished the evidence,[2] but could not show anything conclusive enough to convict. The Puritans had triumphantly proved that the Commission could be successfully opposed by refusing the oath *ex officio*, thus renouncing the jurisdiction of the Court. Of course the Commission could have imprisoned them all for the remainder of their lives or have confiscated all their property for so aggravated a contempt of court. It was not considered expedient, however, to punish them for the contempt, because the whole purpose of the prosecution had been to reveal the truth about the Classis Movement to the general public (the government had long known it) and to demonstrate the illegality of the Puritans' methods before a regular ecclesiastical tribunal by a formal and regular procedure, in order to show that the Church was warranted by law in punishing such

[1] This has been told in some detail, with references to the chief original documents, in Usher's *Reconstruction of the English Church*, i, 62–5.

[2] The original 'brief of the Byl in the Star Chamber' with Whitgift's annotations is Additional MSS. 32092, f. 126.

conduct and was quite capable of doing it by its own machinery. In this the Commission so conspicuously failed that the government judged it best not to create martyrs to the cause by dealing severely with the Puritans arraigned: to imprison them longer would only emphasize the inability of the Commission to handle the original case. The men were therefore soon released. The Puritan attitude towards the Commission found expression in such pasquinades as the following mock epitaph which was floating around the London streets in 1592:

'This is the corps of Roger Rippon, a servant of Christ, and her Majestys faithful subject. Who is the last of sixteen or seventeen which that great enemy of God, the archbishop of Canterbury, with his high commissioners have murdered in Newgate within these five years manifestly for the testimony of Jesus Christ. His soul is now with the Lord; his blood crieth for speedy vengeance against that great enemy of the saints and against Mr. Richard Young, who in this, and many the like points, hath abused his power, for the upholding of the Romish Antichrist, prelacy and priesthood.' [1]

Meanwhile an entirely different sort of attack on the Commission was delivered by Robert Cawdry, who, as we have seen, had already been examined by the commissioners for Puritan practices, and who had finally been deprived by his bishop acting in his capacity of High Commissioner.[2] The new incumbent, inducted into the living by the bishop, was promptly sued by Cawdry in Queen's Bench for trespass.[3] From the first it was

[1] Strype, *Annals*, iv, 186.

[2] The original decree is in Lansdowne MSS. 53, no. 72 (Latin).

[3] The preliminaries, &c., of the case are told in the Articles Original in the Commission which are in Morrice MSS. C, p. 790, an abstract of which has already been given above in chapter iii. The tale is also told at length in Strype's *Aylmer*, 84–97; *Annals*, III, part i, 262. The proceedings in the Queen's Bench we know only from Coke, *Reports*, v, 1.

apparent that the case was a test case. It had already run the gamut of the ecclesiastical tribunals on one plea or another, and it had now come to a common-law court to learn whether or not some grounds might be found which would induce the latter to interfere, and so provide precedent for a sort of appeal from the Commission's sentence which would block the deprivation of Cawdry or any other minister in fact, whether it did or not in law. The chance was slight: the deprivation of clergymen was unquestionably a matter of ecclesiastical cognizance, nor was there a shadow of precedent to show that the Queen's Bench had ever decided what was sufficient cause for deprivation, or what technicalities of procedure were necessary to accomplish it. Yet the only issue in the case of trespass was the validity of the deprivation; if Cawdry had been legally deprived, there could have been no trespass. Cawdry and his counsel fully appreciated the fact that their only chance for victory lay in proving a failure to comply with the letter of certain of the Reformation Statutes. His declaration therefore alleged (1) that the Act of Uniformity authorized deprivation only for the second offence: whereas he had been deprived for the first offence; (2) that the form of the Act had not been observed in his deprivation, for the sentence should have been given 'by verdict of 12 men or by confession or by notorious evidence of the fact', whereas he was sentenced by default, 'in respect he appeared not.' He asserted (3) that the sentence had not been given in proper form, since the bishop had sentenced him 'with' the consent of others, whereas three or more commissioners ought to 'join' in the sentence. He declared (4) that the commissioners were not nominated or appointed according to the Act of 1 Eliz., c. 1, for the sentence did not anywhere show that they were natural born subjects of the Queen, as the Act required.

These technicalities, though far from permitting the discussion of the real offence for which Cawdry had been deprived, did raise an issue of immense significance. Could the common-law courts indirectly but effectively decide upon the technical perfection of so undoubtedly an ecclesiastical matter as the deprivation of the clergy? Were not the Reformation Statutes to be interpreted by the ecclesiastical courts which unquestionably were to enforce them? The logical consequences of such propositions reached to the very verge of ecclesiastical authority and cast doubt upon all ecclesiastical jurisdiction.

The decision went against Cawdry, but the dicta, which were at once recognized as embodying notable and far-reaching constructive propositions, were of much greater importance than the decision in the history of the Commission as well as of the Church. The bishop, said the Court, was not divested of his ordinary ecclesiastical authority by the Statute of Uniformity, nor was he forced by the Act to follow any particular form of punishment. He had full and sufficient power apart from the Act or the Letters Patent to have deprived Cawdry for the first offence. The Court thus cleverly avoided the necessity of deciding the technical questions of procedure raised by Cawdry, because, if he had been legally deprived by any procedure, there could have been no trespass. But though the only issue before the Court was already decided, the judges (according to Coke) proceeded to consider the general issue. They stated distinctly that the Act of Elizabeth could not itself be considered to have described the limits of the Commission's authority by merely affirming the ancient jurisdiction ecclesiastical.

Nor could there be any doubt of the present Commission's legality.

> 'It was resolved by all the Judges that the King or Queen of England for the time being may make such an ecclesiastical Commission as is before mentioned by the ancient prerogative and law of England.'

This opinion the judges who gave it and Coke who reported it conveniently forgot in later days. And,

> 'seeing their authority is to proceed and give sentence in ecclesiastical causes, according to the ecclesiastical law, and they have given a sentence in a cause ecclesiastical upon their proceedings, by force of that law; the Judges of the common law ought to give faith and credit to their sentence, and allow it to be done according to the ecclesiastical law.'

Much was said apparently about the complementary character of the ecclesiastical and common-law jurisdictions, their equal right to respect and authority, and the equal credit each should give to each other's proceedings, assuming always that each best understood the technicalities of its own procedure. The Crown was

> 'instituted and furnished with plenary and entire power, prerogative and jurisdiction, to render justice and right to every part and member of this body, of what estate, degree, or calling soever in all causes ecclesiastical or temporal, otherwise he should not be a head of the whole body. And as in temporal causes, the King, by the mouth of the Judges in his courts of Justice doth judge and determine the same by the temporal laws of England: so in causes ecclesiastical and spiritual, . . . (the conusance whereof belongs not to the common laws of England,) the same are to be determined and decided by ecclesiastical Judges, according to the King's ecclesiastical laws of this realm: . . . so albeit the Kings of England derived their ecclesiastical laws from others, yet so many as were proved, approved, and allowed here, by and with a general consent, are aptly and rightly called, the King's Ecclesiastical Laws of England, which whosoever shall deny, he

denieth that the King hath full and plenary power to deliver justice in all causes to all his subjects, or to punish all crimes and offences within his kingdom: for that as before it appeareth the deciding of matters so many, and of so great importance, are not within the conusance of the common laws, and consequently that the King is no complete monarch, nor head, of the whole and entire body of the realm.'[1]

In Cawdry's case, then, the Queen's Bench recognized the duality of judicial authority in England, and the independence and rightness of the two laws, the law temporal and the law ecclesiastical. There could be no other logical conclusion from the tenet of the royal supremacy. Indeed, both the opinion and the dicta seem to have been received with satisfaction in all judicial circles.

Some little time before this decision was rendered (1591) there were circulated in manuscript two anonymous pamphlets, nicknamed by Cosin *The Treatisour* and *The Notegatherer*, written perhaps by the Puritan lawyers, perhaps, as Cosin hints, by some great dignitary whose name could not be disclosed. These assailed the Commission in a far more fundamental fashion.[2] Their main argument was based upon the evident fact that the Commission was a court and hence fast tied to a definite jurisdiction and procedure, and upon its equally apparent corollary that the Commission was an ecclesiastical court. It should exercise, therefore, they insisted, ecclesiastical authority in ecclesiastical ways, and award ecclesiastical penalties for ecclesiastical crimes, and no more. It drew

[1] Coke, *Reports*, v, 7 a and 8 b.

[2] The quotations in Cosin's *Apologie* and the Epistle to the Reader in that tract make us reasonably certain that the 'Treatisour' is Harl. MS. 5247, 'A briefe treatise of oathes . . .' I am indebted for this identification to Professor C. H. McIlwain, of Harvard University.

this authority from the Elizabethan Statute of Supremacy and ' how generall soeuer the words of the act be in one place, yet are they to be restrained to this particular, viz., none other then such iurisdiction ecclesiasticall as may be lawfully used '. Nor did the pamphleteers find the lawful ecclesiastical procedure a matter of doubt : citation ; procedure by formal accusation or presentment ; the normal procedure at trials in the regular ecclesiastical courts ; and such penalties of excommunication and penance as the practice of the latter had made familiar. The *ex officio* oath, the trial of a man *ex officio mero* whom no individual had sued, the use of fine and imprisonment in particular, the trial of most cases commonly heard by the Commission, all these were simply illegal according to any proper interpretation of the Statute. As for the Letters Patent, they were to be limited by the Statute and the breadth of their language was of small importance and of no legal effect. Nor did one author hesitate to declare that ' the iudgement of heresie now lieth rather in the common law than in the law ecclesiasticall '. The far-reaching but logical conclusions from these propositions were not seen for some years by either the Commissioners or their opponents, and to suppose the writers of these tracts actually had them in mind may be a gratuitous assumption. The strength of their case lay in the fact that the Commission now ranked as one of the ecclesiastical courts, that the ordinary ecclesiastical process was notoriously as described, and that the Commission used other process.

A most significant point, infinitely more fundamental than the statements of the *Notegatherer* and *Treatisour*, appeared in *Th' Appelation of Iohn Penri, unto the Highe Court of Parliament from the bad and injurious dealing of the Archb. of Canterb. and other his colleagues of the high commission*, published in 1589/90. He related at length the proceedings of the Commission against him, which ended in his long imprisonment for contempt. From the High Commission he formally appealed to the High Court of Parliament. Penry did not see in Parliament the legislative and administrative body to which we are accustomed: he saw only the old mediaeval supreme court of final appeal—the King sitting in his Council in his Parliaments—to which any man wronged or without judicial remedy had a right to appeal for relief. The Reformation, argued Penry, had made the Parliament the highest ecclesiastical as well as the highest temporal court. 'They will it may be, alleage the prerogatiue of their Commission to be very large, what then? doe they think, herby to haue libertie to oppresse whom they will, doe they think herby to be aboue the Parliament, whereunto al courts in the land are and ought to be subiect and *from whence the highe commission deriueth al the prerogatiue it hath?*' By the *judgement* of the Parliament as the supreme court of appeal, registered in the Statute of first Elizabeth, argued Penry, the Commission was bound. He demanded a formal trial by the Parliament and an authoritative decision defining more exactly the Commission's jurisdiction and procedure. 'Mine answere unto the high commission is, I appeale unto the Parliament, where I ought to be judged.'

The champion of the Commission soon appeared. Dr. Richard Cosin, one of the ablest and most active of the commissioners, wrote in 1591 and published in 1593 *An Apologie for Sundrie Proceedings by Iurisdiction Ecclesiasticall*, in which, besides considering the jurisdiction and procedure of the ecclesiastical courts in general, he sketched and explained the procedure and organization of the new court and defended its legality, equity, and justice at some length. In the main, his position was the logical development of the dicta in Cawdry's case into a coherent statement of a notion long prevalent among the ecclesiastical lawyers, that the new jurisdiction assumed by the Crown in ecclesiastical causes was as complete, as unlimited, and as necessary to the realm as the time-honoured authority in temporal causes. 'The Queen's Ecclesiastical Laws'—the Canons, Statutes on ecclesiastical questions, judgements of the ecclesiastical courts—were absolutely unrestricted in their scope, and, in one way or another, furnished adequate authority for the decision of every ecclesiastical case which might then or thereafter arise. Like the common lawyers, Cosin declared that this jurisdiction had always been in existence and had now been merely resumed by the Crown. Unlike them, he proceeded to define its limits, to describe its characteristics, and to arrive at the conclusion that only the Crown knew its limits and that whatever the Crown chose to do would be legal. He came, therefore, without difficulty to the conclusion that the Act of Elizabeth was merely declaratory, and that the true limits of the commissioners' authority would be found in their Letters Patent, which, as he and every one else knew, explicitly permitted the use of each and every so-called infringement of the laws.

The issue raised by Penry, Cosin did not discuss *eo nomine*, because he accepted without question (as did all men of the time) Penry's main contention that Parliament was the *highest* court in the realm, and, indeed, based his own case largely upon the conception that it was the highest ecclesiastical court. No one doubted that a new judgement (Statute) by Parliament would decide this dispute about jurisdiction; but he addressed himself to the really debatable issue: whose interpretation of Parliament's previous 'judgement' should in the meantime prevail. Here, again, was a large issue raised, the full significance of which was long in being appreciated. It is hardly likely that this brief tractarian warfare excited much comment outside certain very narrow circles, for nearly fifteen years elapsed before such far-reaching propositions were again enunciated, and we do not in later days find these cases quoted as precedent. According to Cosin, the agitation was the work of 'quick and narrow-sighted fellowes lately sprung up', 'men of Meanest place and reckoning in that studie (common law ?) and such as are knowen to bee overmuch addicted to factitious innovations'.[1] Apparently this phase of the opposition died out as quickly as it appeared.

Two points now raised for the first time, the illegality of the oath *ex officio* and of fine and imprisonment,[2] will appear so constantly in the later history of the Commission that some consideration of their validity becomes a matter of necessity. The chief basis for the former was found in the Statute of 2 Henry V, c. 3, which provided that the libel should be granted to the party in the ecclesiastical court, 'without any difficulty,' 'at what time the libel is grantable by the law.' This was now interpreted to mean that the defendant should see the articles against him *whenever he asked for them*, even before he had taken the oath. If such had been the intention of the Statute, its somewhat ambiguous phrasing had never been so interpreted, and the practice of the ecclesiastical courts had apparently always been (certainly had been for at least two generations) to deliver a copy of the libel *after* the defendant had taken the 'corporal oath', as it was often

[1] *Apologie*, i, 109; and the Preface.

[2] We must distinguish from mere refusals to take the oath, in order to block the procedure of the Commission, as at Cartwright's trial, a claim that the oath was actually illegal.

called, and never before. This interpretation of the Statute seems reasonable and is certainly permissible, for nothing is said as to who shall decide ' at what time the libel is grantable *by the law* ', and upon that point the whole case depends. The commissioners and ecclesiastical judges were not slow in insisting that the ecclesiastical practice was precisely what the Statute intended to confirm.[1]

The question of fine and imprisonment was complicated by the fact that neither was an ecclesiastical penalty in the mediaeval sense; they could not be claimed as part of the ecclesiastical procedure necessarily resumed, and their use by an ecclesiastical body must, therefore, depend upon an authorization from the supreme judicial authority. Henry and his children considered the Crown the repository of all jurisdiction, temporal and spiritual, of any sort, kind, or degree, and saw no reason why they should not allow their Commissioners to exercise authority which every local judicial official in England possessed. Their predecessors had in at least two instances[2] granted by Statute permission to the bishops to fine and imprison, and had thus furnished precedent for another Statute which should make a grant in general terms broad enough to cover all cases. Certainly, the commissioners had hitherto employed both powers without question,[3] though the explicit authorization, begun by Edward, had, by 1570, become a part of the Patent which it was deemed highly inexpedient to omit.[4] The evidence of the frequent use of both fine and imprisonment is overwhelming, not

1 See on this point the elaborate statement by Cosin in the *Apologie*.

2 2 Henry IV, c. 15; 1 Henry VII, c. 4.

3 See, however, *Parker Correspondence*, 447 (Nov. 7, 1573 ?), for what may be a trace of some doubts in Burghley's mind.

4 The clause had been omitted from the Commission of 1570 (now lost), and Parker wrote to Burghley to secure its inclusion: S. P. Dom. Eliz. 74, no. 28. The omission was unintentional.

only in amount but in its conclusive nature.[1] It is also clear that no objection was made by the common-law judges. For some reason the judges and certain other common-law officials were asked, in 1577, whether the commissioners might fine priests and recusants, and replied emphatically in the affirmative. The issue here seems not to have been whether the commissioners might use such a penalty at all, but whether it was permissible in certain cases. The length and breadth of these issues will become clear as the narrative proceeds.

The war upon the oath *ex officio* was vigorously pressed, however, at the next session of Parliament by James Morice, the Attorney of the Court of Wards and an ardent supporter of the Puritans. He introduced a Bill in the House of Commons for the abolition of the oath, which he supported with several warm speeches, directed, however, quite as much against the usage of the oath by the regular ecclesiastical courts as by the Commission. Whitgift wrote strongly in defence of the oath to Elizabeth, who interposed and killed the Bill. Morice, however, told in debate several incidents which shed a good deal of light upon the difficulty the commissioners experienced from time to time in enforcing their authority. He was

[1] Especially the original certificates of fines in the Exchequer Doc. Q. R. Eccles., bundle 12, no. 3; bundle 7, nos. 28 and 30. The formal certificate of prisoners held at the Clink by authority of the commissioners in March 1582/3, is S. P. Dom. Eliz. 159, no. 34. As early as 1560 the Lieutenant of the Tower asked that the prisoners committed by the commissioners might be allowed to eat together at two tables separate from the others (*Parker Correspondence*, 121). One hundred and ten were under bond in April 1580: Harl. MSS. 360, ff. 49–52. See also Morrice MSS. C, p. 653; C, p. 683; M, no. viii; Harl. MSS. 7042, f. 35; S. P. Dom. Eliz. 228, no. 19; *ibid.*, 269, no. 34; *Privy Council Register*, viii, 235; xi, 137, 456; xiii, 276, 327; xv, 196; xxi, 153; xxiii, 357; Strype, *Aylmer*, 56; *Annals*, iv, 308.

once at Colchester when the assize sermon was to be preached. John Knewstubbs, a noted Puritan, mounted the pulpit, despite the fact that the Bishop Suffragan had appointed another man to deliver the sermon. The bishop sent for the bailiff and ordered him to make Knewstubbs leave the pulpit, which the bailiff refused to do. Thereupon the bishop proceeded against him *ex officio mero* in the Consistory Court. The bailiff told him 'plainly' that the proceeding was 'out of mere malice' and not out of 'mere office'; declared him an incompetent judge, and refused the oath as 'ungodlie' and 'against the lawe'. The bishop straightway appealed to the High Commission at London, where the bailiff was long imprisoned for refusing the oath, and was finally released on bond. By increasing his fine, he was at length frightened into taking the oath, but then stuck fast at the questions asked him, all of which, Morice thought, well illustrated the horrible practices of the Commission.

Another incident shows even more graphically how little prompt co-operation the commissioners received from the local officials, upon whom the Letters Patent directed them to rely for enforcing their processes. The bishop's chancellor was sitting at Colchester to collect the fines and fees levied at the last visitation, and, being defied by one culprit, sent him under charge of a constable to the bailiff with an order to put him in jail, giving as his authority a warrant of the High Commission. The bailiff declared the latter insufficient, on the ground that it had expired. Thereupon the chancellor sent for the high constables, who likewise refused to accept it; and, added Morice, the chancellor was the more enraged because he had been accustomed to have a justice of the peace or a constable put men in the stocks on verbal orders given in court or 'even in the open streets as he went from the bench or church '.[1] How far this denial by the local authorities of the legality of the Commission's warrants and procedure was inspired by the opposition just described is not now ascertainable, but it is sufficiently clear that the opposition was by no means confined to a war of words. Undoubtedly the rapid development by the Commission about this time of a staff of pursuivants and messengers resulted from the realization that little was to be expected of the local officials at critical moments. To this extent, this early opposition had an influence on the Commission's growth and position.

[1] Lambeth MSS. 234, f. 103 ff. See also: D'Ewes, *Journals*, 474 ff. (Feb. 27, 1592/3); Whitgift to the Queen, Additional MSS. 28571, f. 172 (Whitgift's draft). The drafts of the two Bills, with some correspondence concerning the incident, are in Baker MSS. (Univ. of Camb.) M.M. 1, 51, ff. 105–24. See also a treatise ' of oathes in Ecclesiasticall Courtes ', Lambeth MSS. 234, f. 100 (1592), probably written by Morice, and the very long treatise in defence of it at the beginning of the same volume. Also papers in Lambeth MSS. 445, ff. 438, 452. The following treatise is hard to date and may belong anywhere from 1590 to 1610, but seems to belong here. Cotton MSS. Cleopatra, F. I, ff. 50–69: ' A brief treatise of oathes exacted by Ordinaries and Ecclesiastical Judges, to answere generallie to all suche Articles or Interrogatories as pleaseth them to propound. And of their forced and constrayned oathes ex officio wherein is prooved that the same are unlawfull.' See also Cotton MSS. Cleopatra, F. I, ff. 1–50: ' A Collection shewinge what iurisdiction the clergie hath heretofore Lawfully used and maye Lawfully use in ye Realme of Englande. Wherein it is manifestly proued that the Prelates or Ecclesiasticall Iudges neuer had anye authoritie to compell anie subject of the Lande to an othe, unless yt were in causes Testamentarie or Matrimoniall or therto appertayninge: with a confutation of such friuolous and unlearned surmises, as haue ben made for the maintenance of the Clergies unlawfull proceadings in these days to the contrarye: whereby they haue sondry wayes incurred the penalties of the statutes of Prouision and Praemunire.' Sidney Lee (*Dict. Nat. Biog.*, under ' Cosin ') calls the former of these Morice's answer to Cosin's *Apologie*. This may be true, but the Lambeth MSS. cited above seems decidedly more probable.

CHAPTER VII

THE COMMON-LAW JUDGES AND THE HIGH COMMISSION, 1535–1607

THE Lord Chief Justice, one of his colleagues, and the Attorney-General had nearly always been members of the early commissions, and had been both active and influential. Under their guidance the common-law forms, whose use the Letters Patent expressly permitted,[1] had been more or less employed; but as the year 1580 approached, the attendance of the common-law members gradually and inevitably fell off [2] as the commissioners became more and more distinctly the judges of an ecclesiastical court of appeals. The moment the transformation was complete, the common-law judges could hardly fail to regard the new court as a rival and 'foreign' jurisdiction. No personal connexion with its past was admitted; if, indeed, they admitted that it possessed any past, and, although their names were still to be found in the Patent, they assumed no personal responsibility for its decisions. Their natural attitude towards the new court was one of hostility, born of the ancient jealousy for the ecclesiastical courts and intensified by the memory of two great victories for the common law.

[1] Letters Patent, 1559, s. iii, 'to enquire as well by the oaths of twelve good and lawful men.' Grindal and some of the common lawyers had tried cases by jury perhaps as late as 1577, and the practice was commoner in the previous decade: Cosin, *Apologie*, i, 108.

[2] This we know from the signatures to formal documents as well as from the reports of trials.

Moreover, the centuries of struggle with all sorts of foes, which the common-law courts had successfully weathered, had not fostered in their judges a frame of mind likely to view with equanimity the existence of rivals, nor likely to admit the legality of their rivals' existence without a prolonged and a severe struggle. The dream of a time when the common law should embrace all jurisdiction whatever is a quite adequate explanation of the searching investigation to which the judges soon subjected the jurisdiction and procedure of the new court.

The differences in procedure were sufficient to suggest illegality to the common-law mind. In the Commission, a case was tried by witnesses and written evidence before judges unassisted by a jury. The oral interchange of arguments and the cross-examination in civil pleas, already dear to the common lawyer, hardly existed. While, at common law, the presumption was in the defendant's favour, in the Commission it was against him. The procedure *ex officio mero* also looked strange to a common lawyer. But it was the effect of the Commission's procedure on the minds of suitors which probably convinced the common lawyers that something was really wrong. We read of case after case pending in the Queen's Bench, the Common Pleas, or the Chancery, which was then impleaded in the Commission upon some excuse in hope of obtaining a final decision. Even cases already heard and sentenced were thus ' appealed '. Litigants would not normally leave the common-law courts, reasoned the judges, and seek ' relief ' from the Commission, unless they were securing something the law did not allow.

The boundaries between the jurisdictions were, indeed, sufficiently vague, and the powers of the Commission abundantly broad enough, to allow in most cases a respectable argument for or against its assumption of jurisdiction, and the differences in procedure between the Commission and the common-law courts must have both helped and hindered the resort of suitors to either. It might be very hard to convince three commissioners, with the whole evidence before them, of the justice of a certain claim; yet by skilful pleading an issue might be developed out of it which could easily be proved to the satisfaction of a jury. On the other hand, a man, who might fare hardly at the hands of a jury, might, perhaps, upon the weighing of the whole evidence, be seen to have the law on his side. Again, at common law, the initial presumption lay on the whole in the defendant's favour, for the plaintiff must first prove a *prima facie* case in order to endanger him at all; but, in the Commission, the presumption was always against the defendant and the initial burden of proof lay upon him. True, in theory, he must be proved guilty beyond any reasonable doubt by both procedures,[1] yet the possession of the initial presumption might be of the utmost practical importance to either plaintiff or defendant. Again, if a man had but one witness, he of course wished his suit tried at common law, where one witness was sufficient. But his adversary, if he had two, was quite as certain to find the Commission preferable, for there his two witnesses would infallibly prove his case and his opponent's one would go for naught. Moreover, in the Commission, every criminal, once he had taken the oath *ex officio* and answered the articles against him, had the benefit of an advocate, a proctor, and process for securing evidence and calling witnesses in his favour.[2] If innocent of a criminal charge or with a reasonably

[1] 'The evidence to convict a prisoner should be so manifest as it could not be contradicted': Coke, *Third Institute*, 137.

[2] This seems to have been true even in cases of summary procedure.

good civil case, this procedure clearly afforded him the better chances. If guilty, however, the presumption in his favour, and the possibility of packing or misleading the jury, made the common law look the safer. Hence it was that many a layman, about to go to law, preferred to sue in the Commission, and that many an ecclesiastic, impleaded in the Commission, desired to be tried at common law. There always existed, too, the possibility, if not the probability, that some one of these differences would cause the court to which the suitor came to take a different view of the case from the one he had just left.

The extreme looseness of jurisdictional lines helped greatly, and here on the whole left the balance in the Commission's favour. In the Commission, where precedent was not as yet firmly established, the Court had no objection to the creation of precedent and to taking cognizance of as many new cases as might appear. At common law, on the other hand, it was necessary to show some warrantable precedent for action. Where, too, the Commission was ready to fit the procedure to the case, at common law the case had to be fitted to such writs and forms of pleading and action as already existed. The differences in pleading and procedure were at that time all-important. To-day substantive law has far outstripped in importance the law of actions and the art of pleading, but in the sixteenth and seventeenth centuries the common law still bore much of the aspect of the old days when the important question was, not what right is there, but what remedy is there? [1] Then no remedy meant no right. Further, the litigant needed to know,

[1] 'So great is the ascendancy of the law of actions in the infancy of courts of justice, that substantive law has at first the look of being gradually secreted in the interstices of procedure': Maine, *Early Law and Custom*, 168, 389.

not only that he had a right and one for which there was a remedy, but as well in which particular court he must seek that remedy. Substantive law existed chiefly as an adjunct of the law of remedial justice. Proof at common law bore still the aspect of the days when the criminal cleared himself by 'going to the water' or by reciting perfectly a formula. Pleadings still were void if not letter-perfect. 'Forma legalis is forma essentialis.'[1] 'People had not yet learned to regard the proceeding before the Court simply as a trial of the question—a reference of it to the judge and jury to know whether the prisoner was guilty or not. Still less had they learned to regard a prejudication of that question as unjust and injurious on the ground that until the case had been openly heard nobody could know.'[2] Litigants strongly believed that, if a man only brought the proper writ, and used the proper form of action, and did so in the proper court, he must infallibly be freed or accorded a judgement. Hence the continual 'appeals', the resort from one court to another, which were perhaps at the bottom of our ancestors' so-called 'fondness for litigation'.

In the Commission, however, substantive law was more prominent than the law of remedial justice. It was not necessary to prove a particular injury in order to secure relief; the proof that the suitor had been unjustly and severely wronged in any way within the scope of the Commission's broad jurisdiction was quite sufficient to set in operation all its authority in his favour. If the jurisdiction of the common law was nominally large, the number of actions available was exceedingly small, and, while the judges interpreted them with great breadth, especially the 'action on the case', the suitor was forced

[1] Coke's *Reports*, x, 100 a.

[2] Spedding, *Life and Letters of Sir Francis Bacon*, v, 284.

again and again to resort to transparent fictions of the boldest sort to obtain even the chance of a remedy. It was naturally easier to prove the truth of an actual injury to the satisfaction of the commissioners than that of a fictitious one to the common-law judges. Nor was it strange that men sought the Commission with wrongs which the common law should have remedied, but for which it provided no writ or action. When all ' clerks ' were legally ecclesiastics in the sight of ' both laws ', and when the Commission and ecclesiastical courts claimed jurisdiction over all cases to which an ecclesiastic was a party, it was not difficult for any man who could read his neck-verse to sue in the Commission for the redress of almost any personal injury. Nor did the Commission hesitate about accepting jurisdiction. In common with all the ecclesiastical courts, it furthermore claimed a sort of territorial jurisdiction over the church lands, which, when broadly interpreted, included not only churches, churchyards, cemeteries, and cathedral closes, but episcopal estates, glebe lands, and the like. We are accustomed to-day to the use of church property only for religious purposes and to the closing of edifices and grounds during the week ; but the men of the sixteenth century lived in their cathedrals and churchyards all the year round, and, in the course of affairs, crimes were often committed in them, whose conusance became, of course, a matter of dispute. Thus, picking pockets in the nave at Paul's, fighting in the churchyard, letting cattle graze upon the glebe land, were, strictly speaking, ecclesiastical offences.[1] Certainly it was quite as logical to insist that

[1] The Visitation Records are full of such cases, and the ecclesiastical courts, as well as the Commission, tried the majority of them without interference from the common-law courts. These classes of jurisdiction were explicitly enumerated by all the later Letters Patent.

crimes by laymen in ecclesiastical precincts were ecclesiastical crimes as to claim that stealing by a clergyman was a temporal crime. As a matter of fact, there were good logical grounds for the extension of either jurisdiction, but neither would have been satisfied to make the test exclusively either the status of the criminal or the character of the crime.

To all these influences was added on both sides the base motive of self-interest. The common-law judges were anxious to increase the competence of their courts in order to increase their own incomes. Their salaries were merely nominal, and their incomes were derived almost wholly from fees paid by the suitors.[1] Naturally, the more suits, the more fees; the greater possibility of suing, the larger probable income. Such considerations did not influence the commissioners, for they were not paid a salary and received no share of the court fees at any time during the Court's history. But the lawyers of both jurisdictions were of course anxious to increase 'business'. Maitland has shown us conclusively how important a part was played by the 'profits of jurisdiction' during the Middle Ages while the common-law courts were developing, and we need to bear constantly in mind the strong influence this fact still had in the sixteenth century.

The possibility of a controversy thus furnished, its probability was no less assured by the fact of the

[1] Reliable information as to the size of judicial incomes is hard to find. We are sure, however, that the salaries of the judges were not more than a couple of hundred pounds, while their incomes were usually several thousand. The judgeships of the Common Pleas were by far the most lucrative: Coke complained bitterly when he was 'promoted' to the King's Bench. The gossip about incomes in the letter-writers is probably as unreliable as the figures they give which we can verify.

Commission's newness as a court. Nothing could disguise the fact that it had not always been a court, and that the Letters Patent and the Statute as well had probably been intended by their framers to sanction only a visitatorial authority, which, however broad in its scope and untrammelled in its procedure, was, nevertheless, meant to be temporary and to authorize the use during an emergency of those residual powers of the State which in a crisis every one was willing to countenance. To claim that under this same Patent and Statute, without the addition of one jot or one tittle to the nominal authority of the commissioners, a law-court could be maintained with a right to recognition from all existing courts, was going far, thought the common lawyers. In addition, the peculiar nature of its procedure and jurisdiction, half secular, half ecclesiastical, gave the Commission a hybrid aspect at which both the ecclesiastical and the common-law judges could not fail to look askance. Clearly, some sort of definition of its position in relation to existing courts, some delimitation of its jurisdiction, some regularization of its procedure, would be necessary before either could receive it on equal terms, or indeed on any terms at all. The fact that a commission was mentioned by the Elizabethan Act of Supremacy complicated the situation and raised the question of its relation to Parliament. In regard to the place of Parliament in the judicial hierarchy, there was by no means agreement. The common lawyers insisted that it was the highest common-law court, whose decision alone was final and which had long been entrusted with the task of assigning jurisdiction to the various courts.[1] It had thus assigned the Commission's jurisdiction, and from the Statute the common-law judges

[1] C. H. McIlwain, *The High Court of Parliament*, 119–24, *et passim*.

must discover what the exact position of that court was Clearly, this view made the Commission subject to the common law, deriving its authority from it and liable to the supervision of its judges. Such a notion the ecclesiastics with one voice indignantly denied.[1] Parliament had become the highest ecclesiastical court, as well as the highest temporal court, by the resumption of the royal ecclesiastical jurisdiction. Its Statutes on ecclesiastical affairs were, therefore, to be interpreted by the ecclesiastical judges. This claim gave the commissioners themselves the right to interpret the eighth section of 1 Elizabeth, c. 1, and hence the right to decide the limits of their jurisdiction, but it was no greater privilege than the common-law judges themselves claimed in regard to their own jurisdiction, and was no more unjust or inequitable. Neither these issues nor the notable constitutional questions which they involved were at this time formally broached or discussed, if, indeed, it was understood that their decision would be a prerequisite to any final adjustment of the quarrel.

It speaks well for the moderation and conservatism of the commissioners that the battle was so long delayed, for, during the twenty years when the Court was assuming final shape, the attitude of the common-law judges was friendly, even if at times a little suspicious. In 1577 some doubt seems to have been expressed as to the right of the commissioners to inflict a fine. Imprisonment was apparently not questioned, nor was any issue made of the general right to fine. The right to fine recusants was the chief point discussed at a conference between

[1] The most elaborate and logical statements of this position are the tracts of Cosin, Bilson, Fulbecke, and Ridley. The ecclesiastical literature of the time is mainly based on it. See a long treatise in Lansdowne MSS. 253, ff. 139–90.

the common-law judges, the Queen's learned counsel, and several doctors of civil law, headed by Dr. Lewes, at that time Judge of the Admiralty, but a man previously very active in the High Commission. The conference concluded that the Statute of 1 Elizabeth, c. 1, gave the commissioners authority 'to inflict any punishment by mulct or otherwise which the ecclesiasticall Lawe doth allowe of. Because all ecclesiasticall iurisdiction and authoritie is by the statute annexed to the Crown. And by the same statute full power is given to hir Majestie to commit ye same authoritie to such persons as shall please hir highnes, and that such Commissioners shall and maie execute ye same according to the tenor of ye said Commission'. The conference also agreed that the ecclesiastical law itself permitted the levying of fines upon recusants, and that *therefore* the commissioners possessed that power.[1] The opinion is perfectly clear: the Commission executed the ecclesiastical law restored to the Crown by the Statute and delegated to it by Letters Patent, and the *ecclesiastical* law permitted the imposition of fines for recusancy. Where this part of the ecclesiastical law was found was not indicated. This extra-judicial opinion is interesting, not only as indicating the friendly attitude which the judges held at this time towards

[1] Attorney-General Gerrard to Burghley, Dec. 3, 1577: Holograph, Lansdowne MSS. 27, f. 46. The men present were Chief Justice Dyer, Justices Sowthrop, Manwood, Monnson, Doctor Lewes, and the Attorney- and Solicitor-General. Garbled extracts from this letter are in Strype's *Grindal*. A paper drawn up from the letter, and perhaps circulated by the Government to make the decision public, is in Caius College MSS. 103, f. 336. Early in 1585 the judges were asked in Star Chamber whether the commissioners might set papists free whom they had themselves imprisoned. The judges replied in the negative, because, once condemned, they were prisoners of the Queen and 'the Commission had no more to do with them': Strype, *Aylmer*, 75.

the Commission, but also in the light of Coke's later statements, that the law permitted none of these things, and that common-law judges time out of mind had consistently so declared. It was, however, significant that the common-law judges should be requested to give opinions upon the limits of the Commission's jurisdiction. It meant either that the Queen and her advisers were by no means as sure of the existence of the Queen's Ecclesiastical Law as the judges were later in Cawdry's case, or that they did not consider it expedient to attempt to exercise the right which the existence of such a law, separate from and independent of the common law, would give them, of defining its limits themselves without appealing to the common lawyers at all. Any consultation with the latter practically admitted all that Coke later claimed. If the common-law judges might decide upon the Commission's competence, why might they not review its decisions and supervise its conduct ?

The only recognized means of formal communication between the common-law courts and the Commission were the time-honoured writs of prohibition and consultation. Both had originated in the dim past, and the prevailing ignorance of history lent colour to many peculiar notions about their early use. It was, however, clear that they had been intended to check the 'usurpations' of the ecclesiastical courts upon the royal courts at the moment when the organization and jurisdiction of the latter were slowly crystallizing. The writ of prohibition was issued by the common-law judge to 'prohibit' the ecclesiastical judge from continuing the trial of a certain case on the ground that it concerned temporal matters. The writ stopped proceedings in either court pending a decision as to the proper jurisdiction ; this decision was awarded by the common-law judge at a hearing, at which the writ was 'returned' by the ecclesiastical suitor or his advocate, and the question of jurisdiction argued at length. If, on 'consultation', the common-law judge concluded that the case contained nothing temporal, he issued a second writ or 'consultation' annulling his prohibition and allowing the case to continue at ecclesiastical law. If, on the contrary, he decided that the case did concern temporality, he simply allowed the prohibition to stand, which put an end to the case at ecclesiastical law, but did not of itself commence any action at common law. Nor was it at all necessary for a common-law judge to be able to claim jurisdiction himself of the temporal matter in dispute; it was enough that the ecclesiastical judge could not try it. Indeed, the common law never pretended to provide a remedy for every grievance, and the mere fact that the plaintiff at ecclesiastical law had seized the only possible method for relief, did not in the least justify the usurpation of the jurisdiction rightly belonging to the common law. That the common law did not exercise it was no reason why some one else should.

While prohibitions had always been in use since the victory won with that writ in the Middle Ages in the matter of real property, they were in 1580 comparatively infrequent and not very well understood by practising lawyers.[1] But the existence of the writ placed in the hands of the common-law judges an excellent offensive instrument: they alone could decide whether or not the prohibition had been justly issued; the maintenance of the writ stopped the proceedings at ecclesiastical law

[1] During the later debates, the ecclesiastical lawyers alleged that prohibitions were not really plentiful till 1592, and hence that they were innovations. See Usher's *Reconstruction*, ii, 75, notes.

completely, even if none were begun at common law; the writ was old, and its very existence lent colour to the statement that the common-law judge was not attempting to increase his court's jurisdiction, but was simply trying to maintain its ancient limits.

The latent possibilities of the old procedure were not long in being discovered, though James I had already ascended the throne before many prohibitions were issued to the Commission.[1] The prompt action of the Privy Council in 1579 had, however, very probably had something to do with this apparent judicial reserve. Giles, a rector of Devonshire, proceeded against by the commissioners for 'certain disorders' 'in the serving of the cure and administracion of Sacramentes and other rites', had stopped the proceedings by securing a prohibition. The Council had summoned him to London at once, and had so treated him as apparently to cause suitors to reflect before asking for prohibitions other than as provided for by strict precedent.[2] Prohibitions were, however, often maintained as early as 1580 in testamentary cases, where the commissioners attempted to execute the will of the deceased by granting or selling land, or to compel the specific performance of trusts or charitable bequests.[3] Perhaps on this account as well as on others, Burghley advised Aylmer not to do anything 'to create more displeasure against them and their Commission', nor 'meddle with many matters by virtue of their Commission but such only as concerned religion'.[4]

[1] The Law Reports contain very few, and most of the later statements treat them as of recent origin.

[2] *Privy Council Register*, xi, 60, 87, Feb. 26 and Mar. 25, 1578/9.

[3] Chief Justice Wray to the Bishop of Chester, July 13, 1581. Copy, Tanner MSS. 79, f. 153.

[4] Dec. 1581. Strype, *Aylmer*, 61.

Probably nothing of the sort was again attempted, for we find record of very few prohibitions during the next ten years, and the form of the judgement in Cawdry's case, as well as its substance (if Coke's report is good evidence), indicates that in 1591 the common-law judges were reconciled to the Commission's existence and conceived it to have found its proper place in the hierarchy of jurisdiction.

In that very year, however, a prohibition was granted by the Queen's Bench, which, while directed against the Commission's position as one of the ecclesiastical hierarchy rather than against its own jurisdiction, certainly revealed a somewhat different animus. A man, who had been sued before the Commission for marrying his wife's sister's daughter, had been divorced by the sentence of that Court. He brought a prohibition on the ground that his marriage was not within the Levitical degrees (which was true) and hence must be valid. The Queen's Bench did not maintain the writ, but issued a consultation on its return.[1] The surprising thing is that it should have interfered at all in what had always been considered so purely an ecclesiastical question as divorce and the definition of a valid marriage. The conduct of the common-law judges in the next few years was aggressive enough to draw from the bishops in 1598 a protest which the judges were probably asked to answer before the Privy Council. The protest was principally concerned with the technicalities of prohibitions to the regular ecclesiastical courts, but the last section was devoted to the High Commission, and enunciated the doctrine of Cawdry's case and of Cosin's *Apologie*. The protest, in

[1] Man's case. 1 Croke, 228, 33 Eliz. Exactly what sort of a plea the plaintiff made is not easy to discover. It was clearly bad.

fact, demanded a reason for issuing prohibitions at all, and hinted that their legality was doubtful since the union of the temporal and ecclesiastical jurisdictions in the Crown. 'And seeing so many and so great personages with some others are trusted to do her Majesty service in her Highness' Ecclesiastical Commission, whether it be convenient, that an offender ready to be censured, upon his own false suggestion, before a conference had with any commissioners thereupon, who knew the truth best, should obtain, and publicly in court throw in, a prohibition to the delay of justice, and to the disgrace and disparagement of those who served freely without all fee therein.' [1]

Whatever the judges had done to rouse this protest, their subsequent conduct was certainly even more hostile to the Commission. Violent assaults upon clergymen, some in time of divine service; scandalous abuse of ministers to their face; adultery; contempt of the Commission's authority; in all these cases prohibitions were issued on one excuse or another.[2] Two clergymen deprived, the one for simony and the other for lack of proper ordination, both secured prohibitions. The former, indeed, was not maintained, but, if the language used by the Court was justifiable, it is hard to see why it should have ever been issued at all. 'And it (simony)

[1] Strype, *Whitgift*, ii, 399–400. The manuscript bibliography of this document is to be found in Usher's *Reconstruction*, ii, 77.

[2] Lansdowne MSS. 161, f. 225. In the case of *Parlor* v. *Butler*, Parlor had said of Butler that 'he was fitter to stand on the pillory then preach in the Pulpit, and that he had taken two orders already, that he lacked but taking the third, which was to have his ears cut off'. 'Les Commissioners ne voilent allower del justification, mes luy censure to ask forgiveness, sur que il port le prohibition. Et fuit adjudge maintainable quia les high commissioners nont a medler ove le cause, si non que fuissoit fait en temps del divine service': Moore's *Report*, 460. Mich. 38 and 39 Eliz.

appertains to the Spiritual Court to determine it, and not to this Court to meddle therewith. And when the Spiritual Court hath so sentenced it, this Court ought to give credence thereto, and ought not to dispute, whether it be error or not.' [1] In another case, the prohibition was maintained with more colour of justice. The Commission had excommunicated a woman for adultery who had continued her practices, and because of her contumacy the Commission sent a pursuivant to apprehend her. The officer arrived at night and was refused admission, but, with excessive zeal, moved perhaps by a hope of taking her *in flagrante delicto*, he broke into the house and forcibly arrested her. The Queen's Bench held such conduct illegal, and remarked that the Commission ought not to arrest men by its own officers, but should certify an excommunication to the chancery and secure a writ which the sheriff would execute.[2]

When James came to the throne the Puritans and common lawyers attempted to influence him to restrict the Commission's authority. At the third session of the Hampton Court Conference, in January 1603/4, the King 'fell into discourse about the High Commission '.[3] He

[1] *Baker* v. *Rogers*. 1 Croke, 788, at 789. Cf. *Love* v. *Prin*. 1 Croke, 753.

[2] *Smith* v. *Smith*. 1 Croke, *Reports*, 741. 41 Eliz. The court's dictum was ominous: the ecclesiastical courts ' are not to meddle with the person of any man, or to send any process to have the body before them '. Coke later cited cases relating to this period, whose existence the commissioners hotly challenged, and, as they are not now forthcoming, the denial was probably true. Something regarding their nature will be said later. The manuscript authority, while it does not give many cases, makes it clear that some existed.

[3] Barlow's is the only account that gives these details. For the bibliography of the Conference, with critical remarks on it, see Usher's *Reconstruction*, i, 317, 318, 330, notes.

had heard that the commissioners were too many in number and too low in station, and that they chiefly busied themselves with small cases which the bishops could have easily decided, and that the diocesan commissions were too numerous and too large. Whitgift urged, in defence, that, without a large membership, the Court could not sit regularly; privy councillors and judges would not attend, and 'some of meaner place as Deanes and Doctors of Diuinity and Law' had to be included among the members because their attendance could be more easily secured. The Archbishop agreed with the complaint that the suits impleaded were in many cases small, but he 'sawe that it could not bee remedied'. Either the high rank of the culprit or his disobedience compelled the bishop to appeal to the High Commission. As for the diocesan commissions, he was in entire accord with the objection, for he did not himself approve of them. The Lord Chancellor suggested that the diocesan commissions might well be limited to the largest and most troublesome dioceses, a suggestion the King thought excellent. In conclusion, James 'willed those to consult to whom should bee appointed the review of the Commission. And here that point had ended but that one of the Lordes . . . pleased to say that the proceeding thereby was like unto the Spanish Inquisition, wherein men were urged to subscribe more then law required; that by the oath *ex officio* they were enforced to accuse themselues, that they were examined upon 20 or 24 Articles upon the sodaine, without deliberation and for the most part against themselves'. Whitgift replied that 'his Lordship was deceived; for if any Article did touch the party any way either for life, liberty or scandall he might refuse to answere, neither was hee urged thereunto'. In regard to the oath *ex officio*, James himself delivered a long statement in answer to the objection, thoroughly approving the procedure. He then required the Privy Council and the bishops to consult regarding the High Commission upon 'the qualitie of the persons to be named and the nature of the causes to be handled therein'. While the suggestions made at the Conference were duly transmitted to the bishops and privy councillors whom the King had appointed to execute them, no special committee was, to our knowledge, appointed in regard to the Commission, nor was any reform carried out. Coke later declared that, at this time, he, as Attorney-General, drew up Letters Patent which reduced the competence of the Commission to 'heresies, schisms, Blasphemy, Idolatrie, incest, polygamy, depravings of the religion established and recusancy'.[1] This practically would have abolished the jurisdiction of the Court as it then existed. A good deal of discussion took place at the Conference between the bishops and privy councillors upon the feasibility and legality of giving the bishops the right to fine and imprison and a somewhat more extended jurisdiction, and of then limiting the Commission strictly to the most serious ecclesiastical offences.[2] Bills were introduced in Parliament to sanction such a change, but were incontinently thrown out by the House of Commons, whose Puritan members were anxious to abolish the bishops' authority altogether, by making them chairmen of a presbytery of ministers where a vote of the majority should decide. The discussions, legal and otherwise, came to nothing. The Letters Patent of 1605 were a verbatim reissue of those of 1601 with a

[1] Holkham MSS. 677, f. 252 ff. Holograph notes by Coke.

[2] Stowe MSS. 164, f. 192; Additional MSS. 28571, ff. 187–92. See also Usher's *Reconstruction*, i, 338–41, where these points are somewhat more fully discussed.

considerably larger membership, including many high dignitaries.

In 1604 the visitatorial authority, still retained by the commissioners, was employed in the coercion and deprivation of the recalcitrant Puritan clergy.[1] The ministers, however, believed that the hostility between the Commission and the common-law courts would enable them to procure from the latter prohibitions, writs of *habeas corpus*, or of trespass, which would block, if not practically annul, their deprivations by the former. Somewhat elaborate directions [2] concerning the common-law process which would thwart the bishop were disseminated in Puritan circles, and one or two of the deprived ministers actually posted up to London in quest of the prohibitions. At this juncture the Government thought it high time to interfere, and so utilized the customary assembly of the judges and privy councillors in the Star Chamber, just previous to the spring circuits, to interrogate them on these points. The legality of the Commission's action was completely upheld in language which events three years later render sufficiently remarkable. The King, agreed the judges, possessed 'the Supream Ecclesiasticall Power which he hath delegated to the Commissioners whereby they had the power of Deprivation *by the Canon Law of the Realm*'. The Act of Supremacy conveyed no new power, and therefore they held it clear that 'the King *without Parliament* might make Orders and Constitutions for the government of the Clergy'. Nor was it illegal to offer the accused the oath *ex officio* before he had been given a copy of the libel.[3]

[1] This incident has been told at length in Usher's *Reconstruction*, i, 403–23; ii, 134–6.

[2] Printed in full in Usher's *Reconstruction*, ii, 362–5.

[3] 2 Croke, 37. Moore, 755.

The extra-judicial opinions of the judges do not seem to have influenced their conduct on the bench at all. A few weeks later we find the Archbishop accusing them before the Privy Council of issuing prohibitions to the Commission, which, according to their own confessions, were indefensible, for they had not maintained them when returned.[1] Bancroft particularly objected to certain cases prohibited on the ground that the Commission had no authority to fine or imprison. Two men, one accused of 'notorious adultery and other intolerable contempts', and the other of abusing a bishop with 'sundry railing termes (no way to be endured)', had been fined and imprisoned by the commissioners until they should enter into suitable bonds for future good behaviour. Despite the evident ecclesiastical character of both offences, one man was delivered from jail by a *habeas corpus* from the King's Bench, and the other by a similar writ from the Common Pleas, both claiming that the Commission had no authority to fine or imprison. Nor were these the only cases, lamented the Archbishop. The judges replied at great length, the sum and substance of their defence being that it was their duty to deliver men unjustly imprisoned. They said nothing at all to the real issue, why the Commission had no such authority. Apparently the protest was of some avail, for we hear in the following year of a prohibition which the judges had denied 'a Puritan', 'until they might have a view of the cause prosecuted before the High Commissioners.'[2] If we can safely argue from these words, the judges

[1] Articuli Cleri, 1605, s. 22. The bibliography of this document, both of manuscripts and of printed books, is in Usher's *Reconstruction*, ii, 78, 79, notes.

[2] From Yelverton's Report to the House of Commons of a conference with the Lords, May 1, 1606: Lambeth MSS. 445.

were now compelling the suitor to bring something like adequate proof that he was injured.

According to Coke, however, the judges' opinions were the same as before. He reports what he says was the substance of an after-dinner conversation among the judges and serjeants at Serjeants' Inn.[1] First, they decided that, whatever the tenor of the royal Patent, the commissioners must 'proceed according to the ecclesiastical law allowed within this realm, for he (the King) cannot alter neither his temporal nor his ecclesiastical laws within this realm by his grant or commission'. And, as the ecclesiastical law did not allow them to fine or imprison, only an Act of Parliament could confer such authority. Coke also tells of advice which Popham and he gave the Privy Council earlier in this same year, to the effect that the oath *ex officio* as used by the Commission was illegal.[2] But that the judges as a whole, or in part, had publicly assumed any such decisive stand up to this time is quite improbable. In fact, the anxiety and astonishment of James, Salisbury, and Bancroft at their conduct in Fuller's case makes it clear that, if the judges had formulated any opinions so definitely hostile to the Commission's legality, they had very carefully kept them to themselves. While they had issued extreme prohibitions from time to time, they had maintained few of them; had in public ostentatiously supported the Commission's authority; and had least of all taken any united stand as a Bench against it. They had certainly provided themselves with ample precedent for any course they might adopt in the future, and were accordingly prepared to advance or retreat as expediency might dictate or opportunity offer.

Nor had they long to wait. Heartened by the readiness

[1] XII *Reports*, 19. [2] *Ibid.* 26.

of the judges to issue prohibitions, and confident that they read in ambiguous phrases an attitude favourable to their claims, the Puritans attacked the administration of the Church in its most vital point—the High Commission. If the power to fine and imprison, to cite men from all parts of England, and the right to use the oath *ex officio* could be taken from that court, the Church would be deprived of its mainstay, and the ardent Puritan leaders could already see the deprived ministers reinstated, the inefficiency of episcopacy made clear, and a king eagerly changing the government of the Church to Presbyterianism. Even if so much were not accomplished, even if the downfall of the Commission were not assured, they might at the very least so cripple it that it could no longer stand in the way of their secret practice of the Book of Discipline. A test case was selected, and a barrister chosen to 'impeach' the Commission before the common-law judges, and to ask the latter to declare its practices illegal.

Nicholas Fuller, the barrister chosen, was already well known to the commissioners.[1] He had for years been counsellor for the Puritans in their attempts to keep within the law and had often held their briefs in the courts. In March 1607, in defence of some Yorkshire men, summoned to London to answer for contempt of the commissioners at York, he had attempted to block the Commission's proceedings by seeking writs of *habeas corpus* both from the Exchequer and the King's Bench. In one or the other court, he had not scrupled to hint at his doubts of the competence of the Commission to deal with cases of contempt, and had declared the use

[1] A full account of Fuller's case has already been printed in Usher's *Reconstruction*, ii, 134–54, where will be found the authorities and critical notes on which these results are based.

of the oath *ex officio* illegal. The Commission had examined him, and released him with a warning that another such offence would result in his own imprisonment. Fuller later declared that he had been actually assigned by the common-law judges themselves the defence of 'poore men imprisoned by the ecclesiasticall commissioners'—a fact which, if true, certainly would explain the extremely bold statements he made before them, and also throw considerable light upon the reluctance of the judges to condemn either him or his opinions. Fuller had also attracted the displeasure of the King by his vigorous opposition in the House of Commons to the King's favourite measures—the subsidies and the union with Scotland. His ready tongue had dilated on the poverty and greed of the Scots, and upon the misfortunes which England would suffer when the hungry horde from the north were loosed upon her, till the King's gorge rose.

The case selected was nearly as ill-chosen as its advocate. Thomas Ladd, a merchant at Yarmouth, had been tried in the ecclesiastical court at Norwich for attending conventicles. He had made some difficulty about taking the oath *ex officio*, and, after he had testified, so many contradictions became apparent in his answers, that he was sent up to the Commission at London to be tried for perjury. He refused now to take the oath *ex officio* at all unless he were first shown his answers at Norwich, and for this refusal he was promptly sent to jail as a matter of course, on March 29, 1607. Mansel, the other client, was a nonconformist minister who had been arrested as one of the promoters of a petition to the House of Commons which the Government thought offensive. He, too, refused the oath *ex officio* and was also incarcerated. Both cases were so clearly cases of contempt, and both were offences for which the commissioners had so often during half a century imprisoned culprits, that the only possible ground for the defence to take was to prove the Commission's procedure illegal. And this ground Fuller promptly took. He had procured writs of *habeas corpus* for both men from the King's Bench on April 30, had secured May 6 as the date for the hearing, and on that day, accordingly, argued that his clients were illegally detained. The Commission was necessarily based, he said, upon the Statute of Elizabeth, which only revived such power as the bishops had possessed before the legislation of Edward and Mary. With copious citations from Statute and Year Book, he proved, to his own complete satisfaction, that the bishops had never had previous to 1559 the power to fine or imprison. Only such powers as the Act expressly sanctioned could the commissioners possess. He read the Act to the judges and analysed it, and pointed out that the extensive powers notoriously exercised by the commissioners were nowhere found in it. What was more, he denied that the Statute authorized a Court at all. 'His Majestie's Commission, which they terme High, is by the true intent of the Statute only a Commission executorie, but for so long time onely as shall please the King, and is no setled court for continuance for ever; as they would haue it, comparing the authority thereof with the King's bench and preferring it aboue it.' The comments which he interjected from time to time were more offensive to the commissioners than the argument itself. The procedure of the Commission he declared 'popish'; its jurisdiction was not of Christ but of Antichrist, and was being used to suppress the 'faith of the Sacrament' and true religion. To his mind, the bishops 'did proceede in these dayes by taking an ell whereby they had but an ynch granted them, and in examining men upon their oathes at their discretion and indiscretion as such their dealings were now lamentable '. The oath they administered tended ' to the damning of their souls that take it '. Men were imprisoned whenever the commissioners saw fit, and ' they detained them in prison as longe as they list '. Having said thus much on May 6, and finding himself on June 13 still at liberty, he launched forth at the second hearing upon further diatribes of the most ' scandalous ' character, not scrupling to hint that the commissioners were embezzling all the fines collected, and were extending their authority so as to embrace every branch of the criminal and civil law. The judges of the King's Bench apparently listened with complacency to this exposition, but gave no decision, and reserved the case for argument before all twelve judges. Fuller's indiscretion, however, had at last roused Bancroft, and he was arraigned by the Commission early in July upon a long list of ' scandalous ' things he had ' factiously and falsely ' affirmed, ' to the slander of the Church, to the hardening of the Papists ', and ' to the malicious impeachment of his Majesty's authority in Causes Ecclesiasticall '. The case was heard by Bancroft, the Archbishop of Canterbury, Ravis, the Bishop of London, and other leading commissioners. Fuller promptly procured from the King's Bench a prohibition, granted by Justices Fenner and Croke in the vacation after the close of Trinity term, which put an end to the trial in the Commission, until the prohibition could be returned to the King's Bench at the opening of Michaelmas term at the end of September. Fuller's rashness had changed the whole issue. The legality of fine and imprisonment was no longer in question. The issue had now become the right of the commissioners to punish slander and the dubious legality of a prohibition issued during the vacation. Ladd, Mansel, and the great case of the Puritans disappeared.

This prohibition, issued to the commissioners on Fuller's own behalf after his impeachment of the Commission's legality, roused James and Salisbury, who were quick to appreciate the fact that the new issue might be even more dangerous to the authority of the Commission than the old, because more indirect and technical. Nor were they blind to that other most significant element in the situation—the attitude of the common-law judges. The accordance of the prohibition with such technicalities of issue as were then being observed, no one seems to have questioned; in any event, the common-law judges had so frequently maintained their exclusive right to decide upon the technical validity of their own writs as to make any plea of irregularity certain of rejection. But that a prohibition should have issued at all to prevent the commissioners from punishing so flagrant a case of contempt of their jurisdiction, seemed to the councillors around the King 'absurd'; and its effect would surely resemble, thought Salisbury, 'fayre fruits gathered from rotten trees.' For the moment, however, the Privy Council waited for the judges' next move. When, at the opening of Michaelmas term, the prohibition in Fuller's case appeared, the judges of the King's Bench, aware of the importance of their decision and of its potential results, took counsel with their brethren of the Common Pleas and of the Exchequer upon the rightfulness of upholding the prohibition or the necessity of issuing a consultation. In any case, they must decide the alleged conflict of jurisdiction.

The issuing of a consultation involved, of course, a tacit confession that the prohibition had been somewhat too hastily issued, a confession which some of the twelve were extremely loath to make. In addition, the ordinary form of consultation not only left the Commission's jurisdiction unscathed, but practically could be interpreted to mean that Fuller's contentions were wrong. Possibly some of those considerations which later so powerfully shaped the law of libel—the right to demonstrate the truth of the libellous statement—were now operating on the minds of the judges. In the end, after much argument, they compromised; and issued, early in October, a consultation, with additional phrases intended to save the jurisdiction of the common law over the case as it had originally appeared. The commissioners were authorized to proceed 'with all due and proper speed according to your ecclesiastical authority against the schism, heresy, impious error, or pernitious opinions of the aforesaid Nicholas Fuller'. In truth, although these phrases seemed to deny power to proceed in the present instance against Fuller, who indeed was accused of slander and contempt and not of heresy and error, they nevertheless did sanction action by the Commission, for several charges concerning heresy and schism had been included (probably by chance) among the counts of the indictment. In any case, if the commissioners were the sole judicial interpreters of the language of the consultation, it would have been plain enough, from their statement, that Fuller's views were, to say the least, 'pernitious opinions.' The gist of the consultation contained, therefore, nothing to hinder the Commission's action.

Having finished the usual form of consultation, the judges added several sentences in the nature of explanation and qualification. 'Nor is there any question by us made, of the authority or validity of the Letters Patent to you and to others directed, nor of the exposition of the Statute of 1 Elizabeth, nor of certain scandals or other matters which, by the Common Law and the Statutes of this Realm of England, are to be punished or concluded.' Technically, of course, these phrases were not part of the consultation and were merely declaratory of the opinions of the judges. The innuendo, therefore, in the last clause, that Fuller could be tried only at common law, even for the slander of the High Commissioners, was of no legal effect; and, if it had been, the two preceding clauses would have completely nullified it, inasmuch as they declared valid the Letters Patent and the commissioners' exposition of the Statute of 1 Elizabeth, from both of which could easily be drawn ample authority to try slanders of all descriptions, whether against the Commissioners or not.[1] In fact, the consultation contained so many mutually contradictory phrases, and so many antagonistic claims, that it could hardly be considered to have placed a limitation upon the Commission's powers. By refusing to support Fuller's 'appeal' and thus assume jurisdiction of the case themselves, the judges had abandoned him to the discretion of the High Commissioners.

Despite the confused phrasing of the writ, the ecclesiastical authorities attempted to follow its very letter and spirit, in order to give Fuller and the judges themselves no cause for complaint. They therefore arraigned him for schism and erroneous opinions, and, probably on October 20 or 21, convicted him, fined him £200, and sentenced him to imprisonment during pleasure.[2]

[1] Just at this time the common-law courts were trying to draw all cases of slander before their own tribunals.

[2] XII *Reports*, 44. This happened before November 14, because on that date Fuller's fine was granted to John Patten of the King's Closet: S. P. Dom., Docquet, Nov. 14, 1607. On October 19 the King wrote to Salisbury to bear in mind Fuller's case (Hatfield MSS. 134, f. 126), and on October 23 Lake wrote

To the astonishment of James and Salisbury, and to the indignation of the commissioners, the judges of the King's Bench immediately made the situation serious by at once granting to Fuller's counsel a *habeas corpus*. If the consultation was valid, the *habeas corpus* certainly was not, for the only issue open to investigation by the latter writ was illegal detention, and, if the commissioners had authority, as the consultation certainly recognized, to punish Fuller for heresy and erroneous opinions, the granting of the new writ looked like gratuitous insult. There could be no doubt that either Fuller or his counsel intended to admit the right of the commissioners to try cases of slander, but to deny the right to imprison. James accordingly believed that the case had now gone far enough, and he directed Salisbury to interfere. The defence of the Commission was placed in the hands of the Attorney-General, Hobart. The King was certainly right: his prerogative would be the real issue discussed at the trial. If Fuller's reading of the Statute was correct, all Letters Patent issued since 1559 were illegal, and the ecclesiastical prerogative of the Crown as Supreme Governor was far less extensive than both Elizabeth and James had believed. The importance of the issue, therefore, far transcended the point ostensibly raised by the *habeas corpus*, and the possibility that the King's Bench might decide upon the limits of the royal prerogative, and hence restrict it, greatly alarmed James. But either Fuller or the judges lost heart, for at the hearing on November 24 only technicalities were discussed. Fuller claimed that the writ of commitment from the Commission

to Salisbury that the King was 'exceedingly well pleased' about the 'prohibition' (Hatfield MSS. 122, f. 150). When Fuller's case came up again it was on a *habeas corpus*; hence this trial would seem to have come on October 20 or 21.

was insufficient in form; Hobart showed that it conformed to the requirements of the consultation, and argued that, if the latter was valid, the *habeas corpus* could not be sustained in face of a writ based upon it. The judges professed themselves completely satisfied, but seemed to the King to raise anew the same doubt of the legality of the Commission's institution by allowing Fuller a new hearing, with the unusual privilege of counsel, which was hardly necessary in view of Fuller's own long experience at the bar. It is not improbable that the judges were anxious to decide against the Commission and were eager to get a case before them whose content would enable them so to do. But they were again disappointed: the only issue properly before them was the rightful commitment of Fuller, who did not apparently dare to deny the right of the Commission to imprison. It is likely that Fuller, and not the judges, lost courage, for the latter did not scruple, in rendering judgement against him, to dilate upon their own importance and dignity, upon the rightfulness of prohibitions in general and the complete validity of those already issued in particular, adding that they fully intended to continue issuing them whenever *they* thought them grantable by *their* precedents.

The State, and not the Commission, had tried Fuller: the State, and not the Commission, proceeded to deal with him. With the judges' professions of independence and rectitude the King was wroth, but was for the present without excuse for interference. After all, the disturber had been silenced, the slander of the Commission punished, and, while its jurisdiction had not been upheld *eo nomine*, the right of the Commission to keep Fuller in jail—which certainly the judges of the King's Bench had tacitly recognized by not maintaining the *habeas corpus*—ought sufficiently to prove to the doubters the weakness of his contentions. The spectacular decision against the Commission, for which Fuller and his friends had hoped, had been made impossible by Fuller's own rashness. The real assault was still to be delivered and was in firmer hands, backed by indomitable courage and the prestige of high judicial office.

CHAPTER VIII

THE ATTACK OF THE COMMON-LAW JUDGES

THE judges had been quick to see the value (from their point of view) of Fuller's arguments, and, not having formally pronounced upon their validity, proceeded as if the case were *res nova*. Coke especially, who had hitherto played the part of mediator between the Commission and the King's Bench,[1] was quick to take advantage of the situation to issue prohibitions himself from the Common Pleas upon such excellent grounds as Fuller suggested. The moderation shown during the preceding twenty years was speedily eclipsed by the rapidity and thoroughness with which the judges, led by Coke, pushed their contentions from a mere attempt to restrain the Commission to its own proper limits to a vigorous assault upon both the jurisdiction and procedure which the judges themselves were thought to have so fully recognized in Cawdry's case.

Within a year after the final remanding of Fuller to prison, the Commission was fairly overwhelmed by prohibitions. Their number was said, by the commissioners, to be infinite ;[2] their reasons, superficial subterfuges ; and the cause of issue, not a desire to right the wrongs of suitors, but a hostility to the Commission which threatened its very existence. The character of the writs

[1] Hatfield MSS. 123, f. 66. Nov. 30, 1607. Holograph, Lake to Salisbury.

[2] The fact was practically admitted by Coke.

issued leaves no reason to doubt the judges' purpose to rob the Commission of as much of its authority as possible. Whatever respect had been shown before to technicalities was apparently thrown to the winds, and with it went the caution hitherto exercised by the judges in not espousing peculiarly scandalous cases. A minister, deprived of his benefice for simony, non-residence, and gross neglect of his charge, obtained a prohibition suspending the sentence against him, although there could not possibly have been any real encroachment in his case upon the common-law jurisdiction.[1] In several flagrant cases of adultery and incest, the parties continued living together under the protection of prohibitions. A man secured a prohibition to prevent the collection of the expenses of a suit in which he had just been defeated in the ecclesiastical court; another was procured by one who had 'scandalously' abused the ecclesiastical courts when summoned by the Commission to explain why he had left his wife without maintenance. Even more extreme cases were aided by the common-law judges without compunction, among them a bailiff who had arrested people in church and dragged them out by force, even when they were kneeling at the altar rail to receive the communion. This feat was eclipsed by a Puritan named Green, who assailed the minister at Burkham on Sunday, and stripped off his surplice; he then carried away all the bread and wine prepared for the communion, so that there was no celebration of the Eucharist that day. The protection of such culprits naturally left in the minds of the commissioners and their supporters no doubts whatever of the animus of the judges and of their determination to clog the wheels of the Commission's work at any cost.

[1] Oct. 27, 1608. Stowe MSS. 424, f. 158, where are most of those quoted and a number more.

The extent of the legal claims advanced[1] by the judges in support of these prohibitions furnished even more explicit evidence, if any were needed. The use of the oath *ex officio*, its exaction before the accused was allowed to see the articles original, the use of fine and imprisonment, the right to arrest culprits by the Commission's own pursuivants, the right to cite any man to appear wherever he lived and the right to compel his attendance, all these were declared illegal on some ground or other, mostly because they lacked explicit statutory authority. These cases, to be sure, opened no questions of jurisdiction, and were concerned simply with procedure. Yet, if the Commission must rely upon the old and inefficient ecclesiastical censures and penalties, its coercive power would disappear, and, with it, the chief function which the Commission had exercised for nearly a quarter of a century, its quasi-appellate jurisdiction in support of the bishop's authority. And upon this coercive power rested at that time, not only the ordinary ecclesiastical routine administration, but the whole scheme of reforms just inaugurated by Bancroft—the enforcing of conformity and uniformity, and the increase of ecclesiastical incomes. Above all, the Commission was now the only weapon the Church possessed for enforcing the jurisdiction which the Church still exercised over the laity. Without it the bishop must fall back upon excommunication, which was not only scorned by the laity and not very seriously considered by the clergy, but which the common-law courts were tending to disregard in what they called 'small matters'—such as refusal to obey the bishop's sentence, or contempt of court. The real sanction behind excommunication for at least a century had been its

[1] See a long list of 'Questions concerning the High Commission' in Tanner MSS. 280, f. 137 (1608 ?).

recognition by the common-law courts as a valid suspension of a man's judicial rights.[1] If, now, the Commission were destroyed, and excommunication were no longer recognized by the common-law courts, the bishop would be unable to enforce his decisions at all, and suitors would eventually be forced to come to the common-law courts for effectual relief.[2] Thus, in Coke's phrase, the Truth would prevail.

But the judges, by no means content merely to destroy the efficacy of the Commission's procedure, began at or about this time the first genuine attempt to impeach its jurisdiction. Roper's case—a simple matter concerning a pension due from an impropriation—furnished (according to Coke's report) the excuse for an elaborate opinion concerning the jurisdiction of the Commission in general, which was, indeed, only a corollary from Fuller's main proposition, that the Commission's power depended upon the proper construction of the Statute of Elizabeth. The Statute, said the judges, limited the Commission to crimes, and, moreover, did not give it power to try any crimes, for

1 'For many are more afrayed of excommunication, for that they can prosecute no action, then of imprisonment, because that course is so chargeable, and so slenderly performed, throughe the corruption of inferior officers and ministres, that men are discouraged to pursue it': Paper drawn up by the bishops, 1584. Strype, *Whitgift*, iii, 129.

2 The Visitation Records contain long lists of persons who 'stood excommunicate' for weeks and months, or longer. The Consistory Court Book for 1605/6 at Ely lists 127, in different parts of the diocese. In Wisbeach Deanery in 1610, 121 were certified as excommunicated. In the previous century the lists were long: between 1579 and 1583 there were 339. In fact, to stand excommunicated became a distinct offence for which the Commission imposed certain regular penalties. In the face of these facts, it is idle to maintain that it was regarded as a severe penalty, or entailed *ipso facto* the loss of any important civil rights.

the Act did not give a right of appeal, and it could not be supposed that the Act would have authorized unlimited power, 'for this should be to dissolve the court of the Ordinary, which is so ancient and inevitably necessary in many cases to the administration of justice, in divers points of it, that without this justice cannot be executed.'[1] Tithes, legacies, adultery, testamentary and matrimonial cases must all be mentioned in the Statute if the Commission was to try them. Practically, this claim meant that the Letters Patent, which did expressly mention most of these categories, were invalid unless explicitly sustained by the Statute; and thus to argue was to condemn all the Letters Patent issued since the Act was passed, and insinuate, into the bargain, that the Crown possessed no ecclesiastical authority beyond the letter of the Statutes. Moreover, the judges further hinted that theirs was the province of interpreting the Statute, of deciding which courts might imprison and which might not, and, above all, of discovering whether the High Commission could receive from any Statute a concurrent jurisdiction which practically superseded the bishop's consistory court. If such an argument as this could be maintained, the contentious jurisdiction of the Commission would be destroyed at one blow.

The hearings upon the return of these prohibitions, as well as the logic of the situation, alone showed the judges the necessity of further definition. If the commissioners might not exercise such jurisdiction as imperilled the court of the bishop, what cases then might they try, for the bishop's jurisdiction was limited but little, if at all? Did it then follow that the Commission had no jurisdiction? When, in attempting to 'assign' to the Commission its due place in the judicial hierarchy, the judges perused

[1] XII *Reports*, 45 at 47.

the Statute once more, they found its phrases uncomfortably broad and inclusive. In particular, they found the Commission empowered to try 'all such errors, heresies, crimes, abuses, offences, contempts, and enormities, spiritual and ecclesiastical, whatsoever'. But few cases ever appeared before the Commission which could not properly have been denominated 'abuses' or 'offences', and the concluding word of the clause, 'whatsoever,' was certainly general and inclusive beyond all doubt. The judges, however, were equal to the emergency, and Coke seems to have been the author of the new opinion that the significant qualifying word in this most important clause was 'enormities'. This word referred back to those just enumerated, and thus empowered the Commission to try all 'errors', 'abuses', 'offences', and 'contempts' only when enormous, or, in more modern phraseology, of an extreme degree.[1] Naturally the judges expected to decide themselves, as they did in Langdale's case, when a given crime was sufficiently enormous to be within the Commission's cognizance.[2] They would have restricted it to what has been already called its original jurisdiction plus its jurisdiction in equity and *in forma pauperis*. Still, if this type of judicial construction was legitimate, its exercise could rapidly limit the Commission to an occasional case or two. The judges seem to have

[1] The word 'enormous' seems to have been common legal usage for a very serious crime, and seems to have already been employed in connexion with the Commission. The bishops used it in 1584, Strype, *Whitgift*, iii, 123; Cosin employed it in 1593, *Apologie*, ii, 47; Cosin also states that the Commission's jurisdiction concerned cases 'being aggrauated (above the ordinarie course of them) by some circumstance of moment', *Apologie*, ii, 48; while Cowell wrote in the *Interpreter*, in 1607, that the Commission was to try 'especially such (cases) as are of a higher nature or at the least, require greater punishment, then ordinarie jurisdiction can afford'.

[2] XII *Reports*, 58.

considered that appeal must lie from every court, and to have overlooked the fact that there must be finality of decision somewhere; but, even if they remembered the necessity of a final adjudication of disputes, they did not find it thinkable that Parliament had given the Commission's decision such finality. Again, they assumed that Parliament could not have intended to create a new court to do something already done by the bishop's court, and so decided that the language of the Statute could not mean what it literally said. Nor could they conceive of the Commission's possessing any authorization but a Statute, nor yet admit that any one but themselves might have a right to interpret the Statute.

All these suppositions the commissioners promptly and flatly declared to be of no value. Why should it not be possible for others besides Coke and his colleagues to construe Statutes? Why, they demanded, was it impossible for Parliament to make the Commission's decision final, or invest it with any jurisdiction it saw fit? And could not the King as fountain of justice, they reasoned, delegate a part of his residuary power to the Commission, just as he had centuries before delegated a part of it to the common-law courts themselves? Thus the arguments, technical enough at the outset, began soon to trench on the mysteries of statecraft, which James thought no subject for the tongues of lawyers. Which construction was correct was not an issue to be decided by precedent, but was a question of constitutional law, and called for the evaluation of the exact legal obligation of a Statute, and of the relations of all courts to the Crown and to each other. The early disputes between the rival judges over these prohibitions and their debates before the Privy Council were rather amplifications of their respective positions than actual arguments upon the real issues involved. Gradually, however, as the debates progressed, it became clearer and clearer that the true basis of the common-law judges' attack lay in their views of constitutional law rather than in precedent.

Certainly the judges received support and encouragement, if not actual enlightenment on the possibilities of the case, from the Puritan attitude, best exemplified in Stoughton's tract, *An Assertion of true and Christian Church policie.* One of the most considerable practical difficulties the Puritans had to meet, in arguing the feasibility of the abolition of episcopacy and the introduction of their Book of Discipline, was some provision for the large contentious jurisdiction of the ecclesiastical courts. There was for the Puritan, however, no alternative, and Stoughton courageously faced the necessity of abolishing all the existing ecclesiastical courts and of making some other provision for the performance of their work. A new set of courts, he declared, might, of course, be created by Parliament, in which the civilians might continue to judge those classes of cases according to civil law ; but such an expedient was clearly unnecessary, for all these cases could be easily handled by the common-law courts. In great detail, and with considerable ingenuity, he discussed the 'pretended' legal difficulties in the way of such a change, and not only insisted that they were really far from serious, but denied that any change in Statute law would be necessary. The existing law, he claimed, was entirely adequate for the assumption of the whole ecclesiastical jurisdiction, including that of the High Commission, by the Common Pleas and the King's Bench. Nor did he hesitate at heresy and schism. The clergy, he maintained, had never had this jurisdiction by delegation from God, or because these were really spiritual offences, but 'by a custome and by sufferance'. These general propositions coincided too well with the ambitions of the judges not to make an impression upon them, and Stoughton's judicial fictions for hearing ecclesiastical suits at common law soon began to appear in prohibitions.

Such arguments as Stoughton's did their work most effectually by breaking down the traditional belief that the ecclesiastical jurisdiction was wholly spiritual and concerned subjects of which laymen did and could know nothing. He insisted that nearly every case heard in an ecclesiastical court was tried by a layman as judge or chancellor, who was no better qualified to comprehend its subtleties than a common-law judge. If such reasoning applied to the ordinary ecclesiastical courts with centuries of tradition and prescription behind them, how much more did it militate against a new court like the Commission, whose existence as a court dated from a time within the memory of the judges even then on the bench!

Such was the serious situation which led James to summon the judges to defend themselves before the Privy Council for their conduct towards the Commission as well as towards most other courts in the realm. The Ecclesiastical courts, the Provincial Councils, the Admiralty, and the Court of Requests had been especially troubled by these same prohibitions,[1] though hardly one of these other courts had had to meet as serious and well-conducted an attack as had the Commission. In February and June 1608 the judges were before the King to answer for their obstruction of administration in Wales and in the North, and it was not till November that the debates touched the High Commission. Sunday, November 6, found judges and commissioners before the King

[1] The ecclesiastical side of these debates has been already treated in detail in Usher's *Reconstruction of the English Church*, ii, 206–45.

in the Council Chamber at Whitehall.[1] But neither was prepared, perhaps because each had expected to bring in a general denial to whatever the other might allege. The King remarked that either the Letters Patent were too long or the judges were too busy to read them, and adjourned the debate till the Sunday following, when he hoped both would be better prepared. To that end he asked them to present to each other their respective gravamina, so that each might be ready to defend as well as accuse. Evidently he thought the question could be finished in one long Sunday forenoon's debate. The maxim which he added—all the Courts were under one God, one King, and one Country—showed that the new prohibitions would be difficult to explain to his satisfaction. Before the commissioners could depart, Coke, the Chief Justice of the Common Pleas, delivered a long and apparently abusive tirade, in which he repeated Fuller's charge that the High Commissioners embezzled the fines paid to them instead of certifying them into the Exchequer.[2] Bancroft, the Archbishop, indignantly replied, and the interchange of words grew so warm that James interrupted and warned them 'to take heade of heat in this business', adding that he should note those who disregarded his wishes. Thus ended the first debate.

Although the King had apparently intended to consider the gravamina of the commissioners on Sunday, November 13, the debate began on the question of the *modus*

[1] The chief authority for all these debates is the holograph notes of Sir Julius Caesar, taken in the Council Chamber when the speeches were delivered: Lansdowne MSS. 160, f. 428 ff.

[2] The contrary was the truth. There are plenty of certificates of fines from the Commissioners in the Exchequer Documents at the Record Office after 1592, and S. P. Dom. Eliz., 228, no. 19, conclusively proves that this was the practice in 1584.

decimandi, and, before it had proceeded far, the King and Chief Justice Coke had come to high words, and almost to blows. Coke finally grovelled on all-fours before James, and was pardoned only after the intercession of Salisbury.[1]

The scene, however, did not in the least damp his enthusiasm for the cause, and on the very next day, November 14, he issued a prohibition to the Commission which easily exceeded in its 'enormity' all previous aggressions.[2] The man who procured the writ was a minister whom the Commission had deprived for simony, ignorance, and insufficiency. The Statute of 1 Elizabeth had limited the Commission, declared Coke, to the reformation of errors and heresies; nor were abuses or offences within its jurisdiction unless they were enormous and serious; he next quoted the clause of Magna Carta that no freeman should be imprisoned except in accordance with the law of the land; and, lastly, he claimed that in any case the minister's offences were condoned by the pardon of 1572. Whatever the law of the matter was, could it not be fairly argued that simony and gross ignorance were, in a clergyman, 'errors' of the first magnitude? Certainly from an administrative point of view they were 'enormous' 'offences'. If Magna Carta, the Act of Supremacy, and the general pardon of 1572 afforded Coke good legal grounds for rescuing such a man from the hands of the Commission and allowing him in consequence to go scot-free, it was clear that the Commission was already defending the last ditch.

In the spring of 1609 an attempt was made by the

[1] The present writer has published the evidence for this debate at length in the *English Historical Review*, Oct. 1903; and more briefly in his *Reconstruction of the English Church*, ii, 213–16.

[2] Stowe MSS. 424, f. 158.

Lord Chancellor, Ellesmere, to settle these difficulties at a conference with several of the judges.[1] As in the previous autumn, such debates and conferences as concerned the Commission were part of a long series of debates intended to compromise the acrimonious disputes between the common-law judges and all the other jurisdictions in England. On May 13, 1609, Ellesmere handed Coke and his colleagues at York House a note of five points of difference of opinion between them and the Commission: whether the Commission might cite any man to appear outside the diocese where he resided; whether it had concurrent jurisdiction with the consistory courts; whether it was restricted to criminal cases; and to them only when enormous; and whether it might inflict fine and imprisonment. Probably on the following Sunday (May 20), the judges replied by demanding the production of actual prohibitions in which they had made such claims. Without insisting upon the point, however, they declared their opinion, that the Commission had not properly cognizance of 'anything concerning meum and tuum as legacies, tithes, and pensions, &c.'; that it might deal 'onely with heresies and schismes and enormious offences and not for every petit offence'. Coke felt it necessary to produce precedent, and cited several cases, among them Atmer's case, where the Commission was not allowed to punish a man for working on a Holyday.[2] Ellesmere, with scarcely veiled sarcasm, said

'it was a pretty case, and vouched a president [precedent] in the queenes time when he was sollicitor; that the High

[1] Holograph notes by Coke. Holkham MSS. 677, ff. 252 and 252 b.

[2] We have even to-day nothing but Coke's own word to prove that these cases were decided, and we can see many reasons for declining to accept them besides the insistence of the Commissioners (who ought to have known the truth quite as well as

Commission did fine one for comitting incontinence in the Court and that so many as were present except two or three resolued the Highe Commissioners might impose a fine. And then the Lo: Chauncelor directinge his speech to me (Coke), sayd, when yow were attorney consideracon was had of the reformacon of the Commission and to reduce it to Certaine heades, and a draught drawne thereof, and that Chatterton Bishop of Chester refused it for that it was not generall. Whereunto I aunswered that it was true and that I drewe a forme and the same was reduced to only heresies, schisms, blasphemy, Idolatrie, incest, poligamy, depravinge of the religion established, and recusancy, and besought the lo: Chauncellor that he would be a meane that such a reformacon might be had, and then all further controversies in that behalf might be ended. And the Lo: Chauncelor said that he thought that 2 highe Commissions in each province were sufficient.'

A few days later the debate before the King on matters ecclesiastical again veered round to the case of the com-

Coke) that they were fabrications. They are all too apposite, and were produced so late in the debates that Coke was hard pressed to show why such excellent precedents had not been found by some one else, or, indeed, been quoted by him at an earlier time. He vouchsafed no explanation. Furthermore, if their dates are correct, they establish legal propositions and phrases at dates decades earlier than other evidence mentions. For instance, Coke cited Leigh's case, reported by Dyer, but (curiously enough!) *not printed,* which denied the commissioners the power to commit for recusancy in 1569. In Lee's case in 1568 and in Hind's case in 1576, both recusant cases, writs of *habeas corpus* were sustained by the Common Pleas, on the specific ground that the Commission might not fine and imprison. But if this was law, what judgement shall we pass upon the judges and learned counsel who declared to the contrary in 1577? What, too, of Cawdry's case? Coke's precedents cannot be said to have any historical value except as parts of his defence. That any such propositions were law prior to 1640 is exceedingly doubtful. But the cases given in the XII and XIII *Reports* and in the *Institutes* (especially iv, 330 ff.) have been the only precedents hitherto cited by lawyers or historians regarding the Commission.

missioners.[1] The clerics insisted that their jurisdiction should not be impeached, and the judges asserted that their jurisdiction limited them to criminal cases, and that Magna Carta forbade them to fine and imprison. Nor were such restraints an impeachment of their jurisdiction. The judges indignantly denied any feeling of hostility towards them; and declared that they favoured the ecclesiastical judges 'as far forth as their duties in their places will giue them leaue'. They also thought that one commission in each province would be sufficient. All this, however, was no more than a repetition in public of their private altercation with the Chancellor at York House. Probably little else was said at the time, and the question was dropped for a couple of months while Hobart, the Attorney-General, prepared the defence of the Commission ordered by the King. During the long debates before the King in July 1609, then, time was allotted to him on July 8.

The objections to the Commission, said Hobart, fell into two classes, jurisdiction and procedure.[2] The argument of the judges, that the Act of 23 Henry VIII, c.9, prevented the Commission from citing any man out of the diocese where he resided, was not well taken, for the Act applied only to the Archbishop and his courts, and could not limit the Commission merely because the Archbishop was a member. At any rate, if the High Commission could not summon men to its bar from any part of England, its power was gone. No Statute ought to be construed so as to have so extreme an effect. Nor was the next point of

[1] Caesar's Notes, Lansdowne MSS. 160, f. 129. Coke does not mention this part of the debate (XIII *Reports*, 37–47).

[2] 'The grounds of Prohibicons to the high Commission and the Answers unto them': Stowe MSS. 420, f. 18. Also in Cotton MSS. Cleopatra, F. I, f. 128; Petyt MSS. 511. 16, f. 117, and 518, f. 86.

the judges more defensible. If the Commission was to be limited to those cases only which the bishop might not determine, it will follow 'that it must meddle with none at all, for there is noe case ecclesiasticall in effect from the highest to the lowest over which the Ordinary hath not Iurisdiction '. As to the claim that the Commission was limited, not only to criminal cases, but to criminal cases of the most serious nature, Hobart said he would ask no better defence than the true construction of the Statute. The basis of the judges' contention was that the commissioners must find warrant in the explicit language of the Statute for any and all jurisdiction they assumed or for such procedure as they employed. It was undeniable, he conceded, that explicit mention was not made in the Statute of most crimes over which the Commission had always exercised jurisdiction, nor of fine and imprisonment, which it had freely used. If, then, the Statute alone was the limit of the Commission's authority, all the Letters Patent issued for sixty years were illegal, and, surely, it was a significant fact that Coke himself, as Attorney-General, had drawn up the three most recent Patents! Such illumination of the judicial mind was rather sudden, thought Hobart. It was strange that the judges had needed half a century to discover such a fundamental difficulty.

But the truth of the matter was, he showed, that the Statute itself explicitly directed the commissioners 'to exercise use and execute all the premisses accordinge to the tenor and effect of the said letters patents, any matter or cause to the contrary in any wise notwithstanding'. The Statute itself declared that the commissioners were to find the definition of their authority in the Letters Patent, not in the Statute. How could such language be held, he asked, to *limit* the Letters Patent?

Thus accepting the judges' own test, no reasonable construction of the words of the Act could prove any restriction in it of the powers the King might grant by his Letters Patent. The Act allowed the commissioners to 'exercise, use, and execute under her Majesty all manner of Iurisdiccon, priuiledges, and preheminences and authorityes in any wise touchinge or concerninge any spirituall or ecclesiasticall power or iurisdiccon within this realme or any other her dominions or Countryes'. 'What can be spoken more generall either for universalityes of causes or extent of place; is there heare any restrainte to Crymes and those enormous? Therefore upon this parte being subiect to noe restraynt, this question is decided.'[1] Further, the Act defined this authority as the right to visit, reform, &c., *all such* heresies, errors, &c., and enormities *whatsoever* which by *any* manner of spiritual or ecclesiastical power, authority, or jurisdiction, can or may lawfully be reformed. Was there here any limitation of the Court to cases which the bishop might not hear, or to criminal cases only, or to enormous and serious crimes? If confirmation were needed, it could easily be found. The Statute of 8 Elizabeth, c. 1, when summing up the power restored to the Crown, cited as amply sufficient the general clauses. The Act of Supremacy itself, moreover, was modelled on the Act of Supremacy of Henry VIII, and the clause from which Coke drew his strained argument regarding enormities was taken verbatim from the earlier Act. The Queen had also been careful to state that she resumed all the powers her father and brother had possessed, and

[1] See Appendix A for the sections referred to in these debates from 26 Hen. VIII, c. 1, and 1 Eliz., c. 1. The clauses of the Commissions are in Appendices B, C, D. This same argument the *Treatisour* had protested against in 1590 and Cosin had made the same answer; *Apologie*, i, 112.

a simple reference to the Henrician Act would show that it restored to the Crown '*all* iurisdiccons and authorityes to the Dignity of the supreame Head belonginge . . . without lymitacon'. The Elizabethan Act, therefore, summed up Hobart, 'is playne for all those purposes, that the word of supreame head implies all iurisdiccon ecclesiasticall of all kyndes,' and covers 'as well causes of interest and instance as Cryminall, and those greate and smale, and all to be exercised by his commissioners'. And, as all these Statutes avowedly restored the royal jurisdiction which had previously existed, and were therefore simply declaratory Statutes, they could not possess any restraining power at all.

Besides, the word 'enormity' did not necessarily mean a great or serious case, and its ordinary usage made such a construction forced at best.[1] Nor could any general rule for judging when offences were enormous be set down, because circumstances of time, person, and place aggravated or mitigated every aspect of the crime. 'And specially as this case is when all the offences in question are spirituall and not subiect to the Iudgment of the Kings Corte; howe shall the Cort that is not Iudge of the offence iudge of the degrees of the offence?'

Hobart then turned to his second head, the matter of fine and imprisonment. The judges here had attempted to define the authority which the Crown had resumed as the ordinary ecclesiastical authority plus the Statutes in existence before 1559. Pope and bishops had certainly never attempted to fine or imprison,[2] and therefore the

[1] *Supra*, p. 185, note.

[2] Cosin declared (*Apologie*, i, 104) that 'an Ordinarie in his diocesse (euen at the Common law) might condemne a man for heresie'.

commissioners could possess such powers only from an explicit statutory grant. The Act did not confer new powers on the commissioners, but simply permitted the Crown to delegate the old powers. Hobart, however, found a recognition of this dilemma in the Statute's direction to the commissioners to follow the letter of their Patent rather than that of the Act, which had then empowered the Crown to grant in the Letters Patent any powers it saw fit. An even stronger argument came from the *non obstante* clause of the Statute, which made void any previous legal provisions inconsistent with its terms—' Where the statute saies that they shall execute the premisses by vertue of this Act accordinge to their Commission any matter or clause to the contrary notwithstanding, can there be a more expresse contradiccon to the statute then to saie they shall not execute but by the former lawe ? '

With this interpretation, reason and logic agreed. Was it not ridiculous that the strongest ecclesiastical authority should be able to try the greater but not the lesser cases, and be unable to fine and imprison as the meanest temporal judges could ? The supreme power included in its nature all lesser powers. In conclusion he dwelt for a few moments on the topic he was to broach next, the exclusive right of the judges of the common law to interpret Statutes.

Coke was taken by surprise and in Caesar's opinion was ' somewhat inclinable to allow of all that ', but he requested time to prepare an answer in writing.[1] The Bishop of London, to prove the care with which the Commission proceeded, stated that no case was impleaded until it had been scrutinized by the Archbishop's chief

[1] Lansdowne MSS. 160, ff. 406, 407, 408. Caesar's notes identify the speech and its author beyond question.

judges. Hobart then delivered his long and important argument upon the right of interpreting Statutes,[1] a topic upon which, as all now recognized, depended the decision of the lawful authority of the Commission. Following the precedent of Cawdry's case as since developed by Cosin and still more powerfully by Ridley, the Attorney-General made a strong plea for the right of the ecclesiastical judges, including the commissioners, independently to interpret such Statutes as they were to execute. A Statute upon an ecclesiastical matter became at once a part of the King's Ecclesiastical Law and was to be executed and interpreted solely by the ecclesiastical judges. If the temporal Statutes were to be construed by the common-law judges on the ground that they alone possessed the requisite knowledge to understand them, the same argument would exclude the common lawyers from the consideration of spiritual matters. Each system of courts should be independent, and each should give the other full credit for its decisions upon all matters particularly within its competence. Of this doctrine Salisbury approved. The judges who should execute a Statute ought to interpret it; besides, prohibitions allowed criminals to escape any penalty, and thus robbed the King's Treasury of fines. The judges, he concluded, ought not to interpret all Statutes, 'bycause some of them concerne other learninge whereof they cannot judge.'

In closing the debate, the King directed Coke to explain in writing the 'unfit and uniust prohibitions' issued to the Commission, and commanded all the judges in the meantime to issue no more prohibitions, but, if aggrieved, to complain directly to him.

[1] A brief summary, with bibliography of manuscripts, is in Usher, *Reconstruction*, ii, 238, 239.

At some time within the following year Coke presented his formal written defence.[1] He first addressed himself to the matter of fine and imprisonment, and elaborated the argument by this time familiar, that, as no ecclesiastic before 1559 could have imposed either by warrant of ecclesiastical law, such a power must be derived solely from the Elizabethan Act of Supremacy. The eighth section must have been included to authorize the Commission, because it did not actually restore the ancient authority to the Queen, but described that part of the ancient authority which the Queen was to delegate to the commissioners. In this section no mention was made of fine or imprisonment, nor were the words, 'accordinge to the tenor of the said Letters Patent,' conclusive; for, plainly, the word 'said' was employed to connote the words, 'the effect whereof was lymitted and expressed before.' The Letters Patent, therefore, ought to include those powers only which were enumerated in the Act. Surely, the Statute never meant the Commission to derive authority from any Letters Patent the Queen might see fit to issue, for then 'as well confiscacon of landes, forfeiture of goodes and Chatteles etc. may be imposed, as fyne and imprisonment'. At the same time, it was not true that the Commission could not fine or imprison at all. Two Statutes, 2 Henry IV, c. 15, and 1 Henry VII, c. 4, had empowered the bishops, in the one case, to fine and imprison for heresy or erroneous opinion 'contrary to the Catholic faith and deturmination of holie Church', and, in the other, to imprison incontinent priests. The final repeal of these acts by this very Statute (section 15) showed that the authority named in them was annexed once more to the Crown. In such cases, therefore, the

[1] Usher, *Reconstruction*, ii, 241–5, notes, for the bibliography of the numerous manuscript copies.

commissioners might fine and imprison. 'The rule in Fuller's Case ympugneth not this opynion.'

As for jurisdiction, the Act 'restored or united' nothing but the 'visitacon of the Ecclesiasticall state and persons and the reformation of the same. And of all heresies, errors, Schisms, abuses, offences, contempts, and enormityes which be Criminall'; nor yet criminal cases unless enormous. The Act permitted the Commission to try only 'such enormous and hayneous Crymes, as by necessity require a more speedy proceedinge than can be had by the Ordinary Iurisdiccon but extendeth not to the criminal and inferior offences nor to any cause of tythes legacyes or other Cyvell cause, for that were to take away from the Ordinary his iurisdiccon and from the subiect his naturall defence of appeale. And then euery man will come to the high Commission Cort to obteyne there an absolut unrevocable Centence in any Cause ecclesiasticall . . .' Thus, this first clause of section viii was general, granting the Commission power to exercise ecclesiastical jurisdiction in the broad sense, and to act generally in such matters as might be specified in the following clauses. The second clause then contained the particular points of the general authority of the Queen with which Parliament meant to give the Commission power to deal. In particular, the word 'enormities' was intended to limit all those preceding; the section in which it stood was to limit the earlier sweeping phrases, while the *non obstante* phrase and the section concerning the Letters Patent, of course, referred back to these earlier clauses, and found their limitations in them. Coke denied, with some indignation, that he had said the High Commission might try only cases a bishop could not hear: the truth was, he insisted, that the Commission might try some, but not *all*, cases the bishops could try. 'We hould that the high Commission grounded upon the act of I Elizabeth doe only extend to such exhorbitant and enormous crymes and offences as of necessity require speedyer proceedinge then by Ordinary Course of Lawe. And that they cannot fyne and ymprison but only in such cases where the Bishop or Ordinarie might haue fined and ymprisoned before the Act of primo Elizabeth. . . .'

CHAPTER IX

COKE'S FINAL ASSAULT

THE King's hopes of forbearance and brotherly love between the rival judges, as the result of these long oral and written arguments, were soon rudely dispelled.[1] The judges not only continued to grant prohibitions but issued them more readily than formerly, probably because they felt that Coke's answer had completely justified their position. In 1609 and 1610 prohibitions were again issued by the judges in cases of adultery and incest, simony, non-residence, incompetence of ministers, assaults upon ministers, and the like. How many writs were issued we do not know, but the Archbishop complained,[2] probably with some exaggeration, that since Coke's promises in July 1609, to stop issuing prohibitions, there had been more of them than ever before. The consequences of Coke's attitude were soon apparent. The nonconformists and all who were discontented with the ecclesiastical laws took their cue from the judges. In 1610 two Brownists obtained writs of *habeas corpus*, but were remanded to jail on the ground that the High Commission could imprison for heresy.[3] Justice Warburton, at the Warwickshire assizes of 1609, released one Gifford, a Catholic, whose house had been searched by the pursuivant of the Commission, and who had been

[1] 'It grieveth me not a little that between my lo: Grace of Cant: and my lo: Chief Justice there should be so long and so lowde an opposition, if it be such as fame reporteth and blazeth abroad terme by terme': Lansdowne MSS. 161, f. 278. Archbishop of York to Caesar, Oct. 10, 1609.

[2] May 23, 1611. Caesar's Notes, Lansdowne MSS. 160, f. 412.

[3] XII *Reports*, 69.

himself imprisoned, giving as his reasons that the Commission might not exercise such powers.[1] A more remarkable case occurred near London as early as June 1609. The Archbishop himself, hearing that some Jesuits were concealed by a certain Christopher Roper, sent his pursuivants to arrest them, and took the additional precaution of sending with his own officers of the Commission the constables of the district. Roper refused to admit them and sent his wife to interview them, that he might be able later to swear (as others had by aid of the same artifice) that *he* had not refused them admission. Lady Roper demanded a warrant under the seals of six of the Privy Council, and, when the pursuivant answered that his warrant was from the Archbishop and three Commissioners, 'shee flurted at it,' wrote the angry prelate to Salisbury. She told the messenger he might come in, if he would not search certain rooms, which the owner of the house (Lord Howard), from whom they leased it, retained for his own use. The ruse was transparent, and the messenger, leaving a guard of forty men about the house, came back to London for instructions. The Archbishop wrote a letter to Roper, 'that he should be better aduised and suffer the search,' and a letter to the justices of the peace and constables of the district, commanding them to guard the house till further notice, and, with these, posted his messenger back again. He sent another man to Salisbury, and begged him either to tell the King of the matter or to send him a letter under the seals of six councillors. The outcome of the matter we do not know, but it is significant that the Archbishop should have thought it necessary to appeal to the Privy Council.[2]

[1] Lambeth MSS. 933, f. 25.

[2] Bancroft to Salisbury, June 7, 1609. Hatfield MSS. 127, f. 67. Original, signed.

In June 1610 Sir William Clifton was tried by the Commission and convicted by several witnesses, '(1) of laying violent hands on Mr. Stoks a minster and publick preacher so as his face was black and blew . . . the said Sir William boasting that he had beaten forty ministers and that Mr. Stoks was the 41st. (2) of reproaching Mr. Stoks to the scandall of his function calling him bald priest, rascall priest, and scurvy priest.' On Clifton's application, a prohibition was issued to the Commission, declaring that, by Magna Carta, no man might be imprisoned but according to the law of the land; that, by the Statute of Elizabeth, the Commissioners might hold plea only of certain matters, 'and the cognizance of the matters aforesaid belong not unto the said Commission by force of that Act;' that such cases as Clifton's were included in the general pardon of 1609, with other similar counts.[1] In a case of adultery, the prohibition cited first, Magna Carta, and the Statute of Articuli Cleri; then quoted 'the statute of primo Elizabeth, saying that Cognitum offensionum predictarum rigore illius actum non spectat ad Commissionarios Reginae quia non sunt lesiones enormes'. It then declared 'that interpretation of all Statutes and also all suites ariseing thereupon belong to the Temporal Judges and not to the Commissioners; that the Defendants being the King's free borne subjects ought to enioy the freedome of all laws and privileges of the Kingdom etc., that they are not bound to answer the articles touching the premisses upon their Oathes; that the Commissioners notwithstanding, contrary to the forme and effect of the said statutes and contrary to the course of the comon lawe, have called and convented

[1] These and various other prohibitions of the same stamp are in full in Stowe MSS. 424, ff. 158–84. Probably a copy made for the Archbishop's use.

the said parties before them and caused them to answer articles upon their oathes touching the premises and besides to endeavor to imprison them to their Great daunger'.

In the parliamentary session of 1610 the Commission formed one of the chief 'grievances' for which redress was asked. In earlier Parliaments, in truth, attacks had been made upon it, and, more often, Bills, introduced for general ecclesiastical reformation, would have affected it seriously,[1] but the agitation had hitherto been half-hearted. In 1606 the Commission had been mentioned in the House of Commons as a grievance, and some debate had taken place *pro* and *con.*[2] In 1607, immediately after Fuller's argument in the King's Bench, there were 'sundry particulars touching the exhorbitant Power and Practice of the High Commission read and opened out of a paper to the House, and a Bill for restraining the same delivered in, but not read at that Time'.[3] Two days later it was read a first time, and the day following read a second time and committed, but stopped there. In 1609/10 another Bill to restrain the Commission was read twice and then was probably abandoned in favour of the Petition of Grievances, presented finally to the King, July 7, 1610,[4] in which the Commission occupied second

[1] See a paper in S. P. Dom. Eliz., 266, no. 24. Jan. 21, 1598.

[2] Mar. 17, 1605/6, *Commons' Journals*, i, 286; Apr. 5, 1606, *id.* 294; May 13, 1606, *id.* 308.

[3] *Commons' Journals*, i, 387.

[4] The Bill was read a first time on Mar. 12, 1609/10, and a second time on Mar. 14 (*Commons' Journals*, i, 409). The Grievance on the Commission was reported from the Committee of Grievances, Apr. 27, 1610 (*Commons' Journals*, i, 422), read a first time May 7 (*Commons' Journals*, i, 425), and passed May 21. 'Mr. D. James against. The High Commission do more service than all the magistrates in the Kingdom for discovering of Recusants' (*Commons' Journals*, i, 430). Very little opposition

place. The Act of 1 Elizabeth was, declared the House, 'inconvenient and of dangerous extent'. Under it a commission might be issued to one man only; a commission had been issued for nearly every diocese in England, thereby depriving the bishop's court of its jurisdiction. The Commission inflicted penalties by fine and imprisonment, 'and exercised other authority not belonging to the ecclesiastical jurisdiction restored by that Statute,' which we conceive to be a great wrong to the subject. By it men were severely punished for all sorts of petty offences. Worst of all, the only limit placed by the Statute upon its jurisdiction was contained in vague words, 'such as pertain to spiritual or ecclesiastical jurisdiction,' which needed definition. The same men possessed both temporal and spiritual jurisdiction: they might 'force the party by oath to accuse himself', or might inquire by a jury, and then inflict for the same offence both temporal and spiritual penalties. Hence a man, committing an offence indictable under one of the penal laws, was liable to punishment, not only as the Act directed, but also at the commissioners' discretion. He might be forced to give bond for appearance or for performance of the Court's orders, though no appeal whatever from any order or decree was possible. Laymen were punished for slander of ecclesiastical subjects or persons; discontented wives were allotted alimony and granted divorces; the pursuivants of the Commission were accustomed 'to break open men's houses, closets and desks, rifling all corners and secret custodies, as in cases of high treason or suspicion thereof'. In view of all these grievances, the Commons humbly prayed the 'reducing'

in the House itself is recorded to this part of the grievances. The petition is in Harl. MSS. 158, f. 172, and has been often printed.

of the Statute and Commission by Act of Parliament 'to reasonable and convenient limits'. This was, in a way, conformable to James's speech to the House of March 21, 1609/10. 'If any Law or Statute be not conuenient,' quoth James, 'let it be amended by Parliament, but in the meane time, terme it not a grieuance . . . Complaints may be made unto you of the High Commissioners: If so be, trie the abuse and spare not to complaine upon it, but say not there shall be no Commission, for that were to abridge the power that is in me.'[1] While the House had, in truth, only declared the Statute inconvenient, and while it had only asked for its reform, it had nevertheless declared the Commission as it existed a grievance. Nothing, however, came of the agitation. The alterations made in the Letters Patent of 1611 were probably not influenced by the complaints of the House of Commons, which, indeed, only echoed what already had often been said by judges and litigants outside.

Coke now issued a number of prohibitions which brought matters to a crisis. A man named Allan Ball had, at some time during the year 1609 or 1610, been arrested and apparently had resisted the pursuivant. In granting him a prohibition, Coke added to his usual dicta, concerning the Commission's lack of authority to imprison, a statement that 'the King by his Commission cannot alter the ecclesiastical law'. Inasmuch as the Letters Patent then in force, like all their predecessors, delegated what Coke declared was illegal authority, the Chief Justice was openly accusing the King of illegal deeds, and arguing that the ecclesiastical prerogative could be limited by his own decisions. He added insult to injury by citing a precedent which had happened, he said, in 42 Elizabeth. According to him, Justices Anderson and

[1] *Works of James I* (1616), 537.

Glanville had decided that the murder of one of the Commission's pursuivants by a man he had been sent to arrest, was self-defence, for the Commission had no power to arrest any man by pursuivant.[1] Such opinions were suggestive, to say the least, to other wrongdoers. In another prohibition, *Rex* v. *the Bishop of Bristol and Hanley*,[2] Coke committed further aggression by declaring that all taxes and dues paid to the King must be assessed according to the actual value of the benefice, and not, as the practice then was, by the rated value in the King's Books. This was really a serious matter, for the ruling would almost double the money due to the King from the clergy, and the greater part of the clergy could barely pay the taxes as then assessed.

Finally appeared in February 1610/11, two prohibitions which ended all belief in the Chief Justice's good faith.[3] Cheekitt, a London cooper and sectary, was presented by the minister and churchwardens of the parish church of St. Botolphe for 'divers scandalous and factious speeches : . . . that there were yet left in London six or seaven churches which had not submitted themselves to the Antichristian rule and government of Lord byshops and popishe and wicked Ceremonies, and that these churches were yet golden candle sticks. That there was noe use for the booke of Common praier nor for the surples and other ceremonies, but that these were putt upon us by the will and at the pleasure of the Byshops, whose authoritye he held to be unlawful, wicked, and contrary

[1] XII *Reports*, 49, Trin. 6 Jac. But Abbot on May 20, 1611, spoke of it as quoted 'this last terme'.

[2] Quoted on May 23, 1611, against Coke: see Caesar's Notes, Lansdowne MSS. 160, f. 41.

[3] Holkham MSS. 677, f. 327. 8 Jac., Feb. 6, dated in Coke's hand. It has been thought that Chancey's case stood alone, but this paper and the letters about to be quoted prove the contrary.

to the word of god'. He refused the oath *ex officio*, and, before his respite, allowed him by the Commission, as usual, to consider whether he would maintain the refusal, had expired, he secured on February 6 a prohibition from the Common Pleas. Coke quoted, as usual, Magna Carta, 2 Henry V, and other Statutes, and repeated several of his well-known points. He then continued: 'Cheekitt is a free man and a lay subjecte and soe hath ben all his life time and ought to enjoy all liberties and customs due to all subjectes.' The action of the commissioners was illegal oppression; Cheekitt had been refused a copy of the articles whereon he was accused, and so had been committed to prison 'contra formam communis legis et statutum praedictum'. 'Therefore the Commissioners are prohibited that they proceede noe further in the matter until they shall deliver unto him a true copie of the said articles.' The case was certainly one of heresy and schism, and such cases Coke had declared were the only ones left to the High Commission. Thus, if Cheekitt's prohibition could be upheld, the High Commission would have in practice no jurisdiction left at all. The case was not one *ex officio*, initiated by the Commission, but a suit brought against Cheekitt by the minister and churchwardens of his parish, and, therefore, a case between party and party, fully justified by several Statutes, and hardly describable as a case of 'illegal persecution'. Probably about this time appeared the prohibition [1] to the Commission in favour of one Chancey, against whom it was proceeding in a case of 'notorious adultery' and desertion of his wife.

[1] This case seems to come in here: (*a*) because there is a clear reference to it in Lake's letter to Salisbury of February 22; (*b*) because the papers we have of Chancey's case in the XII *Reports* are dated in March, and concern, not a prohibition, but a *habeas corpus*.

When these two cases became known, the King was exceedingly angry. They were, he said, 'of a nature extraordinary and shewing more the perversenes of his (Coke's) spirit . . . than anie other prohibitions.' 'It must be very good matter', wrote Lake to Salisbury,[1] 'he must receive from My lo: Chief Justice that shall satisfie him and not a quible of law. His Majesty hauing been alredy so plain with him as your lo: knoweth. Or els his Majesty's resolution wilbe as God speaketh of the wickednes of man. My spirit shalbe no longer vexed with this man; and this disposition seameth to be soe farre imprinted in his Majesty as it must be very good reason that must remoue it.' The Bishop of London was directed to send particulars of these prohibitions to the Attorney-General, who was at once to transmit them to Coke. A few days later (February 27) Coke went to Newmarket and was closeted with the King some time; he assured James that he had not then had any word about these complaints from either the Bishop or the Attorney-General. The King was astonished, understanding him to mean that he did not know any complaint had been made against them; and Lake frankly wrote to Salisbury, that he believed Coke had not told the truth, for 'he hath spoken to others in private that your lo: (Salisbury) sent him word of them'.[2] Coke, however, spoke the literal truth;[3] for, although he undoubtedly knew all the facts when he saw the King, he had not learned them from either the Bishop or the Attorney-General; the papers mentioned were not in

[1] Feb. 22, 1610/11, Lake to Salisbury: S. P. Dom. Jac. I, 61, f. 99, Holograph.

[2] Feb. 27, 1610/11. Same to same: *id.* f. 115.

[3] Hobart's holograph letter is dated March 2, sending them to Coke 'within an hour' after his receipt of them, and Coke's holograph endorsement on the back, 'Recepi 3, die Martis A° 1610.' Holkham MSS. 677, f. 328.

Hobart's hands till March 2, and Coke did not receive them till the day following.

Meanwhile, the Churchmen and the ecclesiastical lawyers had bestirred themselves and had already sent James a petition signed by the most prominent civilians.[1] They dilated upon the reprehensible behaviour of the judges of the Common Pleas in issuing such prohibitions after the care James had taken to settle the matter and after all the promises Coke had made. He had risen to such a 'height of opposition', 'as were not the effect thereof continuallie before oure eyes and eares, we should think such vyolent Coarses against your Majesty's often admonicons to be incredible.' They wished to pursue their occupation 'without feare of losse of libertye *and what other poore fortune wee haue*' and without 'theise indignities and the iust exclamacons and reproches of your Majesty's subjectes, turmoyled in theise Confusions of Iurisdiccons'. And, to that end, they begged James to redress their wrongs and 'sett some certaine Limitts and bounds to both our Jurisdiccons'. They enclosed, for the King's better information, a list of the incorrect propositions Coke had lately delivered from the Bench.[2] These, according to the King's wish, Lake forwarded to Coke on March 1, stating that the King said the complaints touched not only the Court of Common Pleas, but Coke personally, and advised him to return an answer which would satisfy both counts.

The commissioners now took a somewhat important step. They disregarded the prohibition procured by

[1] Holkham MSS. 677, f. 320, copy. The one sent to Coke by order of the King.

[2] Holkham MSS. 677, f. 321, copy. There are two dates on it, prefixed to some of the complaints: Jan. 31, 1610, and Feb. 5, 1610. This is likewise the copy forwarded to Coke by order of the King.

Chancey, tried and convicted him, and committed him to prison on March 19. His counsel at once secured from the Common Pleas a *habeas corpus*, but, when he was brought to the bar, the Warden of the Fleet presented a warrant [1] from the Commission technically so perfect that no repetition of Fuller's plea was possible. The counsel for Chancey then had recourse to another expedient. As adultery was not, he said, an offence 'enormous', it ought to be dealt with by the consistory court, instead of by the Commission, for the Letters Patent could not authorize the commissioners to imprison Chancey for adultery or for denying alimony to his wife, unless the Statute of 1 Elizabeth expressly conferred upon them such powers. The judges agreed with him, maintained the *habeas corpus*, released Chancey on bail, and agreed 'in the meantime to attend upon the Archbishop and to do that which of right and reason they ought to do'.

As the Easter holidays immediately followed this action of the judges, the explanation demanded from Coke by the King was postponed. Coke said later that he delivered to the Archbishop his answers in writing before Easter term.[2] However that may have been, on May 20, 1611, he and the rest of the judges appeared on summons at the Privy Council Chamber at Whitehall to defend their late conduct, before some of the Council

[1] This warrant and the common-law proceedings are in XII *Reports*, 82. The date of the warrant is there wrongly given as March 19, 1611, which would mean 1611/12. This is impossible, not only from what else we know of the case, but from the internal evidence of the paper. Coke mentions Walmesley and Williams as present, but Walmesley retired December 1611, and Williams died January 1611/12 (*Court and Times of James I*, i, 154 and 158).

[2] It seems unlikely that this treatise formed part of his general defence of 1610. The copy in IV, *Institutes*, c. 74, is dated Easter 1611.

as judges, against the accusations there to be brought by the Archbishop, the Bishop of Ely, the Bishop of Bath and Wells, and four Civilians. The King was not present. In reality it was not so much a conference as an arraignment or trial of the judges before the Council. The fact was keenly felt by Coke, who exclaimed during the debate, 'I think this is to be the first tyme that ever any Judges of the Realme haue bine questioned for deliveringe their opinions in matter of lawe according to their conscyences in publique and solempne argyments.' The chief part of the first day's conference (May 20) was occupied with the Archbishop's charge, but Coke began his answer that same day, and finished it at the next meeting on May 23, 1611, at the close of which a more or less general debate took place.[1]

The Archbishop began in the theatrical and wordy

[1] The authorities for this debate are Caesar's Notes in Lansdowne MSS. 160, ff. 409, 410, 412, 411, 256, Coke's account, and the two treatises noted below. Coke's account of the debate is in 'A Conference by the Kings speciall appointment held before the Lords of the Councell touching Prohibitions on the 23 May 1611, where were present both the cheife of the High Commissioners and all the Judges of the Realme': Harl. MSS. 37, f. 125. Also: Cotton MSS. Faustina D, VI, f. 1; Hargrave MSS. 493, f. 111; Hargrave MSS. 278, f. 521; Harl. MSS. 1299, f. 120; Petyt MSS. 511. 16, f. 221; Tanner MSS. 280, f. 119; Tanner MSS. 120, f. 1; Rawlinson MSS. B, 202, f. 209; and a copy in the archives of Trinity College, Dublin. All these are dated May 23, 1611, except Cotton MSS. Faustina D and Hargrave 278, which are dated May 24. See also a paper in XII *Reports*, 84. The argument drawn up for the Archbishop may be 'The Arguments contra for the Archbishop of Canterbury'. Additional MSS. 25270, f. 29. Also: Lansdowne MSS. 211, f. 141; Royal MSS. 18, B, xiii; Exeter College, Oxford, MSS. 154, f. 71; Tanner MSS. 120, f. 141; Harl. MSS. 4892, no. 2; Petyt MSS. 518, f. 51; Cotton MSS. Faustina, D, VI, f. 93; and Cotton MSS. Cleopatra, F. II, f. 287; Hargrave MSS. 278, ff. 726–80; and 493, ff. 272–383; Rawlinson MSS. B, 202, f. 193 b; and C, 738, f. 107.

manner then in fashion, giving thanks to God, to the King, and to the Council for this hearing. These matters were, he said, abuses against God, against the King's royal government, the Church, and the Commonwealth. He rehearsed the now well-worn facts that the Commission rested upon the Statute of Elizabeth; and that the Statute conferred inclusive and not limited powers upon the King. But he shed new light upon the issue when he stated that those best fitted to interpret the Statute were those who drew it. He pointed out that, only two months after the Statute was passed, the first Letters Patent was issued, drawn up by the very men who had drawn the Statute, and including among its members many who sat in the Parliament that passed it. Nor did the common-law judges at the time, he insisted, find any fault with the power to fine and imprison. He showed that Henry VIII and Edward VI had granted to commissioners power to fine and imprison.[1] Moreover, said he, my Lord Coke himself, as Attorney-General, drew up three Letters Patent, and it is hard for him to tax us with illegal deeds explicitly authorized by a document which is his own handiwork. In Coke's own report of Cawdry's case, he continued, the Commission was upheld as lawful, as having the power to fine and imprison, and as having jurisdiction over a long list of offences with which the common law might not deal, including most of those of which the Chief Justice now claimed jurisdiction. According to Coke himself, he repeated, the Commission was founded upon the ancient law of the realm and the King's just prerogative, and might have been instituted by the Crown even if the Act of 1 Elizabeth had never

[1] See Pocock's *Burnet*, v, 456; Wilkins, *Concilia*, iii, 784; Rymer, *Foedera*, xv, 181; *ibid*. xv, 191; *ibid*. xv, 250; Cardwell, *Documentary Annals*, i, 102; Wilkins, *Concilia*, iv, 43.

been passed. He enlarged upon the evil done by prohibitions, saying that there was no villainy, no crime so great, that it was not unpunished, and, after a sort, protected by the Common Pleas. He resented Coke's quoting the precedent of the 'legal' killing of a pursuivant, for 'if so, the hearers were wise to consider what to do in the like case'. He closed his speech with a statement of the goodly revenue of fines which the commissioners might be expected to pay into the Exchequer if their judicial work was unimpeded.

Coke replied in a long and learned opinion, practically identical with his treatise of the previous year. He still found that the whole question hung upon the interpretation of the clauses of the Statute. As to the first head, he asserted that the Commission might take cognizance only of crimes, and not of all crimes, but only of enormous crimes. The first clause of the Statute was, he said, general, granting them power to exercise ecclesiastical jurisdiction in the broad sense and to act *generally* in such matters as thereafter should be *specified.* The second clause contained the particular points of the general authority of the Queen with which Parliament meant to give the Commission power to deal—that is to say, with all 'heresies, errors, schisms, abuses, offences, contempts and enormities whatsoever'. The particularity of this last clause was a restraint upon the generality of the former. This last word 'enormities' was meant to describe and expound all those that preceded it. Parliament did not intend that the Commission should judge all 'offences', for what was there that could not be included under that head? The Commission might deal with the matters enumerated only when they were 'enormous' and horrible crimes. It was not meant to supplant the ordinary ecclesiastical jurisdiction, but to give the Church some extraordinary power for dealing with the popish priests, for whom the censures of the English Church had no fears. As for the power to fine and imprison, he said that the commissioners based their claims upon the clause of the Act which ordered them to proceed ' according to their letters patent ', interpreting the Act to mean, by any Letters Patent which the Queen might issue. Yet the Statute was meant to read, by such Letters Patent as should be in accordance with the limitations just enumerated. In these phrases there was admittedly none which conferred power to fine and imprison, and, therefore, the Commission might not exercise any such powers, except in cases where the bishops had possessed them before the Statute. These were two: for schism and heresy, and for incontinency of priests. In conclusion, he demanded time to answer in writing the complaints which the Archbishop had just made.

The Archbishop replied that, since Coke's earlier offer of peace, he had actually done more injury to the Commission and granted more prohibitions than ever before. The Lord Coke, said he, argued beside the point. The real question at issue was, what were the full powers actually conferred upon the King by Statute, for it was above all necessary to know ' what we may doe by right and not by tolleration '. He charged Coke with attempting to overthrow, ' all upon his owne devise,' the ecclesiastical courts which had existed ' tyme out of mynde '.

Coke replied that he was a true son of the Church and had done nothing that did not tend to its maintenance. ' But I thinke this to be the first tyme that ever any Judges of the Realme haue bine questioned for deliveringe their opinions in matter of lawes according to their conscyences in publique and solempne argyments.' It was, he thought, a very dangerous precedent.

The Lord Chancellor Ellesmere at this point interfered, for the debate was drifting rapidly into personal recriminations between the Archbishop and the Chief Justice. The only reason for this meeting was, he said, to hold a 'peacable and tymeable conference together for the reconciling of theise differences . . . by allowing to every court such jurisdiction as it hath aunciently had'. The King purposed to suffer 'no innovation'.

The Archbishop then briefly summed up his contention. He quoted two clauses of the Statute whose general wording did, in his opinion, 'much fortifie the practice of the Commissioners.' He repeated his former argument that the men who drew both the Act and the first Letters Patent under it were the best expositors of the meaning intended. He pointed out that the Act Books of the Commission proved that, ever since 1559, the Commission had regularly fined and imprisoned without question. This was supported, he felt certain, by Cawdry's case, 'now reported by my lo: Cook.' Lastly, he laid much stress on the injury to the King's revenue done by prohibitions.

Coke followed with the sum of his defence: that the High Commission might fine and imprison any one for heresy and schism, and imprison incontinent priests, and that these fines and this imprisonment were to be understood as 'reasonable'.

Thus the speech-making ended, but not the debating, for the Government was far from satisfied. On June 7 the Judges of the Common Pleas were summoned alone before the Council and took part in a warm debate with the Lord Chancellor, who endeavoured to bring them to 'reason'.[1] All to no purpose: they were not to be

[1] The authorities for these events are chiefly: Coke in XII *Reports*, 84, and an account by Caesar in Lansdowne MSS. 160, f. 256, of a debate and speech by Coke on June 7, 1611.

'convinced'. The Council then called before it nearly all the remaining judges, who, after some debate, agreed with their brethren. So much hesitation and so many repeated demands for time to look into the precedents on the same questions, had, however, by this time thoroughly convinced the Council that the judges intended to disagree in private and invariably present a united front to their enemies. The King was evidently perturbed. He came himself to the Council in all the majesty of state, and found the judges assembled to report as he had directed. The Judges of the Common Pleas were told that they had opposed him, and that they must retire for the present. After they had withdrawn, the matter was debated *pro* and *con* for a couple of hours; the great lords of the Council, Ellesmere, Salisbury, and even the King himself, expostulating with the obstinate lawyers, who felt no doubt that the very existence of the common law depended on their firmness. The King then questioned them separately, with somewhat better success, for it presently appeared that they were far from unanimous. Finally, despairing of ever bringing them to agree in favour of the Church, the King caused the Judges of the Common Pleas to be brought in again. He made a speech to the assembled company, saying, in effect, that he would reform the Commission and reduce it to spiritual causes only; the word 'errors' should be explained; but when the new Letters Patent appeared, he wished it obeyed without further question. After the debate Salisbury was heard to say that the chief feathers had been plucked from the High Commission, 'nothing but stumps remaining.' James went so far as to speak with Coke in private, and endeavoured to cajole him into compliance. In private he was somewhat more amenable, and told the King that the judges would do nothing further till the new Patent appeared, when ' we will, as to that which is of right, seek to satisfy the King's expectation '.

The Archbishop was diligent and prompt, and in August the new Letters Patent appeared, not, however, till after much discussion and debate with James, to whom probably was due the fact that, after all, the new document did not very much curtail the Commission's authority. On August 21 he was satisfied in the main with the Council's draft,[1] ' but dooth mislike a great part of the narrative . . . because he thinketh it tyeth him so as that if hereafter he wold grant a larger Commission he might not and therefore he wold haue it clean left out and instead to say no more but that his Majesty now for causes knowne to himselfe and for his care to save his people as much with good government as may stand, hath been pleased to graunt his commission in form followinge.' This was typical of James's attitude and of the commission which issued. It contained many changes in the direction of the judges' complaints, but it did not rescind the power to take cognizance of small ecclesiastical offences, nor did it limit the commissioners to ' crimes and those enormous ', nor did it take away power to fine and imprison. It rather restated the Commission's position than remodelled it.

It now remained to be seen whether the judges would accept this ' compromise '. The two Chief Justices and six other judges had been made members according to the

[1] S. P. Dom. Jac. I, 65, f. 84, Holograph : Lake to Salisbury. See also *id.* f. 88, probably the draft the King saw ; and Lambeth MSS. Carta Miscellanea, V, f. 3, which seems to be connected with these Letters Patent. On August 26, 1611, the King's doubts were satisfied : Lake to Salisbury, S. P. Dom. Jac. I, 65, f. 86. The Letters Patent are printed with modernized spelling in Prothero, *Select Statutes*, 424. The jurisdictional changes will be treated in detail in chapter xi.

practice of the last thirty years, but it had not been usual for them, or for any of the high officials of the Council, actually to sit. The Letters Patent passed the seals on August 29, 1611, and when, late in September or early in October, the first meeting was announced, the Archbishop summoned the judges and all the great dignitaries of State and Church to attend. They all duly appeared at the Great Chamber in Lambeth Palace on the day appointed, but Coke refused to sit by virtue of the Patent. The Justices of the Common Pleas, he said, were not acquainted with the document as the Justices of the King's Bench were. Therefore he did not know what was contained in it, and, without knowledge, he could not execute it with good conscience, for if the Commission were against the law, the judges ought not to execute it or sit by virtue of it. He had sent to the Rolls for a copy, he asserted, but had found that it was not yet enrolled. If they would give him a copy, he offered either to sit or show cause to the contrary. Salisbury tried in vain to move him from this determination and then conferred with Abbot. The Archbishop was eager to proceed, for 'he had appointed divers causes of heresy, incest, and enormous crimes to be heard upon this day'. He agreed, however, that the Patent should be read. 'And so it was,' says Coke, 'which contained three skins of parchment and contained divers points against the laws and statutes of England, and when this was read all the Judges rejoiced that they did not sit by force of it.' The Lords and Bishops present then took the Oaths of Supremacy and Allegiance, as all commissioners were required to do before taking their seats. But the judges refused to take the oaths as commissioners, though they took them as 'subjects of the King', and refused to sit down at all, fearing that the Archbishop would claim the victory unless they remained standing.

The Archbishop then delivered an oration describing the King's care for the peace of the Church, his desire for the extermination of heresy, and the creation of the Commission and its summary procedure to attain that end. He then called two 'most blasphemous' heretics and interrogated them, hoping thus to convince the judges of the necessity for the Commission and its procedure. All was in vain. Abbot finally promised them a copy of the commission as soon as might be, and the Court was adjourned.[1]

[1] XII *Reports*, 88. Coke is our only authority for this session. The date at the head of the paper is '9 Jac.', but in the body of it the Archbishop is mentioned by name as Bancroft. This is impossible, as Bancroft died in November 1610. There was a Patent issued also in 1608, and it is difficult to say positively that this meeting did not take place at that date; but in the French copy of the *Reports* (Lansdowne MSS. 601, f. 137 b) the date is given as 9 Jac. and the name 'Bancroft' is inserted in the text in a different handwriting. On general reasoning the later date seems better, for, if the account is true at all, it is true of a time when the disagreement had become very acute. See the *Law Quarterly Review*, xv, 283, note, for a very sharp criticism of Coke's law in this paper.

CHAPTER X

THE RELATIVE MERITS OF THE LEGAL ARGUMENTS

THE reason for the discontinuance of the debates and for the failure to reach any conclusion or to publish any decision lay in the realization that behind the legal arguments and their rows of precedents stood very divergent views of constitutional law. Upon these premises rather than upon line and precept the case must ultimately rest, and both sides were beginning clearly to apprehend the fact. After the common law habit, the parties had taken issue upon a very small point of fact to decide a very great matter of principle, and, until some agreement was reached as to the principle underlying the whole question, all arguments regarding the corollaries derived from it were worthless. Given the notions of political theory held respectively by the common lawyers and by the civilians, neither could have come to a different conclusion as to the positive law of the matter. The debating and discussing stopped, not because either was in the least convinced by the other's treatises, but because neither was willing to accept the other's premises or renounce one tittle of its own. In fact, the really vital question—which one of the interpreters had a right to decide the questions raised—was transferred to the political arena for decision, and was to be answered in 1641 by a Parliament which the enemies of the Commission controlled.

The constitutional issues under discussion had attained by 1611 the greatest breadth and significance. The technical arguments had finally brought the rival judges to a deadlock over the interpretation of statutes, but it was soon clear that another issue was also involved, the legal distinction between the royal prerogative and Statutes. Which was of superior obligation? Did the Statute of 1 Elizabeth contain a grant to the Crown by the nation in Parliament assembled, and was it thereby a summary of the total legal powers of the Crown upon that point, or was it a concession by the Crown to the nation, containing merely a record of those powers, which the Crown chose, for the time, with the consent of Parliament, to delegate to the High Commission? Was the Statute declaratory of a right already possessed by the Crown, or was it permissive, creative of powers not hitherto included in the prerogative? Yet this question as surely depended upon a further point: had the King a residual judicial authority, and could he by it have created a new court without consent of Parliament; or did the residual authority rest elsewhere—in Parliament, or in the King in Parliament, or in the people? If the King possessed such an authority, did he possess it by prerogative, by descent from his predecessors, or had it been conferred upon him by the Reformation Statutes? Thus, what seemed to be a purely legal question of the most detailed and technical sort proved to be in reality a most fundamental question of constitutional law. What was the value and authority of a Statute, what was the relation of the common-law courts to the Crown and to the law, how large was the ecclesiastical prerogative of the King, and how might he exercise it? James had been quite right; his prerogative was in question; by declaring that the Statute limited the Letters Patent, Coke was attempting to shear from the Crown extremely important ecclesiastical powers which the Crown had always exercised, and was, moreover, giving expression to a rule of judicial interpretation which would enable him, practically at will, to limit the prerogative in any direction whatever. The struggle over the Commission was only the first engagement of a lengthy battle, and to acknowledge defeat meant virtually the recognition of the right of the common-law judges to allot to the Crown and all administrative bodies such powers as they saw fit.

The constitutional theories of the common lawyers, which governed their view of the issues, had nothing to do with political speculation as ordinarily treated. Bodin and the definition of sovereignty, Buchanan and the rights of kings, were as little regarded as the divine right of bishops. Coke and his colleagues found the basis of the State in 'The Law', which had existed from the very earliest times, and whose basic rules, as applied or interpreted by the common-law judges, were adequate for the decision of any particular case which might arise.[1] The judges did not make the Law: they had but to seek for it and they would find it already existing in custom, Statutes, and the decisions of their predecessors on the Bench. To Parliament, The Law had apportioned the duty of making from time to time such applications of its general principles to large classes of facts as need should require. To the King, The Law had given the duty of administering the State, subject to itself, to Parliament and its Statutes, and to the authoritative decisions of the

[1] Neither Coke nor any of his colleagues ever made any full statement to this effect, and their views must be deduced from the *Reports*, the *Institutes*, and the voluminous manuscript evidence of the controversy.

judges. The royal prerogative was thus an emanation from The Law, necessarily inferior to it, necessarily controlled by it, and limited strictly to such explicit grants as might be found in the customs of England or in Statute law. There could, in fact, be no question but that the prerogative was limited by The Law: the only possible question for dispute was how far, and upon this the decision of the judges would be final. Thus the lawyers tended to regard The Law of the Land as based essentially upon custom. Changes in it by Statute were necessarily abnormal and unusual. They assumed that a Statute was to be strictly interpreted, that it changed the law (the rules which regulated conduct at any one moment; nothing could change The Law) as little as possible, and that every presumption lay in favour of the old law, against change, and, therefore, against any increase of the royal prerogative. Hence, when the interpretation of a Statute fell under dispute, the very first premise of the judges' arguments was that the change was as slight as possible and no greater than the wording of the Statute, as *they* interpreted it, made absolutely necessary.

The civilians and ecclesiastics, on the other hand, regarded the royal prerogative as the foundation of the State,[1] and the law as an emanation from it. Originally the King had possessed all power whatsoever, and he still retained all possible authority that he and his predecessors had not expressly and finally delegated to administrative or judicial bodies. Part of his judicial and legislative power he had, out of grace, and for convenience of administration, delegated to Parliament. Part of his judicial powers he had delegated to the various

[1] See especially the tracts of Cosin, Ridley, Fulbecke, the Canons of 1606, and James I's works and speeches.

courts, which enforced his orders, either directly or through the medium of Parliament in form of Statutes. From time to time, by means of certain Statutes, the King had irrevocably granted away certain attributes of sovereignty; yet each Statute was to be expounded strictly, and all authority, not expressly granted away, remained with the King. A Statute was, therefore, unusual, and changed the law as little as possible, for the real basis of the law of the land, its real residual force, was inherent in the royal prerogative, ample for all possible contingencies. Thus, the decision of the King was the highest in the realm; his judges were merely his satellites, moving in his shadow, 'the lions under the throne.'

Applying these premises to the real moot point of the controversy—what ecclesiastical authority had been 'restored' to the Crown—it became at once necessary to demonstrate the limits of the previous ecclesiastical authority. Nor was it enough to agree upon certain broad propositions; the everyday life of the English people demanded, as the existence of the controversy itself abundantly proved, some clear indication of the exact powers which had been 'lawfully' exercised. To Coke, the assumption that the residual authority remained in The Law made all plain. The Law, he said, had for some centuries countenanced the exercise of ecclesiastical authority by Pope and bishops, until, finding that they abused their trust, it annulled its grant, and conferred upon the King by Statute the true powers which The Law had meant Pope and bishops to exercise. This 'restored' authority, then, was limited to the ordinary episcopal authority *plus* the definite grants by Statutes. The King, as merely an agent of The Law, could not possibly receive any general or sweeping powers.

But the civilians promptly pointed out that these

declaratory Statutes could not, by general and inclusive phraseology, *restrict* the fountain of justice itself; they had merely recognized once more the existence of powers always inherent in the Crown. Where the Crown possessed the residual judicial authority, it was folly to talk about restrictions, and peculiarly puerile to claim that the Crown was limited by a declaration that the King should exercise only 'lawful authority'. The royal authority had from the first been the only lawful authority, and to presume that the King would exercise unlawful authority was an approach to treason. The word 'lawful' merely excluded the jurisdiction which the Statutes continually insisted that the Pope had usurped. In reality, declared the civilians, the Statutes restored all that 'ancient jurisdiction' which the King had possessed *before* the papal usurpation and of which the Pope had usurped a *part.* The extent of an illegal usurpation could not properly serve as a measure of the legal extent of the just authority. As for the Statutes, the union of temporal and ecclesiastical authority in the Crown had created the 'King's Ecclesiastical Law', equal in every respect to his temporal, impleaded in courts as dignified and as worthy of credit, and entitled by reason and logic to the sole interpretation and execution of the Statutes and Canons which composed it. It was reasonable to suppose that these ecclesiastical laws concerned subjects which the temporal lawyers did not so adequately understand as the ecclesiastical; it was logical for each system of courts to decide invariably those questions peculiarly within its own province; it was just and equitable to compromise those difficult matters where the old jurisdictional lines were vague. The practical advantages were obvious: all these troubles and controversies would be ended; the litigious habits of suitors would be checked; and order and system would once more resume their sway in judicial matters.[1]

To all these arguments, the common lawyers replied that reason, logic, equity, and expediency were not the least in question nor of the slightest avail. The very existence of The Law was self-evident proof that there was one law in England and not two. If the ecclesiastical law was not a foreign jurisdiction and hence without any rights at all, it was necessarily part of the common law, and, as such, was to be controlled by Statutes and by the authoritative decisions of the common-law judges. What The Law was had been sufficiently declared, and nothing more was needful but its recognition by the commissioners. The ideas of the ecclesiastics as to what English law was were of no value: it was the exclusive right and duty of the judges of the common law to declare what was law. In 1640 these views were enacted into statutory law, and for three centuries have been accepted as the truth about legal history; yet, while the Long Parliament was clearly capable of *changing* the law, it was hardly capable of changing the facts of history.

If any confidence can be placed in the researches of Maitland and his colleagues in the history of the common law, the ecclesiastics were a good deal nearer right than were the common lawyers. Undoubtedly, the King was the centre of the State during the Middle Ages, and his possession of the residuary judicial power was never questioned. Indeed, from his use of this residuary power

[1] Even a slight acquaintance with the decisions of the eighteenth and nineteenth centuries in both courts, as registered in Phillimore's *Ecclesiastical Law* or in the *Law Reports*, will convince the student that such is now in fact the relationship between the two systems. The ecclesiastical courts now try all temporal matters incidental to the main issue, with appeal to the Judicial Committee of the Privy Council.

in his Council in his Parliaments came the exalted position of Parliament as the chief court of appeals. The *Statuta* were really judgements of a court of law, and not, as was long supposed, legislative attempts to apportion the power between King and People. The common-law courts themselves were not ‘ created ’, but were gradually split off from a royal council in a manner similar to the method by which the Star Chamber, the Court of Requests, the provincial councils, and the High Commission itself were ‘ created ’. Nor is there any valid evidence, in Statute or history, to show that the Crown ever renounced the residuary authority. Indeed, it is doubtful whether any one had ever claimed such a renunciation previous to the days of Coke. There seems to be every reason for believing that the exercise of royal authority was exactly as legal in the sixteenth century as in the thirteenth, and that, as the ecclesiastics claimed, the royal prerogative, and not the Statute, was the true source of the Commission's powers. If the ‘ resumption ’ of ecclesiastical authority was a fiction, it is no less certain that all elements in the State sanctioned it in as formal a manner as possible, and considered it necessary to conceal the essentially radical nature of the change. Such a subterfuge was entirely consonant with English legal thinking. Changes in the law had regularly been declared to be the true law, which had been, for a time, ousted by an illegal usurpation. But whether the statute ‘ conferred ’ or ‘ restored ’, the Crown was meant to possess all ecclesiastical authority which it might ever be necessary to exercise in England, and certainly the Crown was meant to decide how great that authority needed to be at any time.

Under this broad prerogative, Henry VIII and Edward VI issued ecclesiastical commissions without explicit statutory authority, but without thought or question of illegality. Mary repealed the Henrician Statutes, returned to the allegiance of Rome, but, nevertheless, reissued the Edwardian Patent without any judicial opposition that we can now trace. Elizabeth, with her usual prudence, inserted in her Act of Supremacy a direct sanction for an ecclesiastical commission, but certainly without the slightest idea that she was thereby limiting her own authority. The Statute was meant to give the men whom she called upon to perform difficult and unpopular work a solid pledge that they would be supported in their proceedings. It was further intended to limit the commissioners strictly to such Letters Patent as she saw fit to issue to them, and not to give them (even by implication) power to exercise, independent of Patent, the plenitude of the royal authority.

In the light of these conclusions, Coke's position cannot be maintained by the arguments and precedents he himself gave. The Acts he quoted had undoubtedly existed, but his case depended not on their existence, but on their legal effect; it rested upon the suppositions, that a Statute was a statement of the power which The Law had allotted to the Crown, and that, in The Law, and not in the Crown, was the residuary authority. Thus the Statutes concerning the citing men out of their dioceses, the delivery of the libel, fining and imprisoning, and the like were of no importance unless they were restrictive in their operation, instead of being merely administrative regulations which the Crown had itself made, and hence might at any time alter. Certainly, Coke's idea of the origin and history of The Law, and his notions of Parliament, Statute, and prerogative based upon it, find no support in the real development of the common law as we now conceive it. Nor do the common-law judges, prior to the reign of Elizabeth, seem to have had any such conception of legal history or to have espoused such a view of their relation to the Crown and Parliament. Even if the detailed conclusions, which he was defending by this appeal to history and theory, are accurate, or even tenable, it can hardly be maintained to-day that his logic and history will stand the test of modern investigation. But even admitting the truth of Coke's premises, his points seem to us forced. It was, of course, a simple truism that the commissioners might not exceed their lawful authority. They insisted that they were well within the legal limits assigned them, not only by the Letters Patent, but even by the Statute. In construing the latter, Coke proceeded, however, on the assumption that one of the main reasons for passing the Statute was the 'creation' of the *Court* of High Commission. Certainly nothing is farther from the truth. Not only was an ecclesiastical commission still a temporary expedient, but Elizabeth's first commission was not a court at all, nor is there any good reason to suppose she or her councillors contemplated making it one. Elizabeth, least of all, regarded the Statute as necessary to sanction the Commission. In the next place, the student cannot fail to be struck with the fact that Coke's detailed construction of the Statute depended almost entirely on his suppositions as to the *intention* of Parliament. The complicated manner in which each clause deprived its predecessor or its successor of its literal meaning was based on the idea that Parliament certainly did not intend the Commission's decisions to be without appeal. The distinction regarding 'enormous' cases (certainly forced and peculiar, considering the fact that the preceding word is the conjunction 'and') assumed that Parliament could not have intended to supersede the consistory courts.

The phrase regarding the Letters Patent was to be interpreted in the light of the belief that Parliament never meant to allow Elizabeth to issue any Letters Patent she saw fit, nor the commissioners to try any case which might be authorized by the language of the Letters Patent. When Coke found some Statute limiting the ecclesiastical courts in general, he applied it promptly to the Commission on the ground that it was an ecclesiastical court. When, on the other hand, the commissioners claimed to exercise the jurisdiction and procedure belonging to the ordinary ecclesiastical courts, Coke interfered on the ground that the Commission was a special ecclesiastical court with a peculiar position. Apparently, the Commission was to suffer from all the disadvantages and enjoy none of the privileges of the ecclesiastical hierarchy. By employing such assumptions, Coke easily proved the premise from which he started: the Commission was never meant to have such authority, *ergo*, the language of the Statute clearly did not grant it. But the modern student will find it hard to follow Coke in his readings. It may have been highly inexpedient that any court should possess such powers, but it can hardly be gainsaid that both Statute and Letters Patent authorized them.

In reality, while strenuously insisting that expediency had nothing to do with the issues, Coke based his case upon that much-despised point and found in it his justification. The Commission was a hybrid, half ecclesiastical, half temporal in membership; using ecclesiastical procedure, but inflicting temporal penalties; a law court and a visitatorial commission at the same time. Certainly, no such court had ever been seen in England before. When the Puritans complained that its visitatorial powers were superfluous and its existence therefore unnecessary, the commissioners pointed to the admirable judicial work, which so clearly was finding favour with litigants. When the common-law judges declared that this judicial work could be well enough performed by the ordinary ecclesiastical and common-law courts, the commissioners retorted that extraordinary authority and unusual penalties were necessary to make effective the visitatorial powers of the English Church, whose spiritual pains and penalties had for Puritan and Papist few terrors. It was hard for the commissioners' opponents to believe that both such arguments in defence of so anomalous a position could be valid, or to credit the claim that the peculiarly hybrid character of the institution they defended was indispensable. Moreover, the large number of commissioners, their practically unlimited discretion, their extremely broad jurisdiction, the finality of their sentence, all made the possibility of evil deeds astonishingly great. Should such men, vested with such powers, and able to plead at discretion the necessity of their every action to the safety of the State itself, stray ever so little from the task of upholding State and Church, and turn their attention to their own aggrandizement and the oppression of individuals, there was little or nothing they could not do towards destroying the life and liberty of the average man, and practically nothing he could do to save himself. The solid basis of expediency, therefore, on which rested Coke's argument regarding enormities, was the very considerable and probable danger to the individual, if such a court were permitted to deal with cases other than those for whose decision such vast powers were really essential. The residuary judicial powers in causes ecclesiastical could not expediently be vested in men whose chief duty was the hearing of cases, hitherto dealt with by tribunals still in existence, for the very fact that this work had been done before disproved the necessity for their own existence. At the same time, it might readily be conceded that a 'high' and essentially supreme tribunal might be needed for the performance of important work which could not otherwise be accomplished, without in the least admitting that such a court ought to have a competence as great as the whole province of the ecclesiastical law.

Unquestionably sound as these probabilities and potentialities were, they were still matters *in posse*, until it could be shown that the commissioners were within measurable distance of thus abusing their discretion. Whatever Coke's opinion of their behaviour was, he was effectively estopped from using it, because that issue was not in the least judicial. It was a question of state, on which the King considered himself already well informed, and on which he and his councillors continued to hold, as they had in the past, the opposite view from the lawyers. In reality there was little cause for apprehension. The commissioners never had exercised, and did not exercise in 1611, any such unlimited discretion in practice as their Patent legally vested in them. The Privy Council had controlled their actions with the utmost stringency in the past, and knew that it still had the authority to continue that surveillance with even greater strictness, if necessary. Whatever their Patent said, the path of the commissioners was well circumscribed, and they knew it, and the Council was aware that they knew it. To assume, therefore, that the commissioners possessed both the opportunity and the intention to do wrong, was tantamount to assuming that the King and Privy Council would permit them to do it; to say they had done wrong, was to declare that they had been allowed to commit it. Coke, bold as he was, never dared even to hint at such possibilities; but James and

Bancroft thoroughly well understood him to imply them, and, for that reason, treated his assaults upon the Commission as personal affronts.

Nor was this, by any means, all. Coke and his followers did not fail to see that, in default of such a court as the Commission, all litigation, otherwise unprovided for, would find its way to the common-law courts, where some legal fiction or other would easily allow them to accept jurisdiction. The Commission, in fact, was inexpedient because it was robbing the common-law courts of jurisdiction that would otherwise (and hence 'rightfully') be theirs, and because it was rapidly building up a system of law and equity which the common lawyers feared would make inroads upon the position they already held, and make unlikely any expansion of their jurisdiction in the future. If the common-law courts were to become supreme in England, the Commission must be overwhelmed and abolished for all time. It had come forward as the bulwark of the ecclesiastical jurisdiction, to infuse life into the sinking ecclesiastical hierarchy, at the very moment when suitors were beginning to desert the inefficient tribunals of the bishops and flock to the courts at Westminster. To endanger the subject and his birthright was highly inexpedient, and the commissioners unquestionably did threaten him with possibilities which were none the less serious because the commissioners, past and present, had as yet never shown signs of any intention to avail themselves of them. But to endanger the common law, to assume that other methods of settling the subjects' difficulties might be equally efficient, that, to Coke, was more than inexpedient; it approached high treason. And this, too, this most vital of arguments, he obviously could not use!

CHAPTER XI

JURISDICTION, PROCEDURE, ORGANIZATION, 1611–41

THUS ended the period of growth and strife. During the remainder of its life the Commission exercised almost solely its functions as a court of law. The great changes made in the institution in order to meet the needs of the Church, and the bitter struggle for the maintenance of its position had, in fact, defined and crystallized its procedure and jurisdiction as nothing else could, and had greatly hastened the very development which the common lawyers so particularly wished to check. In the Letters Patent of 1611 the procedure and organization of the Commission as a court received their first official sanction. In its second clause appeared the first authoritative statement of what the King and his Council understood the Statute of 1 Elizabeth to mean. After reciting the clause of the Statute, it declared that Parliament had intended 'that such commissions should be of a temporary nature, and that it was desired and meant that they might be accommodated to the accidents and varieties of times and occasions'. This was significant, but not necessarily conclusive. The clause was, in fact, a two-edged sword, by means of which, in the hands of the King, new aggressions might indeed be made for the Commission; but through whose means, if controlled by the judges, that court might quite as surely be shorn of its privileges on the very ground of expediency. All depended, as before, on the question who was to interpret the Statute, and who was to decide what was expedient. James (who was mainly responsible for the form of the clause) had merely restated his former position: he had not altered in the least the aspect of the controversy. Nevertheless, much that the judges objected to had been omitted, and some attempt had been made so to alter the old clauses as to meet the letter of their demands without renouncing any of the Commission's powers. The chief clauses of the old Patent were omitted altogether, and the document therefore lost much of its indefinite and discretionary aspect. The power 'to enquire by the oaths of twelve good and lawful men, as also by witnesses and all other ways and means ye can devise' (s. iii), and the old clause, to 'visit, reform, and redress', with its phrase regarding 'enormities',[1] were omitted, together with the clause giving power to punish by 'fine or imprisonment or otherwise'.

Instead, the subjects within the Commission's jurisdiction were, for the first time, specifically enumerated with a view to attaining completeness in the enumeration. It was to inquire concerning 'all and singular apostasies, heresies, great errors in matters of faith and religion, schisms, unlawful conventicles tending to schism against the religion or government of the Church now established' —apparently the limitation to enormous crimes Coke had desired (s. iii). Then, in other clauses, powers were conferred over all matters concerning recusants and Jesuits; over all libels, acts, or speeches, against the Book of Common Prayer, the 'Doctrine of Religion', the officials, high and low, of the Established Church;

[1] Probably this was not omitted with any idea that it would block Coke's argument as to 'enormities', for his position depended solely on the Statute, which, of course, was still in force.

over all crimes and violent acts done in any church or on any holy ground, or in interruption of divine service; and over all 'simonies, incests, infamous, and notorious adulteries' (s. iii and v). The Commission was to execute the censorship of the press, and reform all abuses in the ecclesiastical courts;[1] and was further to possess 'full, free and lawful power and authority . . . to enquire as aforesaid of all misdemeanors whatsoever committed by any ecclesiastical person within these our realms . . . which in any wise concern the execution of their several offices . . . in any matter of ecclesiastical cognizance, as also of all other misdemeanours, committed by the said ecclesiastical persons for which they may be censured by the ecclesiastical laws of this our kingdom' (s. iv).

The usual grant of power to three commissioners, one of whom must be a member of the quorum of twenty-seven, was not altered. But it was practically nullified by a later clause, which provided that no final sentence should be given in 'any cause or matter determinable by virtue of this commission' without 'the personal presence, hearing and full assent of five or more of you', and which reduced the quorum, one of whom must be

[1] The 'Notes by John Lambe, of the Jurisdiction of the High Commission' in S. P. Dom. Car. I, 474, no. 71, are practically only a quotation of the salient features of these clauses. They were, in all probability, written after the Caroline Patents had restored the earlier form of 1601, which did not enumerate these points. That Lambe should have considered them the definitive statement of the Court's jurisdiction shows both the crystallization of jurisdiction and its virtual independence of the literal wording of the Letters Patent. It further proves that the restoration of the form of Patent of 1601 was not the result of a desire to free the Court from the trammels of its own precedents, or, at the least, that the Court did not in 1625 abandon the definite position already assumed in 1611 because it was now legally possible to recede from it.

present, to sixteen (s. xxv). Nor was this additional restraint upon pronouncing sentence all. Henceforth, all sentences were to be subject to re-examination by a Commission of Review to be issued on petition to the Crown by the aggrieved party (s. xxvii).[1] The commissioners were not only limited to a definite jurisdiction and deprived of their hitherto absolute discretion, but their sentence was to be no longer final. The Court truly seemed to have lost all which had been characteristic of it.

As for procedure, the Letters Patent conferred power to 'enquire, as well by examination of witnesses or presentments as also by examination of the parties accused themselves upon their oath, where there shall first appear sufficient matter of charge, by examination of witnesses, or by presentments, or by public and notorious fame, or by information of the ordinary' (s. iii). By a separate clause, it added authority (s. xiii) 'to hear all the offences and offenders *aforesaid* and to proceed against them either according to the form of the law ecclesiastical or summarily according to the grave wisdoms and discretions of you [naming the quorum] and likewise to order and determine the same, inflicting such censures and punishments *only as are hereafter mentioned and prescribed*'. The following section (s. xiv) then conferred authority to punish offences and contempts of court 'by censures ecclesiastical or by *reasonable* fine and

[1] To our knowledge, none was ever applied for. The explanation probably lies in the fact that the members of the Commissions of Delegates would probably be some of the civil lawyers who were also active in the High Commission. Thus, such a Commission was almost certain to be a rehearing before the High Commissioners. Further, appeals to the Delegates were slow in execution, and exceedingly expensive. On the relations of the High Commissioners and the Delegates see chapter xiv.

imprisonment according to the quality and quantity of their offence, or by all or any the said means according to your discretions'. The commissioners were thus deprived of administrative discretion, and were left little more than a ministerial duty of determining in what category, of those mentioned in the Patent, a particular case belonged or what form of procedure it required.

The Letters Patent of 1611 were, nevertheless, rather a statement of what the Commission had become than a remodelling of the Court, an express authorization rather than a radical change of its jurisdiction and practice. Though in theory it had suffered a very great restriction of its powers, in actuality it could take cognizance, under the new Patent, of nearly every matter of which it had ever held plea as a law-court; nor did the limitations upon procedure rob it of any essential power. It had never used other procedure than 'examination of witnesses' or 'of the parties accused themselves upon their oath', nor had it proceeded except where there was evidence either by witnesses, by presentment, by information from the bishop, or public fame. It had never inflicted other penalties than censures ecclesiastical or fine and imprisonment, and no commissioner would have admitted for an instant that any fine had been laid, or imprisonment ordered, which was not 'reasonable'. Every element of its regular procedure was, in fact, not abolished, but enumerated. A great deal of detail concerning the execution of attachments (s. vii), the awarding of costs (s. xv), the summoning from dioceses only on certificate or complaint of the bishop (s. xvi), the taking of bonds and recognizances (s. viii, ix, x, xvii), the appointment of the Commission's regular officers and the like, was no more than a declaration at length of the ordinary procedure of the Commission, most of which had, in some form, already appeared in previous Letters Patent, or in the administrative regulations of the commissioners themselves. Nevertheless, such a restriction of the Commission to the jurisdiction and procedure expressly stated in a definite document was a change of the very first magnitude. It might now be argued, with some chance of maintaining the point, that it had overstepped its legal bounds.

The Letters Patent of 1611, besides their important changes in substance, differed materially in form from the earlier models.[1] The Edwardian Commissions of 1549 and 1551 had been essentially the same, but their extremely simple visitatorial form had been altered in 1557 so as to meet the administrative needs which were already foreseen. This form was followed, albeit expanded and altered, until 1601,[2] when a somewhat longer and more complicated model succeeded it, on which were framed the Letters Patent of 1605 and 1608. Of this, the model of 1611 was a development, and was itself followed by all the later Jacobean commissions.

Between 1611 and 1641 the Letters Patent, while not literally the same, added few powers of any importance. The Patent of 1613[3] formulated broadly, though definitively, the powers already exercised in cases of alimony and divorce, and required a special quorum to be present at the hearing of such cases. It also gave jurisdiction

[1] Appendices C and D give a comparison of the important clauses of these various forms down to 1641. The bibliography contains indications of the whereabouts of copies of all these commissions.

[2] The Letters Patent of 1584 and 1587 are lost; perhaps the change began in them.

[3] The differences of the Letters Patent of 1613 from those of 1611 are conveniently shown by the italics in Prothero, *Select Statutes*, 424.

over all 'abuses, offences, insolent misbehaviours and contempts being not capital', committed against the Commission or its officers or agents. Further, its last clause directed that all suits pending at the time of the issue of the Patent should proceed to sentence and execution of judgement according to the powers of the Letters Patent of 1611, under which they had been instituted. The Letters Patent of 1625 provided that, while Convocation was in session, the Commission should be in abeyance, and that its powers, and even its usual duties, should devolve upon the bishops of the Commission only.[1] In the Patent of 1613 were also one or two indications of how thoroughly the Commission had become a law-court. In it is the first clear official use of the term 'Our said court of High Commission' (s. iii), which, though common by 1580, only now formally replaced the phrase 'the Commissioners for Causes Ecclesiastical'. The Commission was officially recognized as possessing a place in the hierarchy of ecclesiastical courts by the phrase 'or to any *other* ecclesiastical court'. 'The ecclesiastical laws of this our kingdom' gave formal sanction to the doctrine of the Two Laws. The Letters Patent of Charles I technically contained no new powers, for they were but rather close repetitions of the Letters Patent of 1601.[2] But the change of form practically repealed the clauses concerning the Commission of Review, the exercise of the powers of the Commission by the bishops only during a session of Convocation, and all the definitions introduced in 1611. Thus, the Commission became once more absolute, unlimited, and with-

[1] We know nothing further of this curious proviso to show us either its working, or even the reason for its existence. The clause is in Prothero, p. 435, and in Rymer.

[2] See Appendix, Bibliography.

out appeal, and its visitatorial powers, exercised by Laud in 1634/5 after they had practically been in abeyance for at least twenty years, had probably not been employed to an equal degree since Whitgift's visitation of 1584. While Charles had not in the least changed the powers which the Commission actually exercised, and while ordinarily the commissioners acted in no different way under his patents and under those issued on the model of 1611, he had, nevertheless, made the Commission legally very different from what it had been during the preceding fourteen years. While in reality nothing that either he or Laud did was an innovation upon the precedents of the Commission either in jurisdiction, in procedure, or perhaps in practice, it seemed to many men of the time that illegal innovations had been introduced.

Though the commissioners seem to have frankly admitted that their general jurisdiction depended entirely upon the Statute and the Letters Patent, their jurisdiction in practice was defined and expanded in precisely the same manner in which the jurisdiction of the common-law courts had been developed—by the deciding of cases and the following of precedent. The considerable latitude of decision left to the Commissioners themselves by the early Letters Patent, as to what was and what was not within their jurisdiction, was used, so far as we have record, only as similar prerogatives were used by other courts. When a case appeared, jurisdiction of it was assumed if the wording of the Letters Patent allowed. The actual jurisdiction of the Commission rested, therefore, upon precisely the same basis as did the jurisdiction of all the other courts of the realm: upon a rather indefinite grant of power from the Crown interpreted and fitted to particular cases by the judges themselves. Nevertheless, the Commission's law was not technically judge-made law.

Technically, too, the Commission enforced the law and did not make it, even by the process of following precedent. Actually, however, the Commission probably 'created' law in quite the same manner as the other courts did, though it never issued any official regulations or ordinances which could be regarded as an attempt to fix the substantive law. On the other hand, the majority of the rules of procedure followed in the Commission were contained in administrative orders issued by the court itself. The most important set of these of which we have record was issued, probably in 1616,[1] by the authority of the Privy Council, although there can be little doubt that the Commissioners themselves drafted them. They formed a part of the general settlement of the Commission's procedure, which took place on the dismissal of Coke from the Chief Justiceship of the King's Bench, by far the most important part of which was the order for the erection of a special prison for the Commission and the appointment of a special warder.[2] The declarations of the judges, that imprisonment by the Commission was

[1] The copy we have is undated, but seems, from internal evidence, to belong at this date: S. P. Dom. Jac. I, 89, f. 118, 120. See another very interesting paper endorsed, 'Orders submitted to your Lordships honorable Consideracon whether the same are meete to be established and observed in his Majesties Courte of Commission for Causes Ecclesiastical in all places wheresoeuer throughout the Realme': S. P. Dom. Jac. I, 89, f. 119. If this paper belongs in 1616, the King's Advocate and Procurator would seem to have originated at this time. This would be a very important point to establish, and would, in fact, naturally fit into the general scheme of which the prison and the Orders were a part. Still, the date seems more uncertain even than that of the Orders, and the paper probably contains only a tentative scheme, not at the time executed.

[2] Created by warrant, Nov. 4, 1616. Sign Manual, IV, f. 92. Brian Wilton, Richard Wilton, and John Thurgood appointed to be successively wardens.

illegal, were at last effectively answered. There were to be no more orders from the common-law courts to the wardens of the regular prisons, commanding them to release a prisoner held under the warrants of the Commission.

The Orders of 1616 set forth a number of rather important rules of procedure, chiefly intended to prevent delay and fraud, and to stop collusion between the parties and the officials of the Court. Orders and decrees of the Court should be entered in the Act Books within two days of their making, and all copies, supplied as of right to the parties, should be compared with the original by the Registrar and certified before delivery to the parties or to their counsel. The books themselves might be shown to any judge, but only by the registrar himself, who was to be personally responsible for their safety. A table of fees, approved by the commissioners, should be hung up openly in the registrar's office, and established the maximum charges allowable. The defendant should be examined within at least three days after taking his oath to make a full and true answer, but should not be shown a copy of the articles against him until he had taken his oath. Copies of his examination should be ready within two days. If he made an imperfect answer, he should pay costs 'retardati processus'. No pleadings whatever of any description should be admitted unless first approved by one of the commissioners.[1] It was further provided 'that noe Comission or processe bee graunted against anie particular person whatsoever or in assistance of anie ordinaries or Archdeacon's Iurisdiction unlesse there bee sufficient Bonde giuen for prosecution (by the plaintiff) of articles allowed under the handes of two comissioners, before anie Comission or processe goe out', except by

[1] S. P. Dom. Jac. I, 89, f. 120.

a special command in writing by the Archbishop or the Bishop of London. 'Noe bonde taken either for prosecution, apparance, attendance, or otherwise' should be discharged except in open court, or by warrant from three commissioners, whereof the Archbishop or the Bishop of London should be one. No party should be discharged from any duty, or censured or sentenced for any cause, but in open court. All fines should be paid to the Receiver of Fines and Forfeitures, entered in a book, and an acknowledgement received from him. All holders of general warrants, granted for apprehension of recusants and 'massing stuff', should report once each term at least, and deposit all 'stuff' seized with the Archbishop, the Bishop of London, or the registrar. Its disposal should be regulated by their lordships, and their orders registered 'emongst the secreate directions in the Registrie Booke'.[1]

These orders prove that the procedure sanctioned by the Letters Patent was, by far, more indefinite than the practice of the Court. Where the Letters Patent made permissive the taking of bonds to ensure the prosecution of a suit, the orders made it obligatory in every case. Legally, all bonds might be discharged by any three commissioners at any time, but the orders required action in open court, or by the warrant of three commissioners, of whom the Archbishop or the Bishop of London must be one. The tendency of all orders issued by the Court was clearly to create a just, equitable, and definite judicial procedure.

Among the subsequent administrative regulations of the Commission, some made during Laud's time[2] are

[1] S. P. Dom. Jac. I, 89, f. 118.

[2] See Appendix, Bibliography: 'Procedure.' Note the 'Orders for the regulation of the duties of the Registrar of the Court of High Commission and his deputies and clerks, and also for the regulation of the practice in a variety of specified cases' (in all,

noteworthy because they illustrate well two conflicting tendencies of his administration—the attempt to make more effective the procedure for dealing with obstinate culprits, and the attempt to stop many abuses due to the desire of both parties to 'vex' each other as much as possible. The chief resource of those who wished to block the Commission's proceedings against them was the refusal of the oath *ex officio*. For such obstruction, there was in the early years no remedy but the transferring of the prosecution to the Star Chamber, or imprisonment until he was willing to be sworn. The first was an open confession of the Commission's weakness; the second held the man in durance, but, if he proved obstinate, was no less clear an example of the inefficiency of the Commission's procedure. During Bancroft's primacy there was probably[1] a good deal of discussion of the matter, and a rather general opinion was reached, that the only solution was to consider that he who refused to answer had confessed the affirmative of the question asked him. This view rested upon solid grounds of logic as well as of expediency. If the accused was innocent, it was urged, he could have no reason whatever for refusing to take an oath to tell the truth and the whole truth. Indeed, it was his interest to tell all he knew, and to tell it in as solemn and impressive a manner as possible. Only the guilty had *prima facie* any valid excuse for refusing the

22 articles): S. P. Dom. Car. I, 339, no. 70. 'Articles for regulation of the practice of the Court of Arches and High Commission, arranged under certain heads': S. P. Dom. Car. I, 406, no. 78.

[1] *The Treatisour* (quoted by Cosin, *Apologie*, i, 108) demands that the rule *pro confesso* should be adopted in lieu of imprisonment. This would make it sufficiently clear that such was not the rule in 1590, and its well-established character after 1611 makes it certain that it must have been adopted between the two dates.

oath. If he was guilty and told the truth, he did indeed convict himself. But he had no logical or equitable reason to complain if his refusal to answer was accounted a confession. Gradually this view crept into the practice of the Commission, and in 1631 we find it the established rule.[1] But, being questioned, some official confirmation of the practice was considered necessary. Hence a Royal Letter was issued to the Commission under the Signet on February 4, 1637/8,[2] which formally affirmed the legality of the practice.

> 'After due monition given and intimation made to the said person . . . he shall and may be declared . . . *pro confesso* and shall be held and had so confessed and convicted legally of all those articles and matters to which he so refuseth to be sworn, or being sworn shall refuse to answer, or not to make a full and plain answer as aforesaid.'

Where there were so many commissioners, any three of whom could form a court and exercise all the powers of the Patent, and where there were, in fact, so many small courts of technically the same authority as the Court at London, it was not very difficult for a suitor with a plausible story to procure some warrant or grant from some commissioners, which might virtually annul proceedings begun against him elsewhere. Very considerable abuses in the granting of fines and forfeitures had thus arisen. Probably with the intent of remedying these difficulties, Letters Patent issued on October 15, 1635,[3]

[1] *Cases in Star Chamber and High Commission* (Camden Society), 269. 'This was held no answer, and therefore ordered to aunswere by such a day or be declared pro confesso.' See also Act Book, 1634; S. P. Dom. Car. I, 261, ff. 114 b, 124, 125.

[2] The original, with the impression of the Signet still on it, is in S. P. Dom. Car. I, 381, no. 29. Printed in Rymer, *Foedera*, xx, 190. Also a copy in Lambeth MSS. 943, f. 571.

[3] S. P. Dom. Car. I, 299, no. 70.

providing that no grant or warrant should be drawn relating to any cause of ecclesiastical cognizance, or giving away any fine or forfeiture imposed by the Commission, without the approbation of the Archbishop of Canterbury. This centred the power in one man and did away with the possibility of one writ interfering with another, or a fine being paid twice. It was said later that this order was made expressly for the purpose of vesting the patronage of the Commission in the Archbishop, and that he used it to benefit his private purse, and, also, to defray the expense of repairing St. Paul's Cathedral. Probably the charge was unfounded. There is no evidence now extant to prove that any high commissioner ever made money out of his office, and Laud's accusers did not adduce any *proof* at his trial.[1]

As will be later pointed out in more detail, many abuses in the practice of the Commission arose from acts of the parties to the suit and not from those of the commissioners themselves. The commissioners had no interest in prolonging a case, for they were always overrun with business, and the additional fees were paid into the Exchequer, and not into their own pockets. But the litigants of the seventeenth century firmly believed that the best way to win a suit was to tire out an adversary by delays and ruin him by court charges. Therefore, in 1640, 'the court taking into consideration the inconveniences and disorders daily arising from the neglect of parties and their counsel in not bringing in their briefs in due time after the causes are concluded and assigned to report,

[1] Laud's *Works*, iv. 178 : 'History of Troubles.' If there had been any evidence at all on this point, the Parliamentarians would certainly have found it and have taken great care to preserve it. But they have left nothing but assertions. The Council in the Marches of Wales collected money for the repair of St. Paul's. Bridgewater MSS., 80 ; Welsh Council Papers.

so that they are much delayed,' ordered that the promoter should bring in his brief two weeks after the cause was assigned to report, and that the defendant's counsel should present his within a week after. 'All causes shall hereafter be finally sentenced in the order in which they are concluded and assigned to report.' [1]

Despite the growth of a formal procedure, the Commission never lost its flexibility of organization. In fact, this flexibility made possible the consummation of a most important development during Charles I's reign by the simple expedient of increasing the membership. As in the earlier period, the number of commissioners was an index of the amount of authority and power the Government meant them to exercise. Here, more than anywhere else, we find evidence that Charles and Laud really intended to increase the Commission's powers. The membership of the Commission of 1611 (ninety-two) was a third greater than that of any previous commission, but the first Caroline commission surpassed it with 108 members. The chief reason for this extension of membership lay in the discontinuance in 1611 of separate diocesan commissions. Gradually the number of bishops, deans, and archdeacons on the Commission for the Province of Canterbury was increased, until in 1625, for the first time, all the bishops and both archbishops were members. The archbishopric of York thus came under the jurisdiction of the Canterbury Commission. Scotland was included in the Commissions of 1629 and 1633. This great expansion of membership, however, gave the commissioners sitting at London no further powers or authority. As the Letters Patent had

[1] S. P. Dom. Car. I, 434, f. 208. June 18, 1640. See also *id.* f. 231, July 2, 1640, an order for a Table of Amended Fees to be posted, and other details concerning the approval of the accounts of officers of the Court on Mitigation Day.

not been altered, they could have formerly commanded the services of the older diocesan commissioners with more assurance than they could now demand the aid of their own colleagues. Technically, too, the geographical extension of authority was small, because, in theory, the early commissions of one-fourth the size had possessed precisely the same rights over all England and Wales as did the huge Caroline Commission. In actuality, however, the extension of authority was very considerable, for the powers of the Commission came to be effectively exercised in districts where formerly only their shadow had been seen. A great part of this thirty per cent. increase in membership is thus explained. The increase of bishops and of the general clerical element, the presence of knights and esquires, are both attributable to this inclusion of the diocesan commissions within the general. The increase in the number of Privy Councillors and court officials was, on the other hand, due to a desire to augment as much as possible the dignity and prestige of the Commission, and probably, as well, to have as many parts of the State as possible identified with it and responsible for its acts.

Yet the best index of the authority which the Government expected the Commission to exercise was the size of the quorum. In 1611 the Government meant to reduce the Commission to more conservative proportions. Hence, the quorum was made 32 per cent. of the membership instead of 45 per cent. as in 1608. Further, the presence of five men instead of three was required for any definitive proceeding—a double limitation. But when, in 1620, the movement came to increase the Commission's authority, the quorum rose at once to 52 per cent. of the total membership, became 58 per cent. in 1626, and 66 per cent. in 1633. These figures show quite conclusively that the Commission under Laud was really, as contemporaries claimed, a much more powerful body than its Elizabethan and Jacobean predecessors. Ostensibly there was, and could have been, no considerable increase in power, but this very change in membership contained, and was meant to contain, the increase of power, flexibility, and efficiency. The personnel of this increased total membership and quorum shows how well these changes were calculated to accomplish their purpose. All the bishops, all the important officials of state, a majority of the common-law judges, the presiding official of all the ecclesiastical and prerogative courts, a large number of deans and archdeacons swept into the Commission's ranks all the talent, experience, and authority then in office. The augmentation of the number of simple knights, doctors of divinity, and doctors of civil law, who were without fixed residence and able to travel anywhere, or were open to appointment as diocesan officials by a bishop who lacked a quorum, was probably due to the desire to make the smaller sessions of the Commission *in partibus* efficient. Actually, the number of the clergy was greatly increased, although the proportional increase of the laity, by the addition of so many dignitaries, makes the clerical growth seem smaller than it really was. Both civil and common lawyers increased rapidly in number, though proportionally to the total membership they were somewhat fewer than in the earlier commissions. The clergy and civil lawyers were still greatly in the majority, and were regularly about 60 per cent. of the whole number.

The composition of the quorum was of the greatest importance. In 1620 it contained the Archbishop of Canterbury and fourteen southern bishops, sitting *ex officio*, the Lord Chancellor, the Lord Treasurer, the Lord Privy Seal, the Master of the Rolls, the Chief Justices and Chief Baron, the ecclesiastical judges, the Master of

Requests, and Masters of Chancery, and several doctors of divinity and civil law—in all forty-five. In 1626 it included both archbishops, all the bishops, sitting *ex officio*, the Deans of Canterbury and St. Paul's, also *ex officio*, and all the other members of the quorum of 1620—in all fifty-five. In 1633 it was further augmented by an increase of the doctors of divinity, and of the doctors of civil law—so that the quorum was, in very fact, two-thirds of the total membership. Practically the only members not included in it were the Privy Councillors and administrative judges, who rarely if ever sat, and some of the clergy who would usually sit with the bishop. The power of the Commission was thus almost doubled simply by the increase of the quorum. Here was, in truth, a great development since the first Commission issued under the statutory confirmation. The Commission of 1559 with nineteen members had had a quorum of seven, 37 per cent. of the total membership. The Commission of 1633 had a membership of 108 and a quorum of 68, 66 per cent. of the whole. The growth had been gradual and can hardly be shown to have been illegal or inexpedient, yet, to the Puritan of 1635, 'troubled' by the Commission's activity, it must have seemed an undue extension of authority by illegal methods.

The earlier aspect of a commission created for unusual needs had, indeed, gone far to protect the High Commission in the days of Elizabeth and James I. It was difficult to deny or even to argue that the King did not possess absolute power and discretion to compass the necessary ends of State by a commission composed of such of his subjects as he might select; but it was far more tenable to declare that he might not create a new court of law, outside the old hierarchy, to exercise part of the jurisdiction which the latter ought to have exercised.

The legal recognition of the Commission as a court gave a meaning, and, indeed, a justice, to Coke's arguments, which they had not possessed when he pronounced them. He had not attacked the High Commission as a royal commission, but as a law-court, and the strongest argument against him was the fact that, technically, it was not a court, but a royal commission, exercising by direct authorization from the Crown certain of the royal residuary judicial powers. The arguments of Coke, which had in a sense been misapplied in 1609, became by the action of the Government itself in 1611 thoroughly applicable. The Statute of 1 Elizabeth, however clearly it might have conferred absolute powers upon a temporary commission, had not expressly said anything about a permanent court of law, and whatever its form might nominally be, the Commission was beyond doubt the latter.

The Letters Patent of 1611 having thus strengthened the arguments of the Commission's legal opponents, the Letters Patent of 1625, issued on the older and more indefinite Elizabethan model, lent a similar strength to the Puritan complaints of illegality and innovation. The Letters Patent of 1611, whether they had been legal according to the Statute or not, had clearly supported the form of the Court as it had then existed, but those of 1625, modelled on the Elizabethan patents, where the visitatorial aspect was prominent, certainly accorded a law-court very little express confirmation. Indeed, they imparted to the Commission during its later years an aspect of newness, of innovation upon former precedents. There was now no such answer possible as had once blocked Coke in his triumphant march: the Commission had not always been so. In 1625 neither the Statute nor the Letters Patent seemed to be in its favour. That a visitatorial commission should exercise judicial powers might be inevitable, but that a court of law should exercise the episcopal and archidiaconal functions of visitation seemed by no means so legitimate. The High Commission under Laud was really no more illegal than it had been under Whitgift, Bancroft, and Abbot, but, by a peculiar array of circumstances, it seemed to many men of Laud's day to be both new and illegal.

COMPOSITION OF THE HIGH COMMISSION, 1611–41

	1611	1613	1620	1625	1626	1629	1633
Total Membership	92	82	86	108	98	107	108
New Members	35	11	45	43	21	24	38
Quorum	28	31	45	53	55	29	68
Laity	52	48	56	63	53	60	62
Clergy	40	34	30	45	45	47	46
Bishops	11	12	15	26	25	26	26
Deans, &c.	10	8	7	12	13	14	12
Doctors of Divinity	19	14	8	7	7	7	8
Privy Councillors and Dignitaries	23	24	21	27	25	33	37
Civil Lawyers and Judges	16	14	21	22	18	18	10
Common Law Judges	8	7	7	7	6	5	12
Common Lawyers	5	3	7	7	4	4	3

NOTE. '*Deans, &c.*' include deans, archdeacons, wardens of colleges, bishops' chancellors.

'*Privy Councillors and Dignitaries*,' all great officials of state, officers of the royal household, secretaries, clerks of the Council, and mere knights and esquires.

'*Civil Lawyers and Judges*,' Masters of Requests and of Chancery, all the regular ecclesiastical judges, bishops' commissaries, the Judge of Admiralty, the Attorney of the Court of Wards, and doctors of civil law.

'*Common Lawyers*,' the Attorney-General, Solicitor-General, the Learned Council, and serjeants-at-law.

CHAPTER XII

THE ACTUAL WORKING OF THE COMMISSION 1611–41

THE ordinary routine of judicial business, transacted by the Commission during the last thirty years of its life, was largely concerned with suits between party and party for the remedy against some tort or the redress of some grievance. Only about 20 per cent. of the suits before the Commission seem to have been suits *ex officio*, and of these, half were prosecuted by the Court at the petition of some poor or uninfluential person, and a quarter were appeals from some bishop for assistance. About 5 per cent. of the suits in the Commission were thus originated by the commissioners,[1] and 80 per cent. were ordinary causes between party and party. The plea rolls seem to have been always well filled; indeed, we are told that in 1635 a thousand suits were depending at once,[2] and we know positively that the Court at this time commonly transacted business in a hundred suits on a single court day.

The great majority of these cases were of a disciplinary or matrimonial nature. Suits for alimony, divorce, desertion, abuse, and the like seem to have been the first in point of number. Adultery, incontinency, and other

[1] The idea that the chief work of the Commission was to ferret out cases seems to be a misapprehension. See S. P. Dom. Car. I, 377, no. 149; 313, no. 59; 385, no. 32; 388, no. 35; 388, no. 41; 389, no. 92; 397, no. 91; 401, no. 32; 401, no. 73; 402, no. 55; 406, nos. 64, 70, 75; 446, no. 63; 455, no. 87, &c.

[2] Hackett's *Life of Lord Keeper Williams*, 97.

moral offences, both of clergy and laity, were perhaps the next most numerous class of cases, while the third place was occupied by cases of simony, plurality, drunkenness, and other irregularities of the clergy. These three classes comprised the vast bulk of the business of the Commission.[1] Heresy and schism appeared continually, but by no means as often as we should expect. Neither word possessed judicially the sense popularly attached to it.[2] Just as any misdeed is at common law a tort, and any entrance upon another's land is a trespass, so the quarrelling of two old women in church was schism, witchcraft was heresy, and the failure of the parson to read prayers on a Wednesday, because he was reaping his harvest for fear of a storm, was nonconformity. Neither heresy nor schism was necessarily connected with Puritanism or Roman Catholicism. Nonconformity applied equally to those who broke the rules of the Church through indifference or negligence and to those who refused to perform them for conscience' sake. Nevertheless, the Commission did perform most of the disciplinary work of the Church, and many of the cases against sectaries or holders of conventicles found their way, sooner or later, to the Court at London.

[1] The evidence on this point is very disappointing. The Registers which contained the details of the nature of the case are lost, and the Act Books concern chiefly attendance and a record of formal procedure, and have been preserved for only two years, which may or may not have been typical. Original papers connected with various suits we have in some number, and, while they give us all the information we could ask for regarding the intricacies of procedure, they usually give little about the nature of the suit, and nothing at all about its degree of enormity, as Coke would have said.

[2] In the table on p. 279 *infra* all these terms have been used strictly in the popular sense; not in their technical sixteenth-century judicial meaning.

By 1611 the sessions of the Court had come to be held invariably in London on certain fixed days.[1] Theoretically able to sit anywhere in the province of Canterbury, the Commission had sat in its early years at almost any time and almost anywhere; but, as it became more and more definitely a court, it tended to keep more and more regularly the law terms observed by all the English courts, and, in practice, came to sit only in London—usually at Lambeth, Bow Street, the Consistory of St. Paul's, Doctors' Commons, or the Chapter House of Westminster Cathedral. All very important cases were heard at Lambeth, usually in the presence of the Archbishop. If the Archbishop was to be present, in fact, at any session whatever, the Court would ordinarily sit at Lambeth. If the Bishop of London was the highest official at the moment in London, the session would probably be at Fulham, his episcopal palace. If the Dean of Arches called the session, it would meet at Bow

[1] The only detailed accounts of the arguments and speeches at trials in the Commission are in a volume edited for the Camden Society by S. R. Gardiner, *Cases in Star Chamber and High Commission* (cited hereafter as Gardiner, *Cases*). The first half of these cases that concern the Commission are from the Harl. MSS. 4130, and seem in some respects trustworthy; yet they should be used with great care, for they were compiled from pleadings and oral reports of the parties to the suit, and are not, as they at first seem to be, first-hand reports faithfully made by an eyewitness. The latter half of this volume of cases seems to be almost valueless. The cases are merely abstracts of proceedings made by a Puritan (and therefore by a man hostile to the Commission), of (apparently) what he thought reprehensible in certain nonconformity trials in the Commission. Both sets of cases seem to have been made with an eye to publication by the Commission's opponents. They contain, however, a great deal of valuable incidental material regarding sessions, attendance, places of meeting, and the like, which confirms, and in many ways amplifies, the details of the Act Books and original papers.

Church or at Doctors' Commons. The more informal sessions for the preparation of cases, known technically as 'Informations', sat most often at Bow Church, St. Paul's,[1] or Doctors' Commons.[2] If a case were referred to two members to be reported upon, ordinarily they sat at Doctors' Commons or at St. Paul's.

The full Court sat only on court days, and on those days alone formal and final business was transacted, such as motions to go to report, the submission of articles additional, motions for the examining of a witness, or for a term probatory. Needless to add, the hearing of the case and sentence or decree must take place on a court day. Ordinarily, all Thursdays in January, February, May, June, October, and November were court days; occasionally there were court days in April, July, and December, but the great bulk of the business came up in June, October, and November, or, in legal language, in Trinity and Michaelmas terms. Besides these formal court days, the Court sat frequently throughout the year for the routine business connected with the different formal parts of a suit previous to going to report. At Informations (on the mornings of court days) or for other routine business, only one commissioner usually sat, although several commissioners would probably be carrying on similar business at the same time on the same day. But, on a court day, the presence of three commissioners was required by the Letters Patent, and, under the later Jacobean Patents, five were required to sentence a case. In practice, ten members or more were often present at formal sessions even after this proviso was

[1] Gardiner, *Cases*, 292 (May 8, 1632). S. P. Dom. Car. I, 362, no. 45 (1637); 261, f. 149 b (Jan. 1634/5).

[2] S. P. Dom. Car. I, 430, no. 21; 435, no. 42, ii. Examples of other cases will be found in the Act Books *passim*.

revoked by Charles I.[1] These were most often Laud, the Archbishop, the Bishops of London, Norwich, Rochester, Winchester, Coventry and Lichfield, and the lawyers Lambe, Brent, Caesar, Martin, and Ayliffe.

Ordinarily, upon a court day, between eighty and one hundred suits went through some stage, and we have record several times of as large a number as a hundred and twenty cases on one day. The nature of this business was, of course, in the majority of instances technical. On October 15, 1640, out of one hundred and twenty-one cases appearing before the Court,[2] in thirty-one a day was appointed for a hearing; in nine the defendant appeared and was sworn; in eight the payment of costs was respited for a time; in six the case was deferred to a later day; in seven the publication of the sentence was decreed; five commissions for the examination of witnesses were issued; four conditional attachments were decreed; four men were monished to appear on a day set; three were ordered to put in a defence; three to consider the answers of the other party, and the like. Of the whole one hundred and twenty-one, only twenty-three came up for hearing, and this was an unusually large proportion. As a matter of fact, where the chief part of the procedure in a suit was written, and where examinations took place in private before a single commissioner, there was no need for the hearings in open court required at common law where the procedure was public. Still, it may well be doubted whether the common-law procedure was in any degree more expeditious than that of the Commission. The complaints of delay seem to refer rather to the action

[1] Harl. MSS. 4130. The signatures to certain original sentences would seem to indicate that this was not as invariable an attendance as the recurrence of that number in the cases reported in that volume would lead one to think.

[2] Act Book, S. P. Dom. Car. I, 434.

of the parties in postponing hearings and the like on frivolous excuses than to the lack of opportunity to get the attention of the Court.

As time went on certain parts of the Commission's procedure developed a practical importance far beyond their apparent significance, and of these the most important was 'Informations'. From the very first it had been usual for one or more commissioners to perform, outside the Court, in a sort of semi-official hearing, a good deal of the routine work of signing briefs and approving articles original and additional. Probably, previous to Bancroft's primacy, nothing was concluded at meetings of this sort which had any judicial effect on the decision of the case. Under him this semi-formal hearing at Informations, usually in the forenoon of each court day, began to absorb the consideration of all the details of the case on which the Court must decide prior to the final hearing and final argument. Under Abbot and Laud Informations really did prepare the case for final hearing.[1] Questions of the admissibility of evidence,[2] the decision of any minor disputed point of fact on which the parties might take issue,[3] the amendment of pleadings,[4] the necessity of a fuller reply to the articles of either party,[5] and the taxation of costs,[6] were usually decided at Informations. The articles of either party might there be shortened, if their length seemed vexatious or un-

[1] 'The Proofes were all collected into a breife of the whole cause at the Court of Informations which prepareth alwayes the causes to be heard in this Court': Gardiner, *Cases*, 198 (1631).

[2] *Id.* p. 200, and S. P. Dom. Car. I, 434, ff. 278, 281.

[3] S. P. Dom. Car. I, 434, f. 243. Oct. 15, 1640.

[4] *Ibid.* 434, ff. 272, 272 b, 287 b.

[5] *Ibid.* 434, ff. 272 b, 278.

[6] *Ibid.* 432, f. 24; 434, ff. 277, 287, 290, 300, 306 b, &c. This question was often referred to 'Referrees'.

necessary.[1] Even the question of the jurisdiction of the Court over a suit might be there concluded,[2] a case dismissed,[3] or a party freed.[4] So far as the evidence goes, only decisions of detail were made, and probably of details of fact and procedure only. As the line between law and fact was differently drawn in the Commission from what it was at common law, it is difficult to say whether matters of fact (in the common law sense) were decided at Informations and matters of law at a formal hearing only. Probably no categorical statement of any kind would be correct. Yet, on the whole, no decision upon the legal consequences of a set of facts and no decision of the main issues of fact between the parties seem to have been regularly made at Informations.[5]

Whenever the decision of the legal consequences of a set of facts, or a decision upon the main issues of fact between two parties were made otherwise than by a full Court, they were made by Referees, members of the Court to whom were temporarily delegated its powers. It had early been the practice to refer to one or two commissioners some question of detail whose discussion or proof would occupy too much time at the formal hearing. In time this crystallized into a regular part of the Court's practice, modelled, probably, on the Chancery procedure of referring complicated questions of fact to a master

[1] The Bishop of Rochester said in the Commission in 1631, 'there hath been care taken in this cause to cutt off at the Court of Informations as much as was thought fitt, that we might not in this Court make the cause too longe: we left out a fourth part of the accusations against him': Gardiner, *Cases*, 225. See also S. P. Dom. Car. I, 239, no. 80 (May 1633).

[2] S. P. Dom. Car. I, 434, f. 297. Nov. 19, 1640.

[3] *Ibid.* 434, ff. 272, 297, 297 b; 261, f. 36 b.

[4] *Ibid.* 434, f. 264 b.

[5] See, however, S. P. Dom. Car. I, 434, ff. 297 (1640) and 287; and *ibid.* 261, f. 36 b (1634).

for hearing or decision. The Masters in Chancery had always been influential and often active members of the Commission, and probably were the direct cause of the adoption and extension of a practice at once so convenient, equitable, and rapid, and, at the same time, with proper control, so safe from abuse. Exactly what were its limits it is almost impossible to say, but in all probability it was restricted only by the discretion of the commissioners present when the case was referred. Some commissioner or commissioners performed, as referee or referees, some function of the Court which the Court expressly delegated in set terms. Apparently, too, short of the formal trial, there was no function which could not be delegated. The sufficiency of evidence, the technical perfection of pleadings, the sufficiency of the prosecutor, the payment of costs, the renewal of commissions for the examination of witnesses, the compromising of the difficulty without further legal procedure by securing an agreement of the parties, and, often, the drawing up of the decree in the case and the oversight of the execution of the sentence were referred not only to two commissioners, but even to one.[1] Apparently, the decision of the referee or referees was ordinarily binding upon the Court, and was issued as a decree of the Commission and enforced by its process. The Commission, however, seems always to have been able for cause to set aside the decision. It is possible that the great growth and frequent use of both Informations

[1] Respectively: S. P. Dom. Car. I, 261, ff. 125, 134, 134 b, 125, 126 b, 140, 140 b, 151 b, 159 b, 126, 127 b, 148, 159 b, 161, 173 b, 180. These, and the following additional general references, will show the extent and frequency of the practice. Reference to two commissioners: S. P. Dom. Car. I, 261, ff. 76 b, 78, 79 b, 82, 86 b, 87, 87 b, 98, 102 b, 107 b, 109, 110, 111, 111 b, 115, 118, 118 b, 125, 125 b, 126, 138, 140. To one commissioner: *id.* ff. 78, 80, 87, 88 b, 89, 107 b, 109, 111, 111 b, 115, 117, 126, &c. (1634).

and Referees was hastened by the increase of the quorum in 1611 to five. Yet there would seem to be little probability in the view, for the quorum of five applied only to the delivery of a definitive sentence, and the quorum remained, as before, three for all other purposes. The development of these two characteristics was without much doubt the logical growth for a court so much affected by the civil law practice. So far as our evidence goes, the Commission never attempted to delegate the function of final decree, and, indeed, it probably could not legally have done so.

There seems to be a hint in one document of a committee system in the Commission,[1] but there is no trustworthy evidence to show that the practice, if such existed, was more than some temporary expedient. During the time of Laud at least, there was a King's Advocate,[2] analogous to the Attorney-General at common law, for the prosecution by the State of suits in the High Commission and ecclesiastical courts which no private person could be expected to promote. Many of the cases against the nonconformists, tried *ex officio* in the Commission during the last ten years of its existence, were brought by the King's Advocate in the name of the Crown.[3] The Commission was hardly more responsible for their beginning or conduct than was the Court of King's Bench for the hanging of a criminal prosecuted by the Attorney-General.

[1] Cf. S. P. Dom. Car. I, 290, no. 73.

[2] As already noted, a paper, which seems to be of the date of 1616, would seem to show that he was first appointed in that year. His first definite appearance is, however, in the cases of 1631, printed by the Camden Society from Harl. MSS. 4130. How far he collected information himself and how far he relied on the commissioners or bishops, it is not possible to say. The notices in the Act Books of later years are frequent.

[3] See Gardiner, *Cases*, *passim*.

The Day of Mitigations, the last court day of each term, became, even before 1611, an important part of the Commission's work. Here fines, costs, and even sentences were reduced upon petition. The regular practice was to fine heavily *in terrorem*, and then, at Mitigations, when some evidence of compliance with the Court's order had been shown, to reduce the fine by one-half, by three-fourths, or even to remit it altogether. In the same way deprivations, suspensions, excommunications were lightened for those who showed themselves amenable and repentant.[1]

Fines and imprisonment, while used in the Commission to terrify into obedience a refractory delinquent, and also as a punishment for crime, were in practice chiefly used to ensure the performance of the orders and processes of the Court. A man who refused to obey a summons to appear was served with an intimation under penalty, usually, of £20, which, if disregarded, was followed by another with penalty of £40. A fugitive was 'attached', and, if captured, was imprisoned either by the messenger of the Commission or by the sheriff of the county, who was under special orders to execute the Commission's attachments. For refusal to take the oath *ex officio* or to answer fully the articles against him, the party was commonly imprisoned until he yielded. When a decree was issued for the specific performance of some duty, a considerable fine was added, usually proportioned to the wealth and station of the party, and was meant as a penalty in case the decree was not executed to the satisfaction of the Court.[2] Very few fines indeed were

[1] The Act Books, *passim*: e.g. S. P. Dom. Car. I, 434, f. 119. Feb. 22, 1639/40.

[2] Sir Alexander Cave was several times prosecuted in the Commission in 1619 for adultery with Amy Roe, and gave bond

collected in full, except from refractory persons who refused either to recognize the jurisdiction of the Court or to perform its decree. Ordinarily only a fourth or fifth of the nominal fine was required to be paid, and the payment of the mitigated fine was frequently respited for several years,[1] while many fines, among them all the largest, were remitted outright. The largest fine of which we now have record was one of £12,000 in a case of adultery, which was wholly remitted.[2] One culprit charged with several serious offences refused to answer the articles against him and escaped from prison. Being now out of reach, he was fined £520 for non-appearance, then £500 was added at each of five further intimations, till the fine stood at £3,200. Finally, £3,000 more was added. This having failed to bring the culprit before them, the commissioners demanded orders from the King regarding further procedure, and counselled mitigation, because, as they said, the fine was never meant to be levied, but was only *in terrorem*.[3] Ordinarily fines were graded between £2,000 and £5 according to the rank and wealth of the culprit, the seriousness of his offence, and, most especially, the opinion entertained by the Court of his willingness to perform the order. The vast majority were £500 and below, with a very considerable proportion of these below £100. A fine, once certified into the Exchequer,

to obey the sentence of the Court to abstain from her company in future. Having lived with her for eight years previous to 1634 in defiance of the decree, he was ordered to perform penance, fined £500 with costs, and was committed until he gave sufficient bond and sureties for the performance of the order: S. P. Dom. Car. I, 261, f. 129. Nov. 13, 1634. See, also, on the general topic: S. P. Dom. Car. I, 261, ff. 22 b, 39 b, 111 b, 121, 123 b, 129, 137, 138, 140 b, 141 b, 142, 155 b, 177 b, 185 b.

[1] S. P. Dom. Car. I, 434, f. 119.

[2] *Ibid.* 195, no. 8. June 26, 1631.

[3] *Ibid.* 268, no. 63. May 24, 1634.

could not be mitigated.[1] It should, however, be remembered that, though the Commission certified its fines into the Exchequer, they were not collected by the Exchequer, but by the Receiver of Fines and Forfeitures, who was specially appointed by the King and who ranked as one of the Commission's officers.[2] The 'certifying of fines' was probably only the recording in the King's treasury of the amount of money due.

Few things impress the student of the records of the Commission more than the superabundance of evidence testifying to the consistent care and effort shown by the commissioners, that their powers should be exercised with equity, moderation, and absolute fairness, and that their procedure should be free from undue delay, expense, and vexation. That these ends should have been perfectly attained was not to have been expected, but the commissioners from the time of Aylmer to the days of Laud certainly seem to have striven to obviate as far as possible the evils of administration then apparent in the Commission, in common with all the other courts in the realm. A great many papers have been preserved endorsed by Laud, with orders for a speedy hearing or for the securing of fairness and justice,[3] and there are many similar entries in the Act Books. The commissioners refused to re-hear a case in 1631, giving as a reason that they 'would not have it the scandall of this Court to holde suit upon suite soe that men may have noe end, though it be spoken of other Courtes'.[4] On one occasion the Court ordered

[1] *Ibid.* 261, f. 33 b. June 12, 1634.

[2] e. g. *id.* f. 71 b. July 1, 1634.

[3] S. P. Dom. Car. I, 289, no. 17; 303, no. 103; 313, no. 59; 318, no. 59; 320, no. 45; 321, no. 21; 321, no. 36; 369, no. 93; 371, no. 46; 381, no. 74; 388, no. 34; 397, no. 91; 401, no. 74; 402, no. 54; 402, no. 55; 421, no. 59; 424, no. 18; 424, no. 20; 433, no. 15; 455, no. 87.

[4] Gardiner, *Cases*, 240.

a case referred to two commissioners, one of whom asked to be excused from serving on it, because ' the defendant had seemed to take some exceptions to him '.[1] Such consideration was rare in seventeenth-century courts. The Commission ordered certain ' popish ' vestments and altar ornaments to be defaced, but directed, nevertheless, that the most valuable should be returned to the owners, ' that they may not say that we or any do it for their goods or for lucre.'[2] A Puritan minister, who had given much trouble by his persistent nonconformity and opposition to the bishop's orders, and had, in consequence, been suspended and deprived by the Commission, was soon relieved from his suspension, and merely admonished to ' carry himself moderately and discreetly ', and not to preach in the cures of which he had lately been deprived, nor in London without the bishop's licence. This order, of course, allowed him to preach elsewhere.[3] Laymen imprisoned for attendance at conventicles were released on promise of future conformity without any proceeding against them for their past breach of the law.[4] A man who was unable to find the proper sureties for his bond was freed simply on his own bond and oath to perform the sentence of the Court.[5] Such measures do not seem unduly harsh or severe.

The commissioners insisted that no one should be prosecuted, even *ex officio*, without sufficient bond given to pay him costs, if the promoter failed to prove his

[1] S. P. Dom. Car. I, 261, f. 138. Nov. 20, 1634.

[2] Gardiner, *Cases*, 196; and S. P. Dom. Car. I, 261, f. 126 b, Nov. 13, 1634, for such an order. These two instances at the distance of three years proves that the practice was regular.

[3] S. P. Dom. Car. I, 261, f. 136. Nov. 20, 1634.

[4] *Id.* f. 136 b.

[5] *Id.* f. 148. Dec. 8, 1634. The close proximity of these references is not without its significance.

charge.[1] In many instances the Court ordered a larger bond to be entered, or a new promoter be found,[2] while failure to satisfy the Court in these respects meant invariably the loss of the right to sue and the dismissal of the defendant.[3] A party prosecuted *ex officio* on the presentment of the Bishop of Bristol demanded[4] 'a sufficient promoter against whom to have costs if not found delinquent', and apparently had his request as of right. In another case, in 1634, the plaintiff was a poor minister, unable to pay the charges of the prosecution, and the Court, taking into consideration this fact, coupled to the serious nature of the case, which concerned blasphemy, ordered the Advocate-General to prosecute the defendant *ex officio*, but with the limitation that, if he should not prove the charges against him, the State should pay him costs.[5] Men were sometimes ruined by promoting a suit of office, though, where the Court had really forced a man to accept the position, the expenses of an unsuccessful suit were defrayed by the receiver out of the revenues of the Court.[6] England was infested at the time with a horde of informers who were only too eager to accept

[1] The Orders of 1616 made this a rule.

[2] No sufficient bond having been entered for the prosecution, the defendant was dismissed and his bonds compelling attendance cancelled: Act Book, June 12, 1634, S. P. Dom. Car. I, 261, f. 38. And, on the *same* folio, a more sufficient bond to prosecute to be entered into and a reference to Dr. Wood to report on the state of the case. And again, Order to secure a promoter able to pay costs if he fail to prove the articles: S. P. Dom. Car. I, 434, f. 304 b. Nov. 26, 1640. See, also, S. P. Dom. Car. I, 261, ff. 92, 123 b, 142 b, 159 b, &c. (1634); 321, no. 21. May 14, 1636.

[3] S. P. Dom. Car. I, 261, ff. 172, 100, 108 b, 116 b; and also ff. 28, 38 b, 51, 87 b, 173 b, 184. These and the last note seem to prove sufficiently the frequency of the practice.

[4] Gardiner, *Cases*, 261.

[5] S. P. Dom. Car. I, 261, f. 11 b. Oct. 30, 1634.

[6] See S. P. Dom. Car. I, 321, no. 21. May 14, 1636.

any chance to prove a suit in hope of securing costs from the defendant. No small part of the odium heaped upon the Commission and upon suits *ex officio* is the result of the practices of these men, which the Court was in a measure powerless to prevent.

Not only did the Commission seek to secure the equity and justice of its own proceedings, but it was ready to aid those oppressed elsewhere.[1] Suits *in forma pauperis* [2] and suits *ex officio* in behalf of some poor or oppressed party [3] formed a large part of the Commission's business. Richard Wisedom, a prisoner in the Compter, complained to the Privy Council that one Thomas Hall had alienated his wife's affections, and had caused him to be imprisoned on a false charge so that Hall might live with his wife. He prayed that Hall might be prosecuted in the Commission *ex officio*.[4] A vicar had sued the impropriators of his chapel lands in Chancery, and had procured an augmentation of his living. They promptly sued him at common law and he begged the Commission to rescue him, *ex officio gratioso*, from the warrants out against him.[5] Richard Dixon petitioned to be allowed to answer the articles of one Richardson, a clerk, *in forma pauperis*, alleging that he had once been witness against Richardson, who had ever since vexed him by suits.[6] Boustfield had

[1] On the Commission as a refuge for the oppressed see: S. P. Dom. Car. I, 313, no. 59; 381, no. 54; 387, no. 70; 401, no. 32; 406, no. 75; 435, no. 42; 455, no. 87. There were also cases of hardship and oppression by the Commission itself: S. P. Dom. Car. I, 255, no. 21; 321, no. 21; 351, no. 36; 373, no. 45; 414, no. 39.

[2] S. P. Dom. Car. I, 313, no. 59; 387, no. 91; 388, no. 35.

[3] *Ibid.* 313, no. 59; 389, no. 92; 401, no. 32; 401, no. 73. Petitions to the Commission in such cases: 377, no. 149; 455, no. 87; 446, no. 63.

[4] *Ibid.* 377, no. 149 (1637/8).

[5] *Ibid.* 313, no. 59. Feb. 8, 1635/6.

[6] *Ibid.* 388, no. 35. April 25, 1638.

preferred articles against Morland for blasphemy, whereupon Morland secured a promoter to sue Boustfield in the Commission. The suit was heard when only Boustfield's proctor was present, and Boustfield was fined £500 and 40 marks costs. He had already suffered on Morland's suits from five years' litigation in the Commission, the Chancery, and the King's Bench, and he now petitioned Laud for relief, who ordered that he have every judicial advantage possible.[1]

The equitable aspect of the Commission's jurisdiction and the power of enforcing specific performance became steadily more important. The Court could compel specific performance of a duty, of a promise, of an oath, or whatever the ecclesiastical law might require. It could enforce specific reparation for ecclesiastical torts, such as slander, the defiling of a church or graveyard, declarations by a minister of opinions against the Book of Common Prayer, and the like.[2] Cases of adultery, desertion of a wife without support, divorce, alimony, and testamentary matters, cases where the payment of money or the conveyance of land was often required, the commissioners settled by decrees and exacted a satisfactory bond for their specific performance.[3] It would not be going too far, perhaps, to state that probably three-

[1] *Ibid.* 381, no. 54. Feb. 8, 1637/8.

[2] ' We require you to proceed to extreme punishment corporal or otherwise openly or privately and speedily that our servant may be restored to her good fame ' : the Queen to the commissioners, S. P. Dom. Eliz., Addenda, 13, no. 103. A minister was ordered to read the Prayer Book and do reverence at the Blessed name before the ' second court day of next term or be deprived ' : S. P. Dom. Car. I, 381, no. 63.

[3] Petition to the Commission to restrain J. Davies from maliciously prosecuting him in order to escape fulfilling an order ' either to pay for or yield possession of a house bought by him from Davies ' : S. P. Dom. Jac. I, 104, no. 66.

fourths of the Commission's sentences and decrees affirmatively ordered a man to perform something. Such a power in a court was at that time very unusual, and seemed to many conservative men a real innovation of questionable legality. At equity it was, indeed, just becoming the regular practice to force a man to perform some contract or promise which he had explicitly accepted, but neither equity nor the common-law courts at that time would order a man specifically to perform some duty laid upon him by the law in mere general terms. He might be fined, or imprisoned, or hanged for his breach of the law, but he could not be forced to perform. Apparently, the rule, now associated at common law with the Statute of Limitations, was applied by the commissioners in several cases.[1] It was by no means unusual for an advocate to argue that the Commission had no power to hear that suit,[2] or for a commissioner to declare that no relief could be given in a certain case.[3] Yet, certainly,

[1] The Court referred a charge of adultery, committed nineteen years ago, to a doctor to consider, remarking that it was not the custom of the Court to examine misdemeanours older than ten years: S. P. Dom. Car. I, 261, f. 64 b. June 26, 1634.

[2] Gardiner, *Cases*, 278. Counsel for the defendant urged that certain evidence should not be admitted because 'it was proceeded civilly and not criminally'. Dr. Rives replied that in cases of adultery and cruelty combined the Commission always proceeded criminally: S. P. Dom. Car. I, 261, f. 143 b. Nov. 27, 1634. This is an argument against the jurisdiction of the Court in favour of the defendant.

[3] 'Nor have I any information against him touching any matter cognizable in the Court of Commission for Causes Ecclesiastical': Bishop of Durham to Windebank. Nov. 7, 1639. S. P. Dom. Car. I, 432, no. 20. The Commissioners at Informations on November 19, 1640, decided that 'the matters contained in the articles were not fit for the Cognizance of this Court but might fitly be heard before the ordinary': S. P. Dom. Car. I, 434, f. 297. It was also decided, in 1635, that 'the High Commission had not properly power to break open doors, and take

in practice the equitable function of giving relief in a worthy case, wherever the remedy in the ordinary ecclesiastical courts was clearly inadequate,[1] made these limitations of less consequence than we would otherwise have expected. It was this part of its powers which necessarily took the Commission at times to the very borders of its judicial authority.

Certain positive evils appeared in due time in the Commission's procedure and practice. In its later years the early tendency toward arbitrary decisions and the use of summary procedure seem to have disappeared almost entirely,[2] yet, to modern students familiar only with oral trials at common law, the procedure of the Commission seems in itself a grievance. Indeed, a written procedure might be in many ways less rapid and more expensive than an oral procedure, though it is clear that trials in the Commission were at least as rapid and inexpensive as those at common law. Each party had to be furnished with a copy of each stage of his adversary's pleadings, but the copy, to prevent falsifications and consequent complications, had to be made by some official, who, necessarily, had to be paid. Where so many written stages were possible, each of which needed a commissioner's approval, and some of which required the approval of the Court at a formal sitting, delays were, at times, difficult to avoid.[3] Most of them, however,

forth men's persons, and goods except in cases of heresy and seizing of heretical books': S. P. Dom. Car. I, 303, no. 57. See also *Ibid.* 261, f. 37; 321, no. 43.

[1] *Ibid.* 318, no. 59; 339, no. 68.

[2] Where the records are so scanty and so scattered, it is impossible to speak definitely, but the available material seems to point to this conclusion.

[3] A delay of eighteen months, S. P. Dom. Car. I, 469, no. 93 (1637); suit extending over three years, *ibid.* 410, no. 45 (1638/9); suit extending over two years, *ibid.* 420, no. 49; one year,

and much of the attendant expense were due to the parties[1] and their advocates[2] rather than to the commissioners. The requests by advocates for further delay or for an extension of terms probatory were innumerable, and, on the other hand, we possess a large amount of evidence tending to prove the desire of the commissioners to obviate these practices.[3] They had no reason whatever to permit delay or expense to their suitors: it meant further time and trouble to them with no gain whatever, for, though the registrar, the clerks, and the messengers were paid, the commissioners themselves were not. There is also no trustworthy evidence whatever to show that any commissioner ever took a bribe.[4] At common law and in the Chancery, where a large portion of the fees went to the judges and officers of the Court as part of their salary and perquisites, delays and long suits meant increased fees for the judges as well as for the lawyers.

Many other features, which we to-day feel to be evils,

ibid., 421, no. 59; 424, no. 18; 433, no. 15. See also *ibid.* 381, no. 74; 471, no. 46.

1 S. P. Dom. Car. I, 261, ff. 123 b, 159 b; 303, no. 103; 400, no. 109. A suitor was ruled out of court because of his delay: *Ibid.* 434, f. 219 (1640).

2 *Ibid.* 437, no. 48; Gardiner, *Cases*, 269, 273.

3 S. P. Dom. Car. I, 289, no. 17; 303, no. 103; 369, no. 93; 373, no. 45; 381, no. 74; 383, no. 14; 421, no. 59; 424, no. 18; 424, no. 20; 433, no. 15; &c. The Orders of 1616 *in toto*. The Orders of 1640 (*ibid.* 434, f. 208) were made because of 'the neglect of parties and their counsel in not bringing in their briefs in due time'.

4 The case of Bishop Bridgman of Chester, where there seems to have been some evidence of bribery, cannot be reckoned against the general commissioners for the Province of Canterbury at London. See S. P. Dom. Car. I, 237, no. 78; 240, no. 44; 254, no. 47. Sir John Bennett, convicted of receiving bribes in 1622, was convicted as Judge of the Audience, not as High Commissioner: see *Commons' Journals*, i, 580–91; *Lords' Journals*, iii, 87–197.

the Commission shared with all the other courts of the realm, especially with the common-law courts: the free use of vituperation by attorneys and proctors, barristers and advocates, the oaths and violent denunciations of the prisoner used by the judge, the heavy costs, the severe penalties and fines. As for the procedure to which posterity has objected—the examination upon oath *ex officio*, the written procedure, a trial largely in private before the formal hearing—this the Commission possessed in common with the Star Chamber, the Chancery, the Admiralty, the Court of Requests, all the ecclesiastical courts, the Councils of the North and in the Marches of Wales.

Other evils in procedure and practice were due to the propensity of men in the seventeenth century towards litigation. It was distinctly a part of the tactics of an advocate or proctor to cause his opponent as much delay and expense as possible, to 'vex' him by as many frivolous suits as he could in other courts, to gain slight decisions which should entail costs upon him, to aggravate his fine so as to force him to go at least to the delay and expense of attendance at the Court of Mitigations. The longer his own articles were, the greater the cost to his adversary of a copy, and the greater chance of finding that the answer left something important unnoticed. Equally, the longer the pleadings, the larger would be the proctors' and advocates' fees.[1] Then, as now, the Court costs were a minor part of the expense of a suit. John Fabian, a vicar, petitioned Laud in 1636 for aid from the Commission against Sir Francis Popham. Fabian

[1] In the Bibliography are references to examples of processes and pleadings in the Commission. For the number of papers in a single suit, see S. P. Dom. Car. I, 383, no. 47; 246, no. 13; 268, no. 63; 278, no. 65; 388, no. 41; 432, no. 27.

had recovered from the latter by suit in the Commission the churchyard of Dundry, which Popham had long used as his own land, and was at once made defendant in several suits at law by William King, one of Popham's tenants. Popham himself preferred a bill against Fabian in Chancery for the same land, and had taken out three commissions returnable in that very term. Bird, another tenant of Popham's, had sued Fabian in the Commission, and had caused a vast number of depositions to be taken, on articles not mentioned in his brief, to the number of one hundred folios of paper, the whole volume of depositions amounting already to three hundred and thirty folios, which had put the petitioner and his witnesses to the cost and trouble of sitting twenty-two days before the commissioners sent down into the country to examine them. At that moment the case was being further delayed. Laud ordered it to be attended to at once.[1] The petition of a prisoner in the Fleet informed Laud that he had been there for five years under a judgement secured by a man who had ever since been living in adultery with his wife. The two had been sued in the Commission, but had succeeded in postponing the hearing. Presented to the Court of the Chancellor of the Bishop of Norwich for this same crime, they had procured from the Court of Arches an inhibition to the Chancellor. They were then presented to the Court of the Archdeacon at Bury, confessed the crime, but secured the right to prosecute the churchwardens, who had presented them, in the Arches, where two suits were thus pending, besides the one in the Commission. The petitioner begged for a settlement of the whole case by the Commission.[2]

[1] S. P. Dom. Car. I, 320, no. 45. May 7, 1636. Petition of Fabian to Laud. Endorsed by Laud.

[2] *Ibid.* 313, no. 59. Feb. 4, 1635/6.

A minister, Davies, had refused to 'church' a Puritan's wife after childbirth unless she wore a veil as the canons required. Her husband sued him at once at common law for a battery, had him arrested in the churchyard, and dragged forcibly through the market-place. Davies, thereupon, prosecuted them both in the Commission, and they, in turn, procured warrants from a justice of the peace to bind him over for good behaviour, and even brought him to Quarter Sessions, where, however, he was dismissed. The suit then proceeded in the Commission.[1] One man was prosecuted at the same time by the same parties in fifteen different suits before the Commission, the Star Chamber, and the Assizes.[2] The promoter in a case of simony had begun two suits at law upon precisely the same facts.[3] Frequently such suits were brought out of malice,[4] in hope that the defendant would be unable to meet the expense of so much simultaneous litigation. It seems clear that these suits, just cited above, were not in the least based upon doubts as to the jurisdiction of any of these courts, but upon a determination to win the case at all costs, and upon the litigant's thorough belief that, if he only persisted long enough, he would find the right writ and the right court, and would, thereupon, be infallibly awarded the decision.[5]

1 *Ibid.* 388, no. 41, ii. April 26, 1638.

2 *Ibid.* 315, no. 29 (1635/6).

3 Gardiner, *Cases*, 239.

4 e.g. S. P. Dom. Car. I, 387, no. 93.

5 See also on this topic: *Ibid.* 303, no. 7; 312, no. 1; 313, no. 19; 320, no. 59; 320, no. 60; 321, no. 21; 322, no. 29; 339, no. 59; 373, no. 61; 387, no. 70; 387, no. 93; 392, no. 23; 406, no. 69; 406, no. 70; 410, nos. 45, 371; 425, no. 12; 443, no. 86. William Faunt threatened a vicar, Carter, that he would vex him with all manner of suits at law, 'till he make him glad to yield to what he shall think fit': S. P. Dom. Car. I, 321, no. 3. May 12, 1636.

There were, however, certain undeniable abuses among the officials of the Commission. There were cases of proctors charged with taking bribes from their client's opponent to delay the suit.[1] Messengers were discovered taking money in considerable sums to release men whom they had been sent to arrest. The Commission punished several, who had apparently compelled a poor wretch to pay them several separate times for threats supported with the same attachment.[2] There were charges of collusion in the hearing of suits, in the entering of pleadings, and the referring of cases back to bishops and to other courts.[3] Many of these cases were discovered and severely punished by the Commission. How much more of the same sort happened undiscovered we have no means of knowing, but we have still preserved certain blank warrants signed by Laud himself, and certain warrants, signed and sealed[4] and only needing to be filled in by the possessor to be valid. Do these point to other abuses of a deeper sort, or are they merely relics of a sort of secret service very common indeed in the seventeenth century?

1 Gardiner, *Cases*, 269, 273; and S. P. Dom. Car. I, 437, no. 48.
2 Gardiner, *Cases*, 316.
3 *Calendar S. P. Dom.*, 1637, p. 568. Nov. 25, 1637.
4 S. P. Dom. Car. I, 255, nos. 23, 24; 406, no. 57; perhaps explained by the following:—An order issued, November 6, 1634, to send a commission into the country to examine a witness, with a blank bond to be sealed by him for his appearance when summoned: *Ibid.* 261, f. 118.

NOTE A

THE CHARACTER OF SUITS IN THE COMMISSION

	Number of cases in year April 1634 to April 1635.	*Number of cases in year Jan. to Dec. 1640.*
For or concerning Alimony	24	17
Adultery	12	6
Incontinency	1	2
Incest	4	0
Disagreement of husband and wife	9	4
Irreverent behaviour of laymen in church	8	3
Irregularity of the clergy	4	1
Simony	7	1
Clergy questioned for sermons	7	1
Questioned on account of books	2	2
Abetting the spreading of unlicensed books	2	4
Drunkenness and swearing	1	1
Repairing the church or chancel	3	3
Slander	1	1
HERESY	2	1
NONCONFORMITY	5	4
CONTEMPT OF ECCLESIASTICAL AUTHORITY	1	1
BLASPHEMY	3	0
SCHISM	1	0
Concealing massing stuff	3	0
Bad printing of the Bible	1	0
Detaining the key to the church books	1	2
Encroaching on the church land	2	1
Leasing of lands by ecclesiastical corporations	0	2
Refusal of churchwardens to pay the parish clerk's wages	0	2
Non-payment of the curate's wages	0	1
Revenue of a free school	1	0
Advowson	1	0
Money bequeathed *in pios usus*	1	0
Dispute over seats in the church	0	2
Irregular marriage	0	1
Undue procuring of a licence	0	1
Pretending to be an ordained minister	1	0
Dilapidation of the goods of Manchester College	1	0
Question of producing letters of Institution	1	0
Many years' absence from church	0	1
Rhymes on the Lord's Prayer	0	1
Restoration of a bell to a chapel	0	1

NOTE B

Formal Proceedings on Court Days

	1634 June 12	1634 Oct. 9	1640 July 2	1640 Oct. 15
Hearing	5	0	4	23
Day appointed	18	6	2	31
Appeared and sworn	11	16	2	9
Cause referred till later day	16	3	0	6
Case continued	0	5	0	0
Publication of sentence decreed	2	0	0	7
Respite of costs or fines	2	0	13	8
Fines or bonds to be certified	2 (bonds)	2 (bonds)	7 (fines)	3 (bonds)
Imprisonment ordered	6	1	1	0
Party licensed to depart	5	1	0	1
Case dismissed	1	2	2	0
Extension of time allowed	7	11	0	0
Monition to appear or bring in papers	7	1	0	4
Referred to Informations	2	0	0	2
Witnesses to be examined	6	13	0	7
Witnesses examined	4	0	0	1
Witnesses discharged	4	0	0	1
Witnesses produced	3	0	0	3
Depositions of witnesses published	5	3	0	0
Attachment ordered	5	22	2	5
Formal papers read	0	9	0	0
To go to report	0	1	0	0

Note. This table is by no means as satisfactory as might be wished: it is exceedingly difficult to tabulate *briefly* the very numerous stages possible in so complicated a procedure. The list does not contain either all the cases contained in the records of a single day. The count made by some one else who did not use quite the same classification might differ slightly. Still, it is probable that the list as it is gives an impression which is substantially correct.

NOTE C

Sessions of the Commission

In the year April 1634 to April 1635, the Commission sat on the following days, those in parenthesis were court days: May 3, 5, (8), 12, 13, 14, 29; June 3, 9, 10, (12), 14, 16, 18, (19), 21, 23, 24, (26), 27; July (1), 2, 7, 8, 21; October 2, 3, 8, (9), 11, 13, 14, (16), 17, 18, 21, (23), 24, 28, 29, (30); November 3, 5, (6), 12, (13), (20), 24, 26, (27); December 1, 8, 12; January 19, 26, 27, 28, (29), 30, 31; February 3, (5), 9, 10, 11, (12), 17, 18, (19), 23, 24; March 9, 26.

The following are the number of actual entries in the Act Books for each Court day:

May 8	105	Nov. 6	79
June 12	124	Nov. 13	86
June 19	95	Nov. 20	82
June 26	88	Nov. 27	85
July 1 (Mitigation Day)	21	Jan. 29	93
Oct. 9	104	Feb. 5	102
Oct. 16	106	Feb. 12	115
Oct. 23	88	Feb. 19 (Mitigation Day)	46
Oct. 30	81		

NOTE D

Fines

For non-appearance, £50 (S. P. Dom. 434, f. 229 b) and £40 (*id.*).
Contempt of Court, £50 (*id.* f. 228).
Not appearing on Intimation, £50 (*id.* f. 121).

Sentence Fines, to secure Performance

Heretical Doctrine, £1,000 (434, f. 119), (261, f. 68 b).
Adultery, £12,000 (mitigated to £2,000 bond and no fine, S. P. Dom. Car. 1, 195, n. 8).
Adultery, £500 (434, f. 121), (and 261, f. 71).
Adultery, £400 (*id.*), (mitigated to £100).
Adultery, £2,000 (261, f. 71), not mitigated.

Incest, £500, respited.
Contempt, £100, certified.
Contempt, £100 (mitigated to £10).
Contempt, £150, certified. } (261, f. 71).

Anabaptism, £500 (434, f. 120).

Slander, £2,000 (261, f. 25, May 8).

Affronting ecclesiastical jurisdiction, £100 (mitigated, £40).

Preaching on Toby's Dog, £200 (434, f. 120).

Drinking healths near the Communion table, £40 (mitigated, £20).

Disturbance in Church, £50 and £30 (mitigated, £20 and £10).

Unduly procuring a licence to preach, £200 (434, f. 121).

Many years' absence from Church, £100 (mitigated to £50) (*id.*).

Importing popish books, £100 (mitigated to £10) (*id.*).

Profane rhymes on the Lord's Prayer, £100 (mitigated to £40).

Scandalous words against the King and Queen, 500 marks, remitted for twelve months (261, f. 77).

Publishing fanatical pamphlets, £3,000 (*id.*).

Disturbing Divine service, £2,000 (*id.*).

Maintaining heretical opinions on the Sabbath, £1,000 (*id.*).

Respiting of Fines

The following fines were respited from October 1633 till February 1640, and then were certified: £300, £3,000, £2,000, £100, £1,000, £1,000, £1,000, £100, £20, £1,000, £200.

NOTE E

Costs

Total costs: 20 marks (434, f. 99 b); 40 marks (381, n. 54); £3 (434, f. 231); £4 (434, f. 124 b, 278); £7 (261, f. 28 b); £8 (375, n. 101); £10 (434, f. 30, 33 b); £16 (261, f. 25); £24 (261, f. 64); £30 (434, f. 17); £50 (434, f. 37; 261, f. 29); £100 (434, f. 61 b; 434 a, f. 24); £160 (434, f. 230 b).

Bonds. To appear, £20 (434, f. 53); £100 (434, f. 120, f. 230); £200 (434, f. 235). To perform orders, £40 (434, f. 16); £500 (434, f. 24).

INTIMATIONS. To appear, £20 (261, f. 28 b, f. 39; f. 65 b, 67; 434, f. 8, 10, 24, 36, 295, 304, &c., &c.); £30 (434, f. 110 b); £40 (434, f. 67, 89 b).

ATTACHMENTS. For non-appearance, £40 (434, f. 53); £100 (434, f. 105, 109).

To answer articles, £50 (261, f. 61).

COMMISSION FOR ANSWERS, 13*s*. 4*d*.

PROMOTER'S DEPOSIT AT BEGINNING OF SUIT, 20*s*. (434, f. 60).

RETARDATI PROCESSUS, 40*s*. (434, f. 303 b); £7 (434, f. 259).

MESSENGERS' FEES, 20 marks, £16, £18, £17, for one term's service.

These were the regular and ordinary costs. These examples cover both extremes.

CHAPTER XIII

SPECIAL AND DIOCESAN COMMISSIONS

THE relegation to a single chapter of the consecutive account of all commissions except that for the Province of Canterbury depends for its justification upon the correctness of styling the latter 'the' High Commission, and of thus placing all other commissioners and commissions in an inferior position, which their number and ubiquity apparently contradicts. Their legal position was the same as that of 'the' Commission, for their Letters Patent came from the Crown, and did not explicitly subject the commissioners named to the Court of High Commission or declare their inferiority in definite words. The formal language of Letters Patent is, however, an unstable basis on which to found an opinion: no comparison of the Patents issued to the Canterbury Commissioners would establish the undoubted existence of a court of law or the moment of its appearance. The usage of contemporaries, which has been followed in other matters as a trustworthy guide to the actual situation, employed the terms and assigned special and diocesan commissions a very subordinate place indeed. At the same time there is something to be said for the contention that the history of these smaller commissions is not, and naturally cannot be, a part of the history of the court of law which sat at London, and for the belief that, though these commissions, like the ecclesiastical courts, had relations with that court, they were not parts of it. Until Elizabeth's reign, it must be admitted, a clear relationship usually existed: the general commission was in most cases the parent of the smaller bodies and controlled them. After 1559 the relationship was not so clear. The Crown, in fact, issued patents granting authority to other men, which had already been conferred upon the commissioners for the Province of Canterbury. The position of these special and diocesan commissions was, therefore, peculiar and anomalous, since the commissioners at London could, and not infrequently did, supersede their authority by warrant of their own Letters Patent. This fact seems to be the key to the situation : the Canterbury commissioners were not expected to perform regular ecclesiastical routine business in the dioceses, even though their Patent vested in them the requisite authority; if the Crown deemed expedient the regular exercise of such authority in any part of England, a special patent was issued for a single case or for a certain district, defining with exactitude the powers to be employed and naming the men who were to use them, among whom were usually several of the Canterbury commissioners. But the Court of High Commission itself (as distinguished from the general body of the Canterbury commissioners) was clearly expected to supervise these commissions and to supplement at discretion by its own broad authority their very limited powers. In course of time these smaller commissions became, in practice, additional ecclesiastical courts or visitatorial bodies, from which an appeal lay to the Court at London. They formed, in fact, a sort of hierarchy of small high commissions of first instance.

The history of such small commissions as persisted after 1559 records so many varying types, that any single conclusion as to their character becomes difficult. We have a copy of the original record of one appointed in 1562 to examine the validity of the marriage of Edward Seymour, the Earl of Hertford, with Lady Katharine Gray, a marriage which might have had serious political consequences had an heir been born while Elizabeth was still of marriageable age.[1] This special commission, however, was, unlike the Henrician and Marian special commissions, issued by the Crown and not by the Commissioners for the Province of Canterbury, though its members already belonged to that body. The trial was exceedingly technical and carefully followed every vestige of formality required by canon law for the annulment of a marriage. The explanation is simple. Elizabeth realized that only by the utmost care in observing all possible judicial forms would the trial serve her purpose. Evidently, then, this case cannot be considered valid evidence proving the use of a regular judicial procedure by the Canterbury Commissioners or the issue of special commissions by the Crown as a regular expedient. The commissions issued by Parker to visit the hospitals[2] were, perhaps, special commissions of the older model; possibly the commissions for uniformity of religion, which seem to have existed in most counties between 1570 and 1590, were also of that type.[3] On the other hand, the justices of the peace of Gloucestershire were directed by the Privy Council in 1585/6 to reform the ecclesiastical courts in that shire, but were also told to refer cases that exceeded their commission to the High Commissioners.[4] It is evident that the Crown and Council took an extremely liberal view of the right to delegate ecclesiastical authority, and certainly created an astonishing variety of jurisdictions in the first few decades after

[1] Harl. MSS. 249, f. 45 ff. [2] Strype, *Parker*, i, 202–3.

[3] *Privy Council Register, New Series*, vi, 102; viii, 173, 208 (1573); S. P. Dom. Eliz., 247, no. 5 (1594). Perhaps those referred to in Petyt MSS. 538. 52, f. 1, are of this date. See also *Privy Council Register*, viii, 271; x, 295.

[4] *Ibid.* xiv, 39.

the Reformation. Nothing could make clearer the fact that Coke's interpretation of the Statute of 1 Elizabeth was not that of its framers.

At the same time there is no good reason to doubt that the early type of small commission gave way soon after 1559 to commissions granted to a bishop and others for his diocese only.[1] Some such commissions had been issued by Mary, and Elizabeth issued one for Chester in 1562, another probably in 1567, and, in the following year, one for the Province of York. The desirability of such an ecclesiastical body wherever the Church was hard pressed, coupled with the clear physical impossibility that the general commissioners could always respond in emergency, suggested another expedient. The lost Commission for the Province of Canterbury of 1570[2] and that of 1572 named some score of men who were to exercise authority solely in certain dioceses—Canterbury, Winchester, and Chichester were specified in 1570, to which were added, in 1572, Worcester and St. Davids. But this expedient was immediately discarded in favour of separate commissions with territorial limitation, which were certainly issued, between 1575 and 1580, for the dioceses of Canterbury, London, and Chester, for the Province of York, for Wales and the Marches (to the Lord President and Council in the Marches of Wales), and probably for Ireland.[3] The Commission in the diocese of London seems to have been soon discontinued, but the others were renewed, and by 1590 commissions had also issued to the Bishops of Winchester, Norwich, Salisbury, and Durham, and by

[1] A list of the Commissions referred to in the following paragraphs is in the Appendix.

[2] *Parker Correspondence*, 370 (Parker Society).

[3] *Report on the MSS. of the Earl of Egmont*, I, part i, 21. This petition of Nov. 6, 1590, mentions the Lord Chancellor of Ireland as head of an ecclesiastical commission.

1611 to those of Exeter, and Lincoln, and, not improbably, to those of most of the other English dioceses. It is extremely likely that these special commissions covered between them the whole of England, Wales, and Ireland from about 1580 to 1605.

The detailed evidence about these commissions is extremely scanty, but thoroughly reliable. They were all limited in jurisdiction and in duration. So few men were named as members that a few deaths would void the patent. The Letters Patent of 1572 for the Province of Canterbury named only twenty-eight to exercise jurisdiction in four dioceses and the whole of Wales. The Letters Patent of 1579 for Wales, issued to the Lord President of the Council in the Marches of Wales, the Bishop of Worcester, Vice-President of the Council, and eighteen others, applied to the four English marcher-counties and all Wales. Four commissioners were usually necessary for the transaction of business under these special patents, but any four could act, for in the earlier patents often no quorum was named. Elizabeth's later commissions, however, on which the Jacobean were modelled, often named twenty-five or thirty commissioners, reduced the number necessary for business to the usual three, and named a fairly large quorum. No such unlimited discretion was granted these commissioners in jurisdiction as was accorded the general commissioners, though much the same discretion in procedure was theirs. The Welsh Commission of 1579 directed them ' to enquire, not only by the verdict of twelve good and lawful men but also by all other good and lawful means whatsoever, of all misdemeanours, misbehaviours, trespasses and offences whatsoever, and them to see reformed and amended from time to time according to such articles of instructions as ye shall receive from our Privy Council in writing signed with six of their hands'. A commission for Norwich[1] empowered the Commissioners to try 'as well by the othes of Xii men as also by witnesses and all other lawfull wayes and meanes, of all offences and misdemeanours' against the Acts of Supremacy, Uniformity, and the Act of 1572 concerning ministers. They were also to 'enquyre of all and singular hereticall opynyons, sedyciouse bookes, contempts, slaunderouse wordes publyshed', and to commit to ward all recusants. The later commissions, for example that for Winchester, nearly approximated to the scope of jurisdiction allotted to the Canterbury Commission, while, under James and Charles, there was practically no difference between them. The taking of bonds, the right to attach, to fine, and imprison, were usually granted *eo nomine*, and the Patent named a Registrar, a Receiver of Fines and Forfeitures, and provided for the certification of fines into the Exchequer.

What little we know of the actual work carried on by these commissioners tends to show that their practice did not differ materially from that of the Canterbury Commission, except in degree of 'enormity'. Certainly they copied the latter's procedure with great alacrity, and as early as 1579 began to try suits between party and party. The Commissioners for the diocese of London tried a case of forgery as early as 1579,[2] and in 1581 the commissioners for Chester were prohibited by the Queen's Bench from attempting to compel the specific performance of certain bequests.[3] The Exchequer Records contain bonds, certificates of fines, and the like from many of these commissions, and make clear the fact that

[1] Cotton MSS. Vespasian, F, IX, f. 269.

[2] *Privy Council Register*, xi, 322. Nov. 30, 1579.

[3] Tanner MSS. 79, f. 153.

they, too, insisted upon specific performance of their decrees.[1]

At the same time, the correspondence of the bishops abundantly proves that the diocesan commissions were used chiefly to perform the visitatorial work which the episcopate was tired of trying to accomplish by visitations and ecclesiastical censures. It might, therefore, be reasonably contended that the functions, exercised by the general commissioners until 1580, were delegated to diocesan commissioners when the general commission had become clearly a court of law. Would it not then follow, that the Court of High Commission, instead of being an evolution from the earlier commissions, and a result of their gradual development, was a new body superimposed on the older commissions to exercise an entirely different type of authority, and, only as a matter of expediency, 'created' under a form of patent already in use, and merely by accident denominated 'the' High Commission? Thus, we should have a hierarchy of small commissions as the legitimate and natural successors of the earlier commissions, and, quite apart from them, a law-court.

[1] See on the working of these commissions during Elizabeth's reign, Exchequer Doc. Q. R. Eccles., bundle 7, no. 14; bundle 12, no. 4, schedule of fines received by Henry Best on behalf of the Ecclesiastical Commissioners in the diocese of Norwich, 40 and 41 Eliz. *Ibid.*, Bundle 12, no. 2, bonds for recusants and others from the commissioners at Durham, 37 Eliz., &c. J. Waddington, *The Track of the Hidden Church*, 157, note, prints a certificate into the Exchequer of fines for non-appearance imposed by the High Commissioners at York. S. P. Dom. Eliz., 141, nos. 3 and 28, contain notes of the proceedings of the commissioners at York in 1580, and Morrice MSS. C, pp. 766–88, contains formal papers, &c., relating to the same commissioners' proceedings in 1586 and 1587. See, also, S. P. Dom. Eliz., 262, no. 25, i; and *Hist. MSS. Com. Report*, viii, 375, where there is a letter from the commissioners at York to the Mayor of Chester asking him to collect a fine and forward the money (Aug. 5, 1593).

Unfortunately, the facts do not permit us to accept so logical and satisfying a suggestion. The Court of High Commission was by no means merely a law-court; its Letters Patent always permitted the exercise of visitatorial authority, not essentially different from that exercised by the Edwardian and Marian commissioners, and the Court was not slow to use it in 1605 and in 1635 in support of the metropolitan visitations. It is this anomalous aspect of the Commission's history which it is so hard to comprehend: it was in the very earliest days something more than a visitatorial body, and, in its later years, unquestionably something more than a law-court. The special and diocesan commissions did exercise similar authority to that possessed by the Commissioners for the Province of Canterbury, but they did not supplant or dispense with the latter's prerogatives.

The relation of these minor commissions to the Privy Council was, in most cases, probably closer even than that of the London commission. Whatever their Patents said, they were not allowed to undertake anything besides ecclesiastical routine without explicit orders, and they were, of course, likely to be called to strict account at any time. Cases were referred to them and explicit directions forwarded as to procedure, sentences, &c.;[1] nor was the Council above appointing their messengers and other officers.[2] Technically, the Court of High Commission possessed no authority over them,[3] but the breadth of its own jurisdiction became the excuse for some sort of constant oversight of whose precise nature we know nothing.

[1] *Privy Council Register, New Series*, xi, 315, 362, 386, 445; xii, 59 (1579).

[2] *Ibid.* viii, 395 (1575).

[3] Mary's Commission of 1557 to the Archbishop of York had explicitly provided an appeal to the Canterbury commissioners. This was omitted by Elizabeth: Pocock's *Burnet's Reformation*, ii, 557.

The common-law courts did not scruple to prohibit the suits of the smaller commissions, but do not seem to have had much occasion. At times we hear of the commissioners in some diocese calling for the aid from the local officers which their Patent authorized, but we are entirely ignorant as to what their relations to the latter really were. Slender as these indications are as to the work actually performed by these commissioners, they point indubitably to a very considerable activity.

A vigorous opposition to their existence, probably proportional to their own vigour, became evident in 1603, and was supported and fomented by the delinquent clergy and laity, who had felt their pressure, as well as by the Puritans, who saw in them the chief obstacles to the transformation of the Church to the New Discipline. Moreover, their opponents found not only the Lord Chancellor, but the King and the Archbishop in agreement with them in their complaint that there were too many such commissions with too large a membership and too great powers. Whitgift declared that diocesan commissions had often been granted despite his opposition, and, at times, without his knowledge; Coke later said that, about this time, he drew up, as Attorney-General, a scheme which provided for one commission only in each province;[1] but nothing was done; except, perhaps, to discontinue the commissions already existing in some of the less disorderly dioceses. Probably the Archbishop was jealous of the diocesan commissions, because they interfered with his power as metropolitan, or, at the least, enabled the bishop to do himself what he could not otherwise have accomplished without assistance, which would, in time, have created precedent in favour of the archi-

[1] Barlow, *The Summe and Substance of the Conference*, The Third Day.

episcopal right to interfere in such cases. Nor would it afterwards be always easy to distinguish between aid given by the Archbishop as metropolitan and as member of the Canterbury Commission. Perhaps, too, the Canterbury commissioners regarded the issue of diocesan commissions as an attempt to subdivide their authority; and certainly in visitatorial work such was the result. In any case, we hear little more from Puritans, lawyers, or bishops against these commissions till 1610, when they were given prominence in the counts of the 'omnibus' bill of grievances presented to the King by the House of Commons.[1] The chief objection to them was, according to the House, that they deprived the bishop of his jurisdiction—a sufficiently humorous plea from a Puritan House anxious to abolish the bishop's jurisdiction altogether. The House did not desire it supplanted, however, by a jurisdiction far broader and more efficient. Alexander Searle had already suggested to Salisbury an expedient (though both were probably ignorant that it had been already tried in 1572) by which these diocesan commissions might be abolished and yet retained. He pointed out how necessary a commission's authority was to supplement the bishops', how convenient it was for suitors and those accused to have a court near them, which would free them from the costly and time-consuming journey to London, rendering them readier and better able to pay the large fines which would accrue to the nearly empty treasury. All the inconveniences could be avoided and the amount of fines increased by simply making members of the general commissions for Canterbury and York such men as ought to sit in the dioceses.[2] As any three

[1] Petyt, *Jus Parliamentarium*, 319–31. Prothero has printed long extracts in his *Select Statutes*, 302–7.

[2] S. P. Dom. Jac. I, 49, no. 2. Nov. 1, 1609.

commissioners, one of whom belonged to the quorum, could legally transact business, and as they might sit wherever they pleased, the only limitation on the number of courts that might do business would be the size of the quorum.

Whether or not in pursuance of Searle's scheme, the new Letters Patent for the Province of Canterbury in 1611 did, in fact, include the important diocesan commissioners, and the total number of members was gradually increased and the quorum enlarged, until, under Charles I, commissioners probably sat simultaneously in all the dioceses of England and Wales. These courts were literally the London or York Commission itself sitting *in partibus*, and no further questions of subordination or inferiority could technically arise. At the same time the commissioners of the Court at London never lost their position as superiors, did constantly oversee the others, and regularly heard 'appeals' from them, or assumed jurisdiction over cases which they had already begun. Usually, behind these appeals, we find some such obvious convenience as the presence of the culprit in another part of England; but at times the magnitude of the offence or the rank of the culprit made it expedient to transfer his case to London. Probably, in practice, a division of power took place between the commissioners at London and their colleagues in the country: the former seem to have confined themselves almost exclusively to their voluminous judicial business, while the latter tried minor cases and, above all, exercised the visitatorial powers.

The only one of all these 'diocesan commissions' of which we now have any considerable information is that branch of the York Commission which sat at Durham from 1625 to 1640. Of its proceedings, indeed, we have the fullest evidence we possess for any section of the Commission's history: Act books, articles original and additional, depositions, formal papers of all sorts, not only in sufficient number to show us the whole range of the Court's procedure, but enough to give us the full history of almost every case impleaded before it.[1] We have literally all we could ask, and the evidence greatly strengthens the results of our inquiry concerning the Court at London; for, by establishing the practical identity of the jurisdiction and procedure of the northern and southern commissioners, it furnishes us by analogy with a much greater and more consistent body of evidence about the procedure of the Court at London than exists for that Court's own proceedings, and enables us to interpret the latter's scanty records with some assurance. In many ways we would prefer to have had the record of some other diocese, for Durham was a border bishopric, and the peculiar authority exercised by the Bishop Palatine, the influence of the Marcher Lordships, and of the Council of the North since the reign of Henry, besides the undoubted retention by the Bishop of many of the administrative habits of centuries, render it highly probable that the commissioners at Durham exercised far more power and possessed much more discretion than those in any other diocese. The Letters Patent of 1630

[1] These have been carefully worked over by W. H. D. Longstaffe for the Surtees Society, and *The Acts of the High Commission Court within the Diocese of Durham* (1858) contains almost all the information of any value in the records. The proceedings in all important cases have been published together with extracts and summaries from the articles original and additional and from depositions and examinations. By no means all the cases have been even recorded, and no statistics of any value can be compiled from the volume, but examples of every sort of case ever tried at Durham and of all stages of procedure are included. The printing of samples of the ordinary formal documents, citations, attachments, decrees, and the like would materially have added to the value of the volume.

for the Province of York,[1] under which most of their acts were performed, were of the model of 1601, and contained all the broad inclusive clauses, as well as specific grants of the *ex officio* oath, and of fine and imprisonment. The procedure used in practice, even to Informations, Mitigations, the use of referees, and the like, was the same as at London,[2] and, indeed, was probably copied from it. Some points find no counterpart in what we know of the London practice. The commissioners at Durham at times waived the formalities of service of intimations or other writs, and assumed that the culprit had had constructive notice sufficient to warrant further proceedings.[3] We find them issuing a commission to a single commissioner with power to hear and determine a case.[4] We see the Bishop settling a case out of court, and the Court accepting his act as a formal legal acquittal.[5] At times traces of Coke's arguments appeared in the forms of sentence, which stated that the matter decided was an enormous and horrible crime.[6] One peculiar survival appeared in the acceptance by the Commission of twelve compurgators, who swore, in good old fashion, that they believed a woman told the truth in denying a charge of adultery. Twice the commissioners accepted this as a full legal

[1] Long extracts from it have been printed in *The High Commission of Durham*, 258–65, from Hunter's rare tract, *Illustrations of Mr. Neal's History of the Puritans*, where it is printed in full.

[2] *High Commission of Durham*, 8, 9, 10, 14, 15, 16, 70, 193, &c.

[3] *Ibid.* 52. This had long been the practice at London.

[4] *Ibid.* 168.

[5] *Ibid.* 182. 'Objected that he kept an ayle house and disorders were done about his house. Gave his Lordship satisfaccion after the court was ended, and the Rev. Father, by note, required he should be dismissed, paieing costes': Sept. 19, 1637.

[6] 'For all his enormous and unparalleled offences,' p. 68; 'After mature deliberacionn . . . of the great and enormous crimes, offences, and misdemeanors of Richardson,' p. 99.

acquittal.[1] This is an interesting confirmation of the extent to which the commissioners attempted to follow the practice of the ordinary ecclesiastical courts, for the latter had, during the Middle Ages, continued to accept the compurgators in certain classes of cases.

The chief departure from the practice at London lay in the lack of the same formality and regularity of sessions. The Court at Durham never sat more than eighteen times in one year, and averaged about once a month,[2] though it usually sat two or three times in one week and then did not meet again for two months.[3] Indeed, so irregular were its sessions that we find the court itself formally excusing men for non-attendance, or declining to appoint a day for attendance on account of the uncertainty of the sessions.[4] The Letters Patent allowed the northern commissioners to sit at seven places—York, Bishopthorpe, Ripon, Cawood, Southwell, Durham, and Auckland, of which the Durham commissioners used only the two latter. Usually three, four, or five men (almost invariably the same ones) sat in Durham in the Galilee, or Western Chapel of the Cathedral, between one and three o'clock, on Tuesday or Thursday afternoons. But they also met at the Bishop's Palace, in the High or the Low Dining Room, in the Cathedral Library, and other similar places, at all

[1] *High Commission of Durham*, 14, 138.

[2] Hunter transcribed in a note-book the court days and attendance from 1625 to 1640; Longstaffe published his transcript, 269–73. A tabulation gives the following number of sessions from January to January: 1626, 20; 1627, 12; 1628, 18; 1629, 6; 1630, 6; 1631, 8; 1632, 8; 1633, 17; 1634, 15; 1635, 11; 1636, 7; 1637, 13; 1638, 12; 1639, 11.

[3] 1626: Jan. 12, 13, 16; Feb. 14; Mar. 9, 30; Apr. 20; May 11; June 8, 25; July 13, 18, 20; Sept. 22, 28. 1632: Jan. 12, Feb. 9, Mar. 8, Apr. 12, May 3, May 31, July 5, Oct. 25, Nov. 22.

[4] *High Commission of Durham*, 21, 29.

hours of the day (once at nine in the evening), and on any day of the week, including Sunday. The other chief differences between the procedures at Durham and at London were the smaller costs and fines, and the number of times (amounting, perhaps, to nearly half of the total cases) in which both were entirely remitted. At London both were often mitigated or the fine remitted; but costs were more rarely remitted at London than at Durham.[1]

The cases heard at Durham were chiefly of a disciplinary nature, usually in support of the episcopal jurisdiction.[2] There were several hundred cases of 'contempt' of all varying degrees of that elastic ecclesiastical offence; exceedingly numerous cases of adultery, incest, and incontinence, which, with alimony, made up the most numerous class of cases; many cases of slandering, abusing, or beating the clergy; numerous instances of beating the commissioners' messengers or failing to assist them; and, then, the usual profanation of the church and churchyard, brawls, blasphemy, slander, drunkenness, and the failure to pay rates, or assessments, or to repair the churches. There were apparently no Puritans in the diocese, and only seven ministers were tried for failure to conform to the requirements of the law, most of whom were scandalously ignorant, drunken, or immoral. Recusants must have been plentiful, but we find fewer than we should expect indicted as 'Popish seducers' or for clandestine marriages, burials, and baptisms.[3] The most striking single fact is, perhaps, the number of cases where

[1] *High Commission of Durham*, 20, 31, 32, 33, 34, 48, 49, 51, 72, 77, 80, 108, 146, &c. [2] *Ibid.* 9, 21, 22, 42, 51, 80, &c.

[3] In the notes to pp. 260–2, Mr. Longstaffe has collected the references to the various classes of cases. It must be remembered that the number of cases in the book is no indication of the frequency with which that type of case appeared before the Commission.

the extreme penalties at the commissioners' disposal were employed against refractory culprits,[1] the length of time before the parties submitted, and the very large proportion of cases where the parties never submitted at all.[2] How many of the latter were tried at York or London, it is impossible to say.

We get from Hunter's Note Books our only glimpse of the formalities employed at the granting of a new Patent.[3] Five of the commissioners, headed by the Bishop of Durham, assembled on October 20, 1625, in an upper chamber of the Manor House at Auckland, before whom appeared a notary public and presented to them the new Letters Patent. The men present then took the oaths of supremacy, allegiance, and fealty, and assumed the execution of the Patent. The following month three of them met in one of the prebend's houses within the cathedral precincts at Durham, and there administered the oaths to nine others. There is no reason to doubt that this identical ceremony was in use in London. No formality could well have been less formal.

It would be most interesting to know precisely what relation the Durham commissioners bore to those at London and at York. The most important case impleaded at Durham was promptly summoned to London; another was on petition of the parties transferred to York; the fact that a man had been already punished for a certain offence by the Council of the North caused the Commissioners to dismiss his case at once.[4] But these few facts

[1] *Ibid.* 18, 19, 22, 23, 29, 31, 62, 64, 65, 68, 256, &c.

[2] *Ibid.* 18, 19, 49, 52, 54, 68, 71, 75, 107, 109, 110, 111, 131 139–41, 168, 169, 175, 178, 180, 184, &c.

[3] *Ibid.* 269.

[4] *Ibid.* 21, 81, 109. These points the original records would undoubtedly make clear, but the present writer has not had access to them. Probably, however, there are only a few scattered bits

seem to be hardly a sufficient basis for any theory of relationship, beyond the undoubted fact that the commissioners at London and at York considered themselves the possessors of superior authority. Besides, the peculiar freedom the Bishop of Durham had always had from any control except from the Crown, the peculiar liberties of the bishopric, as well as of the Dean and Chapter, were of such a nature as to render any regular control by any other authority unlikely and the interference of even the London commissioners hesitating and infrequent. In regard to the Consistory Court at Durham, however, the evidence is ample and clearly proves a very close relation between it and the commissioners at Durham, not unlike that now obtaining between a court of first instance and its superior court. Many cases were 'remitted to the ordinarie jurisdiction' on the ground that they were outside the commissioners' competence;[1] cases were frequently 'appealed' by the Bishop or his chancellor; one case was referred to the Consistory Court for the decision of a single point, with orders to return the case for further proceedings in the Commission;[2] other cases were sent down for settlement in accordance with the action already taken by the Commission;[3] but usually the cases were left to the Chancellor's discretion.[4] At times the same crime was impleaded simultaneously in the Commission and in the Consistory Court, and in such cases the Commission

of evidence, or Mr. Longstaffe's attention would have been attracted by them. It must be remembered, moreover, that the commissioners at Durham were the colleagues of those at York and London and individually possessed the same legal authority, for all were named in the same patent.

[1] *High Commission of Durham*, 28, 34, 44, 52, 74, 123, 154, 155, 167, 172, &c.

[2] *Ibid.* 153. [3] *Ibid.* 52, 82, 168, 181.

[4] *Ibid.* 146, 115.

usually dismissed its suit.[1] One case of contempt was remitted to the Consistory Court where the contempt was committed; the defendant was then required to give bond to the commissioners to obey the Consistory Court's sentence; the latter Court certified to the commissioners his discharge of the contempt, whereupon the bond was cancelled.[2] Cases were also referred, usually by request, to the Archidiaconal court,[3] to the Vicar-General,[4] and to the Dean and Chapter.[5] The common-law courts seem to have paid very little attention to the Court at Durham, but there are a few prohibitions recorded.[6]

With one exception, there was no opposition to the Durham commissioners, except of that type which Church and State were determined to crush.[7] As already remarked, the number of cases in which the process of the Court seemed inadequate to bring the culprit to terms were numerous; many men fled the diocese and seemed then to be safe;[8] the Roman Catholics and their sympathizers no doubt were responsible for most of this opposition, as well as for the beating of messengers. One man named Brandling, probably a Puritan, gave the commissioners more trouble at various times than any man in the diocese; locking up the chancel of his parish church so that the minister and congregation had to climb through a hole in the grill to celebrate the com-

[1] *Ibid.* 124, 174, 176, 182.
[2] *Ibid.* 130.
[3] *Ibid.* 123, 129, 172, 180.
[4] *Ibid.* 181.
[5] *Ibid.* 185.
[6] *Ibid.* 12.
[7] *Ibid.* 18, 19, 22, 23, 29, 31, 62, 64, 65, 68, &c. Chiefly disregard of process, slander of the court, beating or resisting the messenger, refusals to pay costs or fines.
[8] This shows the reality of the territorial restriction in practice, for the legal authority of these commissioners ran throughout the northern province.

munion, collecting customary money payments in service time in a disorderly way, and the like. He was also apparently the only man in the diocese who scorned the commissioners' authority. He came to court 'with a greate train of people', and thus addressed the Advocate for the Office: "'You officers have gotten a trick to call manie poore menn unto your courtes and thereupponn to excommunicate them, and then to bring them into the court of the High Commission." And he further said that "the Kinge's people and wee all doe suffer and groane under the burthen thereof, but (quoth he) if ever I be a parliament man", and then he contained himself, yet examinate conceived and he thinketh that the rest whoe were present did the like, that Brandlinge meant that if he were a parlyament mann he would labour utterlie to quash the authority of the said Commissionn Court' (p. 62). At another time he was abusing the ecclesiastical courts, and the bystanders warned him to beware of the Commission. 'Whereunto Brandlinge answered he cared not one pinn for them of the High Commission, for it was the most wicked court in England' (p. 64).

The only case we have, in which was displayed any consistent attempt to impeach the jurisdiction or block the procedure of the commissioners at Durham, by a clear attempt at judicial opposition, was Smart's case, the most important by far ever heard at Durham.[1] The Cathedral had been the scene of one of the most elaborate Arminian 'innovations' which up to that date had been made, in which candles, vestments, and incense had been freely used, with genuflexions and gestures, which

[1] The whole documentary evidence for this case has been printed by Mr. Longstaffe, pp. 197–250, and includes all the correspondence and the proceedings in the House of Commons, as well as the legal documents.

seemed to the indignant Smart, the senior prebendary, to be only so many relics of the Mass. He accordingly denounced them with more warmth than discretion in a public sermon at the Cathedral, and was, in consequence, arraigned by the High Commissioners that very Sunday afternoon. Before the case had progressed very far towards a hearing, it was transferred to London, whence it was soon referred to the commissioners at York, by whom he was sentenced more than two years after the offence was committed. He was required to recant according to a form which the commissioners should dictate, was then suspended, and fined £400 and costs; he refused to pay and was committed to prison; and, for his continued refusal, was excommunicated and his livings sequestrated. Finally, because of his failure to recant and pay his fine and costs, he was 'degraded ab omni gradu et dignitate clericali'.[1] Already he had brought an action of false imprisonment in the King's Bench against two of the York Commissioners and their pursuivant. The action hung on for seven terms, and finally ended in a long plea by the defendants and a demurrer by Smart, which was never argued. In 1632 Smart sued his successor in the prebendal stall at the Durham Assizes for the income from the property, alleging that his lease was to last till 'death, resignation, deprivation, cession'; and that degradation and sequestration were not of the same effect as deprivation. Smart's lawyers brought forward some of the old pleas of the previous generation; that the commissioners could not use a seal, and hence their sealed documents were not evidence; that his prebend was his freehold, of which he could be deprived only by action at common law;

[1] These words of the sentence afterwards were the basis of the proceedings at common law.

that, when sentenced, his plea for a *habeas corpus* in the King's Bench had placed him outside the Commission's jurisdiction, so that he had never been legally sentenced at all. The judges, however, did not think much of these pleas, and even Smart's own lawyers were apologetic in manner and very far from displaying the assurance that had made Nicholas Fuller an effective barrister under such circumstances. It is significant that none of Coke's most characteristic arguments were used; the case, however, afforded little opportunity for them. The action failed; Smart lost his income; but the London Puritans collected for his maintenance a handsome stipend of £400 a year, a sum far larger than the value of his prebend. In due time came the Long Parliament, where his case was one of the first taken up, and his sentence one of those most solemnly quashed and branded as illegal by resolution of the House of Commons. Probably no small part of the onus of hatred and hostility which the Court of High Commission bore was due to the acts of commissioners in the dioceses, whose attempts to administer the law as the State understood it, effectually hid the moderation, equity, and fairness which were such conspicuous traits of the judicial work of the Court at London.

CHAPTER XIV

THE COMMISSION IN ITS RELATION TO OTHER JUDICIAL AND ADMINISTRATIVE BODIES

TECHNICALLY the Court of High Commission had no definitely assigned relations with any other judicial or administrative body. It stood alone and apart. In the early Letters Patent no mention at all was made of any officers other than the commissioners' own, except the justices of the peace and other local officials, who were commanded by the Letters Patent to assist the commissioners in the execution of their decrees. In later Patents the decrees of the Star Chamber regulating the publication of books were mentioned very much as were Statutes of Parliament: the commissioners were to enforce them, but there was no hint of any relation between the commissioners and the Star Chamber other than the *prima facie* conclusion that the one made the law which the others enforced. The language of the Patent of 1611, mentioning 'the other ecclesiastical courts', recognized the Commission as one of them, and presupposed some sort of connexion between them and the Commission, yet certainly no Letters Patent created that relation, nor sanctioned it by express words, nor even formally recognized it. All relations between the Commission and other courts were part of its practice, not of its formal institution.

The position which the Commission came to occupy in the State, ecclesiastical and temporal, grew, like most of its other important attributes, out of the judicial and administrative needs of the time. The ecclesiastical commissions, from which it developed, were really used by the Privy Council, during the first thirty years of their existence (1535–65), as an arm of the supreme administrative power of the State, and they had relations with other bodies, not of themselves, but through the Council. The acquisition of institutional strength, coupled to freedom from arbitrary control by the Council, gave the Commission a permanency of institutional life and a settled jurisdiction, which necessarily required a connexion of some sort with the courts and administrative bodies already existing in the State, which forced the Commission into relations with the hierarchy of law and administration, and into relations, too, which became of necessity definite and well recognized. But the Commission's position, however inevitable and legal, being the result of circumstances, of judicial decisions and administrative rulings, the evidence of it is not to be found in some ordinance of the Privy Council, or in Letters Patent, or in Statutes, but in the daily work of the various courts. The scantiness of the authoritative records tends to leave an impression that the relation itself was one rather exceptional than ordinary, and that it was of small importance in the daily work of the Commission. Although it would be rash to say that such a view is not conservative and possibly correct, the very nature of the evidence seems, nevertheless, to prove the contrary.

Indeed, the relation of the Commission to other judicial and administrative bodies was probably of constant importance in its daily work, and through it perhaps its chief influence was exerted. The history of the early commissions is little more than a study of their relations to the Privy Council. The disputes between the Commission and the common-law courts were, in last analysis, based upon two very different ideas of their mutual relations, as well as upon a different notion of the relation of the Commission to the other ecclesiastical courts. The odium heaped upon the Commission by the Puritans was due almost entirely to its relation to the visitatorial powers of the bishops. Much of the hatred felt for the Star Chamber became attached to the Commission by reason of the close relations between the two. In short, from one point of view, the history of the Commission is merely a study of its relations to the other judicial and administrative bodies in the realm, plus a statement of what contemporaries thought those relations should have been.

It is a rather striking fact that the officers of nearly all the other courts in the realm were *ex officio* members of the Commission after 1601:[1] a large number of the Privy Council and, of course, of the Star Chamber; many of the common-law judges; the Attorney-General and Solicitor-General; all the Masters of Chancery, the Masters of Requests, the Master of the Rolls, all the chief ecclesiastical judges, and the Judge of the Admiralty. The Commission was thus connected, *ex officio*, with every court in England, for, in each, one of its own members presided. Yet the only result of this union of functions seems to have been some influence on procedure. It is highly probable that 'Informations' and the practice of referring a case to a single commissioner for a report on its merits were copied from the analogous practice in the Chancery and the Court of Requests. Sir Julius Caesar and Sir Charles Caesar, both learned Chancery lawyers, were influential commissioners, the former during the years when the Commission's procedure was forming,

[1] See the list of commissioners in the Appendix.

the latter during the years 1620–40. The influence of the ecclesiastical judges was even greater in crystallizing the regular procedure of the Commission and bringing it into general conformity with that obtaining in their own courts. They sat more often as High Commissioners than as ecclesiastical judges, delegating the lesser function to commissaries. On the other hand, the common-law judges, the Privy Councillors, and many ecclesiastics seldom, if ever, sat in the Commission after it became openly a court,[1] and, while Coke and many other judges, before and after his day, were actually members of the Commission, whose actions they prohibited, their other sympathies far outweighed any incipient loyalty to it, and it is improbable that they ever exercised much direct influence on it or ever were influenced by it.

The breadth of the Commission's jurisdiction, its discretionary procedure, with the temporal penalties of fine and imprisonment, its right to exact specific performance of its sentence, and the finality of its decision, made it *ipso facto* the court of last resort in the ecclesiastical hierarchy, and this relationship was further defined by the delegation to the commissioners of the duty of overseeing and reforming the ecclesiastical courts, and by the function, so often employed, of reprimanding, or even displacing some lesser ecclesiastical judge. While unquestionably this was a part of the supreme visitatorial authority, exercised by the members of the Court as commissioners rather than as judges, nevertheless it could not fail to influence the court's relationship to the rest of the ecclesiastical hierarchy from a purely judicial point of view. The visiting and reforming marched closely with correcting and amending; in fact,

[1] Probably they did not sit without summons, such as issued for the meeting of September 1611.

the line seems never to have been very accurately drawn between visitatorial and judicial functions. Nor did the aspect of emergency, which the Commission early bore to the episcopal authority in its significant attempt to sustain the bishops' tottering disciplinary jurisdiction, disappear as quickly as might have been expected from the rapid development of its judicial relations with the ecclesiastical courts. Previous to 1611 cases were referred to the commissioners by the bishop, more because the ecclesiastical censures at his disposal were insufficient to bring the culprit to terms than because he recognized, in that fashion, his own lack of jurisdiction or the superiority of the Commission's authority. Even when one of the parties to the suit transferred it to the Commission, no definite judicial relation could be inferred with the court from which it came. Something more than this was necessary and appeared in the last phase of the Commission's development. A definite line was drawn, soon after 1611, between the Commission's jurisdiction and that of the bishop, based not upon the need of coercive measures, but upon the nature of the case. The evidence is too scanty to admit of more than a rough determination of the place where this line was drawn, but apparently it approached very nearly Coke's test of the enormity of the case, though it probably was applied to individual cases with considerable elasticity of interpretation. Upon this basis we frequently find the Commission refusing to assume jurisdiction, and, what is vastly more significant, remitting cases, already impleaded, to the Arches or to the bishop for trial or sentence.[1] At the same time we do not

[1] For instance: the Commissioners at Informations decided that 'the matters contained in the articles were not fit for the cognizance of this court but might fitly be heard before the Ordinary': Nov. 19, 1640. S. P. Dom. Car. I, 434, f. 297. A note by Sir John Lambe: 'To advise whether action will lie

find the commissioners hesitating to call before themselves, on no better judicial basis than their own information, some case which an ecclesiastical court had already begun.[1] Official cognizance was taken of the earlier procedure in the case,[2] and perhaps its previous history was regularly investigated.[3] The bishop's sentence in a case was a valid defence in the Commission against action for the same offence, and, if the case was already impleaded, prevented further proceedings, thus proving that, in certain classes of cases at all events, the commissioners were prepared to affirm the bishop's sentence without further hearing, thus making that sentence in practice final.[4] As a matter of course, evidence and depositions, already taken by the regular ecclesiastical courts, were accepted as valid by the Commission, but there is no clear evidence to show that the Commission sent down a case for trial or retrial with orders for the decision of a disputed point, which the lower court was forced to follow.[5] Nor is it likely that the Commission allowed the lower courts to decide facts and reserved to itself only what would be called, at common law, matters of law. It is quite clear that the Commission did not

in the Ecclesiastical Court, or to be called into the High Commission; against the churchwardens or inhabitants': S. P. Dom. Car. I, 385, no. 91; *ibid.* 261, f. 37; and many cases in *Calendar*, 1634/5, 109, 110, 114.

[1] e.g. S. P. Dom. Car. I, 381, f. 62. Feb. 9, 1637/8.

[2] *Ibid.* 261, ff. 34 b, 40, 43 b, 64 (of proceedings in Arches), 61 b (proceedings by bishop); *ibid.* 434 A, f. 43 (Council in Marches of Wales).

[3] *Ibid.* 261, f. 50.

[4] *Ibid.* 261, f. 88 b. Oct. 16, 1634.

[5] A suspension by a bishop, appealed to the Commission, 'was ratified by this Court': S. P. Dom. Car. I, 261, f. 179 b; an appeal from an order of the Bishop of Bath and Wells was 'reaffirmed' by the Commission: *ibid.* 434, f. 218; defendant ordered to defend himself in a case remitted to the Bishop of London: *ibid.* 261, f. 37.

scruple to retry cases as if they had never been heard.[1] In fact, all the limitations which the commissioners voluntarily placed upon their supreme authority over the ecclesiastical courts could at any moment be suspended by the same discretion which created them. Nevertheless, as time elapsed, the commissioners made less and less use of this discretion.

The connexion of the Commission and the Court of Delegates was probably very much closer than a conservative study of the scanty evidence reveals.[2] In most cases the Commission of Delegates was composed entirely of those High Commissioners who may be called the High Commissioners *par excellence*, the most active and efficient, whose attendance was most regular.[3] Whenever another person appeared among the delegates, he was almost certain to be some less energetic commissioner. Although nearly all the most prominent doctors of civil law were members of the Commission, there were a large number of capable men, who were not members, who could have filled the post acceptably. Appeals to the delegates were chiefly in cases of slander or cases of a testamentary nature heard on appeal from the Prerogative Court. The reason why there were practically no appeals on doctrine or discipline to the delegates, previous to 1660, is probably

[1] *Ibid.* 261, f. 64. June 26, 1634.

[2] Rothery's Return, in *Parliamentary Documents*, 1867/8, vol. lxvii, whence most of this information is drawn. Mr. Rothery calls attention to the close connexion of the Commission and the Delegates, but did not note the fact that the Delegates were High Commissioners.

[3] Nathaniel Brent to Laud: 'I purposed to have been in London the first day of term. . . . We never have anything to do on the first court of the Delegates, because Mr. Freeman does not use to come up so soon, and in the Court of High Commission your Grace will be abundantly assisted': S. P. Dom. Car. I, 441, no. 117. Jan. 13, 1639/40.

to be found in the existence of the High Commission, just as the use of the delegates for such appeals after 1660 can be explained by the lack of a High Commission. The latter was far more rapid in its procedure than was the delegates, immeasurably less expensive, and, in fact, was composed of the very men who would probably have been appointed by the Commission of Delegates. Further, the decree of the High Commission was final, and the seventeenth-century litigant was seeking above all else for a decision which could not be reversed. Nothing could so 'vex' his adversary as to have the case decided against him and be unable to get it reversed. This fact in part explains the remarkable resort of suitors to the Commission. Probably the unimportant and inconspicuous part played by the delegates in history was due in no small measure to the existence of the High Commission. The personnel, the procedure, the jurisdiction of the two courts, were so similar, that many cases, besides those of doctrine and discipline, which might otherwise have gone to the delegates, were decided by the Commission because the parties concerned preferred it.

The Star Chamber was related to the Commission in several ways. In many respects it was an equal; in others it rendered assistance of much the nature which the Commission itself gave to the ecclesiastical courts. The relation of equality most frequently appeared in practice. The Star Chamber executed the temporal sentences of the Commission; the Commission executed the ecclesiastical censures and orders of the Star Chamber. Bishop Williams was ordered to be suspended from his office by a decree of the Star Chamber (1637). The order was executed by the High Commission,[1] not by the Archbishop as Metropolitan. At still other times the Star Chamber

[1] S. P. Dom. Car. I, 364, no. 42 (1637).

was the Commission's superior. The licensing of books, the suppressing of forbidden books, the search for them and for secret presses, such as those from which the Marprelate tracts were printed, the destruction of these books when found, all were performed by the commissioners virtually under the Star Chamber's supervision and direction.[1] The jurisdiction of the High Commission was affirmed by a decree in the Star Chamber.[2] The connexion was, however, so close between the Star Chamber and the Privy Council that it is difficult to know which was responsible for these decrees. Probably so much of the Star Chamber business bore outwardly the aspect of Council proceedings, that until some close study is made of the relations between the two we shall remain in ignorance of the real relations of the Commission after 1611 to both.[3]

That the Commission's relations to the Privy Council were still close and important is abundantly clear. The Council maintained after 1611 theoretically the same supreme control over the Commission which it had so often exercised in the early years of Elizabeth's reign. Yet, in practice, it seldom did more than refer to it some case brought to its own attention by some petitioner or official.[4] It still aided the Commission with its own process; it still punished stringently those who assailed it; but its orders to the Commission after 1611 seem to have been rather requests than commands, and did not

[1] The State Papers teem with material of this sort. See *Calendar*, 1633/4, 158, 412; 1635, 565; 1636/7, 546; 1637/8, 145; 1638/9, 55, 258, 547.

[2] Decree of July 4, 1637. Rymer, *Foedera*, xx, 156.

[3] Miss Scofield's *Star Chamber* by no means performs this function. Though a useful book, it really gives very little information on any points other than the institution of the court and its growth prior to Elizabeth's reign.

[4] S. P. Dom. Car. I, 261, f. 35 b; 430, no. 21; 432, no. 76; Gardiner, *Cases*, 241.

contain, as formerly, peremptory directions to act at once according to the tenor of this present letter and to report proceedings for further order.[1] Nevertheless, there was a real and very present power of 'appeal' from the Commission to the Privy Council, which, though often utilized, rarely met with success. While, in the earlier years, it had been a common thing for the Council to reverse the commissioners' proceedings, to our present knowledge this was never actually done after 1611. If the Council meant to interfere at all, it probably did so directly or indirectly before sentence had been pronounced.

There had always been, and continued to be, some connexion between the commissioners and the local officials. The earliest forms of patent provided abundantly for assistance to the commissioners from sheriffs, justices of the peace, mayors of boroughs, and the like. In the early days the commissioners' processes and decrees were executed either by the messengers of the Privy Council or by the local officials, on special order from the commissioners, and, in some cases, from the Council itself. Gradually this sort of aid became less important, for the commissioners in the majority of cases were able to enforce their own process by their own pursuivants without aid. In special cases, however, local assistance was asked for and given.[2] In two classes of the commissioners' regular functions the local officials were constantly employed: in the search for forbidden books, presses, and persons charged with offences against the Ordinances for Censorship of the Press; and in the search for Jesuits, altar ornaments, and vestments of all kinds.[3] Here the local

[1] See, however, S. P. Dom. Car. I, 355, no. 43.

[2] e.g. in Roper's case, 1609.

[3] S. P. Dom. Car. I, 265, no. 6 (1634). For the Council's part see *ibid.* 308, nos. 65–9, and the *Calendars of State Papers, Domestic*, index under 'Catholics'.

officials acted under warrants, both general and special, issued by the Registrar of the Commission on order of the Court. The books, ornaments, and vestments found and collected were put in charge of the registrar, and were usually destroyed by him, according to the Court's orders.[1] Some formal judicial relationship with the local officials did exist, because we find the justices at Quarter Sessions referring cases to the commissioners,[2] and the latter in turn remitting cases to them.[3] A papist, found by the commissioners, was turned over to the assizes for trial. The Privy Council ordered the Justices of Gloucestershire in 1585/6 to refer to the High Commissioners ecclesiastical cases 'that exceed the Commission of the Peace'.[4]

With the various civil law-courts, like the Chancery, the Requests, the Admiralty, and the provincial councils, the Commission was on the most amicable terms, and, in general, accorded them the same privileges allowed to the regular ecclesiastical courts. Their decrees and proceedings were apparently accorded full credence as of right. We also find arguments offered that the Commission had no jurisdiction, because the case properly belonged to Chancery, or to the Lord Marshal's Court,[5] or to the jurisdiction of the Tower of London.[6] The latter jurisdiction the Commission refused to recognize.

[1] S. P. Dom. Car. I, 424, f. 231. Orders of 1616, S. P. Dom. Jac. I, 89, f. 118.

[2] S. P. Dom. Car. I, 312, no. 45. Jan. 26, 1635/6.

[3] *Privy Council Register*, x, 174, 1577. S. P. Dom. Car. I, 434 A, f. 9 b. Apr. 23, 1640.

[4] *Privy Council Register*, xiv, 39. Perhaps explained by the abnormal government of that county.

[5] Gardiner, *Cases*, 278, 1632.

[6] *Ibid.* 322, 1632.

CHAPTER XV

THE OPPOSITION TO THE COMMISSION, 1611–41

THE student might have reasonably expected to find the only part of his subject which had previously attracted any considerable attention teeming with important and interesting events, for whose elucidation more direct evidence existed than for any earlier period. Yet, not only is it true that the opposition to the Commission from 1611 to 1641 cannot be compared in interest or significance with that of the earlier years, but it is also clear that the indirect evidence of the existence of an opposition (usually the more valuable) is not greater in amount nor more trustworthy in character, while most of the direct evidence, if somewhat more voluminous, certainly bears, even more clearly than in the earlier period, the marks of having been manufactured with a purpose. In fact, whether or not the result of design, the loss of the records of the Commission has made the charges of its opponents the chief evidence in most cases of the existence and character of any opposition at all. The evidential difficulties are the more serious because the Commission's opponents have brought against it charges of oppression and tyranny, whose truth is not substantiated by even the most conclusive demonstration of the details of a few cases. Only a thorough investigation of the Commission's records, resulting in the discovery of a very considerable number of cases similar to those already notorious, could justify the historian in rendering a final verdict against the Court of High Commission.

Nothing short of a conclusive demonstration from those same records, that the cases, whose history we know, were so few in number as to be exceptional, could justify the student in giving a final verdict in the Commission's favour. In short, nothing approaching finality can be attained until the official records are found. We do possess, however, enough trustworthy evidence to enable us to express with some confidence a tentative opinion upon the subject.

On the whole the opposition to the Court of High Commission after 1611 resembled that of the period from 1580 to 1592 rather than that of the years from 1592 to 1611. The common-law judges gave up any direct attack, and acquiesced, albeit in a somewhat jealous and disapproving spirit, in the Commission's continued existence and activity. Prohibitions still issued in considerable numbers,[1] and, while Coke remained on the bench, displayed a tendency to stretch the claims of the common law to the utmost.[2] Many of the writs were clearly justifiable, like the one which concerned a contract to repair the pews in a church.[3] Others were not so clear: in a case in 1616 the common-law judges seem once more to be trying to apportion the jurisdiction between the Commission and the ecclesiastical courts.[4] In 1629 a procuress was freed by a prohibition based on a new reading of the Statute of Elizabeth. The Commission,

[1] Laud declared that they were as numerous in his day as in Archbishop Abbot's; which may very well have been true without their reaching a very large total: *Works*, iv, 140.

[2] See an opinion by Coke, 11 Jac., in 2 Bulstrode, 183.

[3] S. P. Dom. Car. I, 432, no. 13. Nov. 4, 1639.

[4] 'Donques quia il fuit sue pur un pencon devant les hault Commissioners queux nont jurisdiction de ceo, coment que le Court Ecclesiasticall ad, un autre prohibition fuit a luy grantus': Moore, *Reports*, 917.

said Hutton, might fine and imprison for an actual offence, but not for contempt, nor for a failure to perform the orders of the Court, nor for a failure to give bond. Furthermore, he continued, suits for adultery were to be tried by the bishop, except when enormous, and no cases of alimony at all were within the Commission's cognizance.[1] But after 1630 prohibitions were rare. Finch wrote to Laud in 1638 that a motion for one, then pending before him, was the first presented in the four years he had been a member of the Common Pleas. 'I assure myself you are very confident that no man ever sat on a bench that was more tender how he invaded the jurisdiction of other courts especially those of ecclesiastical cognizance: and for the High Commission Court, I know (as I then openly said) that it is a court of a high and eminent nature, and it behoved us to be very wary of granting prohibitions to stop that court.'[2]

About 1631 an action was begun in the King's Bench by a Mr. Huntley against several members of the High Commission for false imprisonment. The Attorney-General, the Advocate-General, and the Archbishop failed to reach an agreement as to whether the Letters Patent were, in themselves, a sufficient defence, and appealed to the King. The case hung fire for years, apparently because the lawyers feared to incur royal displeasure by taking Huntley's brief. In 1634 we find him importuning the Attorney-General to take it, and presenting him with what he claimed was an order to

[1] 3 Croke, 113, 114. See also 2 Croke, 321, 335; and two cases quoted by Longstaffe in the *Court of High Commission of Durham*, 256, not elsewhere traceable. In one case the plaintiff in the Commission was ordered to give a heavy bond not to sue the defendant at common law while the suit was pending in the Commission: Gardiner, *Cases*, 239.

[2] S. P. Dom. Car. I, 381, no. 24. Feb. 3, 1637/8.

that effect from the King's Bench. He promised Noy a large fee, and declared that £100,000 could be secured from the commissioners in fines. Noy scorned his offer, and told him he would consult with the Archbishop and the judges of the King's Bench.[1] The outcome of this interesting case we do not know. Perhaps the Commission of 1631 to settle the jurisdiction of courts was in some way connected with it.[2] We have, however, no record of any decision about the Commission's jurisdiction. In addition to the attempt in 1637 to strengthen the oath *ex officio*, Laud deemed it necessary to secure a formal opinion from the common-law judges in the Star Chamber that Bastwick had been legally tried and sentenced; a decree was then issued by that Court, and also a proclamation describing the opinion and decree.[3] Certainly such action would point to a very insistent opposition to the Commission, and one which it was necessary to meet. Moreover, it is likely that Laud's declaration of February 1637/8, forbidding all common- and civil-law judges from interfering with any ecclesiastical court without his approbation, was partially made on account of the Commission.[4]

The Puritan opposition after 1611 was probably the work of individuals; there seems to have been no recurrence of the earlier attempts at a systematic assault upon the Court's jurisdiction. Individual Puritans endeavoured to block the Commission's proceedings by the methods initiated in Elizabeth's reign, chiefly by refusing to take

[1] S. P. Dom. Car. I, 205, no. 104; 275, no. 35; Laud, *Works*, iv, 135.

[2] Patent Roll, 7 Car. I, part 20, no. 46, dorso. Printed in Rymer, *Foedera*, xix, 279.

[3] All printed in Rymer, *Foedera*, xx, 143, 156, 168.

[4] S. P. Dom. Car. I, 383, no. 49. This was one of the articles against him in 1645. Laud, *Works*, iv, 89.

the oath *ex officio*,[1] but they rarely attempted to show that the Commission's jurisdiction or procedure was illegal. Yet the men who 'scornfully' and 'derisively' defied Laud seem to have been no more 'insolent' or 'stiff-necked' than those who dared Grindal and Bancroft to do their worst;[2] nor were the prohibitions they brought more extreme than those of earlier years. Laud, when later charged with having 'laid by the heels' all who brought him prohibitions, replied that they 'were commonly brought by bold impudent men picked out of purpose to affront the court'. One man, indeed, brought him a prohibition nailed to the end of a long pole, and, to show that he would not touch the Archbishop with a ten-foot pole, threw the pole into the court-room with such violence that it bounded from the table and hit Laud on the breast. 'If the Court made their imprisonment as common as they their rudeness, where 's the fault,' said Laud in 1645. But his own impatient remarks seemed to the Puritans worst of all. Two raked out against him in 1645 were: 'Doth the King give us power, and then we are prohibited? Let us go and

[1] There seems to be only one case to the contrary. Laurence Snelling, on trial in 1637 for not reading the Book of Sports, objected to the competence of the court. The case was promoted by the King's Advocate, Dr. Rives: Rushworth, *Collections*, ii, 459. There were of course the usual contempts and rescues from the Commission's officers: S. P. Dom. Car. I, 261, f. 31; Gardiner, *Cases*, 245; S. P. Dom. Car. I, 283, f. 10; &c.

[2] Laud's Report for 1637 to the King quotes the case of Brewer, a Puritan, who 'is taken again and was called before the High Commission Court, there he stood silent, but in such a jeering, scornful manner as I scarce ever saw the like': Rymer, *Foedera*, xx, 195. See also Gardiner, *Cases*, 301. Most of the cases in this volume are of that stamp, and others can be multiplied from Rushworth and the State Papers, Domestic. This phase of the subject has been so often treated at length that it is hardly necessary to repeat the familiar details.

complain.'[1] 'You desire an order of the Court that you may have it to show and get a prohibition, but I will break the back of prohibitions or they shall break mine.'

The opposition on legal and judicial grounds was, in all probability, abandoned by the Puritans because of the determination, reached by the leaders in 1605 and 1606, that the direct assault upon the Church had failed and could never succeed under such conditions as then prevailed. The letter of the law was against them and must be changed before any permanent success would be possible. They therefore transferred the battle to the House of Commons, where their party was already strong. By the common-law judges and lawyers, the attack was abandoned, because they had no means of compelling their adversaries to accept their view of the law. So long as the State supported the Commission, and so long as the judges must depend upon the officers of the State for the enforcement of such of their writs as the Commission refused to recognize, even Chief Justice Coke had no alternative but to forgo the empty satisfaction of issuing writs which he could not, single-handed, compel the commissioners to observe. The removal of Coke from the bench in 1616 unquestionably sapped the courage of the existing judges and practising lawyers; and James and Charles were careful to appoint to the bench, in the future, men whose views were more consonant with the law as the King understood it. The common-law opposition gradually disappeared because the complexion of the bench was completely altered by the action of the State. It ceased, also, because suitors refused to desert the Commission. Neither the common-

[1] Laud, 'History of Troubles,' *Works*, iv, 137 ff. He admitted the remarks, but denied the deductions his accusers drew from them.

law judges nor the commissioners ordinarily acted unless a suit was instituted by some party, and the advantages of the Commission's procedure and the breadth of its jurisdiction, the possibility of obtaining there remedies impossible at common law, no less now than in the years when its judicial work was beginning, caused suitors to resort thither in large numbers. No prohibition could be issued by the common-law judges without the assistance of one or the other party to the suit before the commissioners. Without the co-operation of the litigants, even Coke was powerless, and, when the litigants learned, as they soon did, that a prohibition, if maintained, only put an end to that particular suit, and did not at all pledge the judges to afford the plaintiff a remedy themselves, or free him from further liability before the Commission or elsewhere, they ceased of their own accord to apply for such writs. The same forces which had brought the Court of High Commission into being enabled it to survive.

The significance of this period of the Commission's history for the student lies in the necessity of explaining in some way the existence and truthfulness of the charges of tyranny and oppression, so loudly trumpeted forth by the Long Parliament, and so dramatically insisted upon by Laud's accusers in 1645 at his trial for high treason. The establishment of the fact that the opposition was not essentially different in character from that of other epochs is, if anything, perplexing. Historians have seen in the High Commission's existence and character one of the chief causes of the Revolution of 1640, one of the most cogent explanations of the popular distrust of Charles I. They have found it the only adequate explanation of the strength of the Puritan movement, which enabled it for a time to abolish the English Church altogether, and which must have rested (it has been supposed) upon a widespread popular hatred of the institution as it then existed. Indeed, a description of the cases of Bastwick and Prynne, an appeal to the principles of freedom of press and of conscience, together with the quotation of the charges in the Grand Remonstrance and in the Statute of 1641, have been often the only account of the Commission's history given even by the standard authorities. We must, indeed, admit that a demonstration that the Commission did not deserve unpopularity would not alter the very general conclusion that the Puritans' hatred for it and the belief in certain quarters in its illegality were significant causes of the hatred of King and Church in 1640. The ideas about the truth held by great bodies of men are far more potent forces in history than the truth itself. The historian of the Commission can, at best, establish merely the existence or absence of adequate cause for such conceptions. While the loss of the records makes any conclusion which we may reach only tentative, there seems to be excellent reason to doubt the existence of a real basis for the charges of tyranny and oppression so often made.

The indirect evidence of the popularity of the Court of High Commission under Laud's régime, as well as in the previous four decades, is overwhelming. Only five per cent. of its cases seem to have been initiated by the commissioners themselves, and the bulk of its business was almost entirely the hearing of suits between party and party, initiated by some individual. Its sessions would therefore hardly have been crowded with lawyers and clients, one hundred-odd cases would scarcely have been the ordinary number in which some action was taken on a single court day, had its methods been seriously disapproved by the English people as a whole or had they attached suspicions of illegality to its jurisdiction. The large number of petitions filed with the commissioners for aid *ex officio*, for suits *in forma pauperis*, for assistance in cases of hardship or oppression, in cases where there was no remedy at common or ecclesiastical law, all point to its wide popularity and to a thoroughly well-accepted idea of its useful function in the State. While it is easy to stretch such a presumption as this too far, it seems clear that the disapproval of the Commission must have been limited rather to a section of the people (even though a numerous section) than widely diffused throughout the whole community.

If, moreover, we compare its procedure and decisions in the cases we do know with the procedure and decisions of other courts of the period, we can hardly avoid the conclusion that their barbarity and severity have been exaggerated. There were undoubtedly cases where the Commission's decrees worked great injustice and hardship;[1] there were cases where men were punished far beyond their deserts, very few of which acquired, then or since, any notoriety;[2] there were clearly instances of the imposition of imprisonment or fines because of some fancied unruly bearing of the nonconformist;[3] all this it would be idle to deny. Yet it seems to be difficult to sustain many statements that have been written about the excessive fines, imprisonments, and other penalties meted out by the Commission, without so much qualification as nearly to destroy the statements themselves.

Practically all of the large fines were 'mitigated' to small sums or remitted altogether. Suits were not longer

[1] For instance, S. P. Dom. Car. I, 414, no. 39; 373, no. 45; 400, no. 109.

[2] For instance, *ibid.* 351, no. 36; 402, no. 55.

[3] See some cases in Gardiner, *Cases*, 268.

nor costs greater than in most other courts of the period. Certainly the imprisonment imposed for refusing the oath *ex officio* will bear comparison with the pressing under lead weights, till the culprit pleaded or died, used at common law for the same purpose, or with the torture so usual on the Continent. The criminal code at common law, with its hundreds of capital crimes, its burning of witches, its whipping and nose-slitting for the very smallest offences, was more barbarous, according to modern ideas, than any sentence we know to have been imposed by the Commission. Indeed, it is improbable that we could find a case in the annals of the Commission which would present to the modern mind so many aspects of unnecessary severity as one heard on 'appeal' by the Commission about 1638. Two poor men, Cock and Harrison, had threatened to indict a merchant of adultery with a certain woman, and, in revenge, the merchant had presented them at Quarter Sessions for a petty offence. For this they were thrice whipped from the jail to the pillory, stood thrice for eleven hours in the pillory, were then forced to beg forgiveness before all the spectators, and were then thrice whipped back to jail again. 'By the extremity of which execution, the petitioner lost his speech and almost his understanding, and Cock was carried home dead in the Cart.'[1] The famous sentence of the Star Chamber upon Prynne had certainly no such fatal results; nor had these poor men openly defied Church and State, nor publicly broken the law after repeated warnings of the consequences.

Let us place beside this common case Bastwick's famous petition to the House of Commons. He complained of a 'long and expensive prosecution' in which 'he was fined £1,000, excommunicated, debarred the

[1] S. P. Dom. Car. I, 406, no. 75, 1638 (?).

practice of physic, his chief livelihood, his book ordered to be burnt, and he to pay costs of the suit and be imprisoned until he should recant, all which was only for the said book '.[1] If we examine the book, we shall hardly be able to agree with Bastwick's plea of its entire innocence. If we examine the official record of his trial,[2] we shall find that the length of the suit and its expense were due, apparently, to his own contumacy, and that, in reality, he was treated with unusual leniency. On October 9, 1634, he appeared in court, refused to take the oath *ex officio*, and was committed to the Gatehouse, whence he was released on bond (contrary to the practice of the Commission), because of the approaching childbed of his wife. On October 23 his answers were voted ' scandalous ' and he was ordered to answer ' plene, plane, et directe ' upon pain of a fine of £100. He refused, however, to give any bond for further appearance or answer, declaring that he stood before them as did Paul before Nero ; yet, on petitions from his wife and in consideration of her condition, the Court admonished him to appear next court day, and dispensed with the usual bond. On October 30 he was not ready, and the case was ordered ' peremptorily ' to be ready for final hearing and sentence on the last court day in November. On November 20 the hearing was postponed until the first session in Hilary term (January), and he promised then to appear and make satisfactory answer. That the delay was entirely on Bastwick's part, is clear from an order of January 29 that, unless Dr. Merrick, Bastwick's advocate, presented

[1] S. P. Dom. Car. I, 473, no. 71. Dec. 17, 1640. If we view this sentence from the point of view that Bastwick's book really was objectionable, it seems very moderate.

[2] *Ibid.* 261, ff. 82 b, 97, 107, 132, 150, 159, 171 b, 177, 178. Bastwick tried to convey away all his property before the fine could be levied. See f. 183, Feb. 19.

his brief that Thursday night, the case should go to sentence without it. On February 5 the case was again before the Court, but no progress was made, and on February 12 the situation was unchanged; but, by suspending other business and breaking the rule of the Court against considering the same suit twice in one court day, sentence was finally given. Surely no blame can attach to the Commission for the length or the expense of the procedure, for the Commission was ready to give sentence in the case on the 1st of November, and probably would have been ready much earlier, if Bastwick's own delays had not clogged proceedings. In any event, four months was by no means a long time for the trial of a law-suit. On the whole, the procedure in Bastwick's case seems to have been swifter and more lenient than usual. If such is the result of a comparison of the Commission's records with the Puritan accusations in a case which the Puritans themselves chose as a particularly horrible example, is it not probable that an examination of the full record of cases previous to 1641 might compel us to modify the usual verdict of the barbarity and severity of the Commission's procedure as compared with that of other courts at the same time?

Nor is it necessary to accept the truth of the charges, brought by the Commission's enemies, to understand their hatred of it, and to explain the fact that it has been a byword of reproach, synonymous with tyranny and oppression, for nearly three hundred years. After all, the vehemence of the Puritans was caused less by the Commission's methods than by its objects. It was hardly to be expected that a Puritan, who saw in Laud an emissary of Antichrist, maintained in office by the temporal arm in the face of God's direct commands, would approve of the instrument by which the Archbishop's jurisdiction was made effective and by which his continued existence was ensured. Nor could the Puritans and lawyers, who believed Ship Money oppressive and illegal, fail to consider unwarrantable the punishment by the Commission of Richard Powell of Northampton, who had preached against Ship Money so effectively that all his parishioners determined not to pay it. The oath *ex officio*, the citation of a man out of his diocese, the extortions and delays of the pursuivants were, after all, merely corollaries of the main proposition, that the object of the Commission's jurisdiction and procedure was itself iniquitous. The oath *ex officio*, however, became the chief bone of contention, and with the imprisonment which followed its refusal by the accused, its hardships, and illegality, most of the complaints are concerned.[1] That these complaints were in any way just, the commissioners indignantly denied. How could an innocent man do himself any injury, temporal or spiritual, they demanded, by answering truly questions concerning his knowledge of a crime he did not commit ? The fact was, they insisted, that the Puritan, who was haled before the Commission, was usually guilty of the charges against him,[2] but he not

[1] Typical cases are those given in Gardiner, *Cases*, 285, 292 ; and in S. P. Dom. Car. I, 261, f. 37 b, and f. 64. On Oct. 15, 1640, three persons were admonished by the Court to appear and 'certify of their conference with Dr. Featly touching the lawfulness of the oath *ex officio* ' : S. P. Dom. Car. I, 434, f. 241. A good many students have been influenced by such phrases of the letter-writers as this : ' Sir Giles Allington's wife, that he was fined so horribly for in the High Commission, being his niece, is dead of the small pox ' : Strafford, *Letters*, i, 359 (Dublin, 1740). Even though Wentworth wrote this sentence, it is still merely hearsay and an expression of individual opinion.

[2] Laud wrote of one man who refused the oath : ' But the truth is he was too guilty to appear ' : *Works*, iv, 120. ' This I am sure of,' wrote Laud in 1645, ' both the High Commission and myself have been quick enough against all ministers which have been

only was averse to suffering for them, but conscientiously believed that they were positive merits in the sight of God. He objected to the procedure, not so much because the fine was too heavy had he been liable to punishment, or the imprisonment in itself too harshly imposed, or because the oath *ex officio* was improperly used, but because he felt that he ought not to be questioned at all for that offence in any court, much less fined and imprisoned on account of it. His disapproval of the law he transferred to the agent of the law against him.

A study of even the famous cases shows this to have been the real situation.[1] Prynne and Bastwick had really published in their books the passages considered so objectionable, but regarded them as particularly meritorious. Sherfield had deliberately broken the stained glass in the church window, because he believed it to be a superstitious relic of the Scarlet Woman. Mr. Vicars had really held conventicles and preached irregular doctrines, and was prosecuted by the inhabitants of his own parish, headed by the town clerk. He confessed his nonconformity and promised to obey in the future. Chancey had refused to obey the order for the erection of a communion rail, and admitted the refusal, but alleged in defence that he had set up one in his new parish.[2] The real clash of opinion in every case came over the nature

proved to be debauched in their life or conversation. And he says nothing against me, but " that I sided with his adversaries ", which is easy to say against any judge that delivers his sentence against any man ' : *Works*, iv, 166. Case of Hunsford.

[1] In Laud's ' History of Troubles ' there is a long account of the debate between him and the Parliamentary lawyers in 1645 over these cases, in which, it must be owned, the Archbishop had far the better reason and logic on his side : Laud, *Works*, iv, *passim*, but especially 105, 233, 234, 239, 255, 263.

[2] The Commission doubted the truth of his justification. S. P. Dom. Car. I, 302, f. 16. Nov. 15, 1635.

of the case itself, not over the manner by which the Court should establish the fact of its commission. In most cases the Puritan had deliberately and wittingly committed the act as a challenge and reproach to the enemies of God. To suppose that the procedure of the Commission was the essential point in these cases is, therefore, a mistake in emphasis which cannot fail to have serious consequences.

The insistence by the Puritans upon the illegality of the Commission may be explained by the use of the Letters Patent of 1601 as a model for those issued by Charles I. By 1625 the few commissioners sitting in the Court at London had so long stood for 'the Commission' in the minds of contemporaries, and they had so long devoted the major part of their time to the trials of suits between party and party, that there were few men alive who could remember the day when a much larger body of men had frequently exercised visitatorial functions of a peculiarly supreme nature. When, therefore, Laud enforced his visitation by the commissioners' authority, the Puritans insisted vehemently that 'the Commission' was a court of law, and not merely a substitute for the Archbishop's visitation, a place to prosecute suits, not to try presentments by the churchwardens.[1]

[1] At his trial, Laud was accused of having renewed the Letters Patent and 'put in many illegal and exhorbitant clauses which were not in the former': the jurisdiction over peculiars and exempts, fine and imprisonment, the *non obstante* clause, and 'that by this Commission I took greater power than ever any court had because both temporal and ecclesiastical': *Works*, iv, 178. Even the slightest investigation of any early Letters Patent would have revealed the entire falsity of almost every item; the Parliamentary lawyers were not only hard put to it to make out a case, but either totally failed to look into the history of the Commission, or realized that no one would dare challenge anything they saw fit to say about it. Would they have done this had they not believed that the evidence, which could disprove their statements, had been destroyed?

The lack of information about the Commission's past outside official circles; the vague wording of the Letters Patent, which failed explicitly to define the Commission's position, either as a court of law or as a visitatorial body; the undoubted fact that the Statute authorized 'commissioners', but said nothing about judges of a law-court; the assumption that, if the Commission was legally one, it could not be also the other,—all combined to convince the Puritan that he was not bound 'by law' to recognize either function. The situation of 1590 was exactly reversed. The Puritans had then denied the Commission any rights as a court of law, on the ground that its true functions were administrative and visitatorial. Now they declined to recognize the legality of its visitatorial powers because it was, and always had been to them, a court of law. Coke had claimed that the Commission was illegal and against the Law of the Land; the Puritans declared it wrong and contrary to the Law of God.

Undoubtedly, too, they were right in insisting that the Caroline Commissions were more powerful than their predecessors. According to the Letters Patent, the Commission of 1625 possessed almost identically the same authority as the Commission of 1601, but the great increase in membership and in the quorum made possible a subdivision of the commissioners into many more courts, sitting in many more places, a good deal more frequently, than ever before in its history. Special and diocesan commissioners had been common enough; they had more than once, as in the time of Charles, been included in the general commission, and so could have legally exercised the full authority granted by the Letters Patent; but the opportunity does not seem to have been utilized to any considerable extent before Laud's accession to the

Archbishopric. However good a technical defence can be made, therefore, the Puritans were certainly right in claiming that the Commission was more active than formerly, and exercised 'new' powers. Was it not strange, moreover, to know that the Court of High Commission had regularly sat in London for forty years, and then to learn that it was holding court in the next town; nay, what was more, to discover that the Canterbury Commission was simultaneously 'oppressing' the brethren in a dozen places at once, at the very same moment that the judges, who had always transacted its business, were still holding court in London as usual? This, cried the Puritans, was certainly oppression. Could a law-court be one and at the same time twenty; did the King's Bench or the Court of Arches sit on the same day at Lincoln, Wells, and London; was it not a farce to talk about 'the' High Commission, when there were notoriously as many high commissions as the total membership divided by three? Where was there anything in the Statute to sanction such proceedings? Where was there precedent of any kind to show that such things had been done before? Was not this the crowning wickedness?

There can be little doubt that much odium has been heaped upon the Commission by historians through failure to distinguish between it and the Star Chamber. Prynne, Leighton, and Bastwick were tried in the Commission, but the proceedings now so celebrated took place in the Star Chamber, which imposed the sentence executed upon Prynne for the cropping of ears, slitting of nostrils, and standing in the pillory. The Commission never to our knowledge imposed such a sentence, and possessed no power so to do. The fact that Laud was a prominent member of the Privy Council and of the Star Chamber; was Archbishop and judge of the archiepiscopal courts;

was possessed besides of visitatorial functions as Metropolitan, tended at the time and has tended since to lead men to confuse his acts in one capacity with his acts in other capacities, and, in particular, with the acts of the High Commission. Such considerations as these seem to make it possible to believe that the Commission was legal as the law was understood prior to 1640, and its work in most cases beneficial and equitable, and, at the same time, permit us to understand the reason for the vehemence of the opposition accorded to it by the Puritans and the common lawyers in the Long Parliament.

By 1640 the opposition was unblushing, but of these last dramatic scenes in the Commission's life we can catch only a glimpse here and there. One lawyer actually announced readings at the Middle Temple against the Commission's authority for Easter term 1640, and was stopped only by order from the Privy Council.[1] Mr. Lapthorne, when suspended by the Bishop of Durham, threatened him to his face to 'get even with him at the Parliament',[2] and, barely ten days before the Long Parliament assembled, a great crowd of some '2,000 Brownists' (as Laud wrote to Ussher) attended the session of the Commission at St. Paul's, and, at its close, amid much shouting and disorder, tore down the benches in the consistory, 'crying out that they would have no Bishops nor High Commission.' 'I like not this preface to the Parliament,' added the Archbishop.[3] The last sessions of the Commission were probably those of Michaelmas term 1640, for before Hilary term the Archbishop was in prison, the Earl of Strafford impeached,

[1] S. P. Dom. Car. I, 447, no. 33. Mar. 6, 1639/40.

[2] *Ibid.* 436, no. 22. Dec. 22, 1639. For his earlier trial in the Commission, see Act Book, S. P. Dom. Car. I, 261, f. 83, Oct. 9, 1634.

[3] Laud's *Works*, vi, 585. See also iii, 237.

and the Lord Chief Justice in flight. Then followed dramatic scenes: petitions, speeches, books, denouncing the Commission;[1] Bastwick, Prynne, and Smart led back to London in triumph by a shouting populace. Finally, after Strafford's death, the legislation of June and July 1641 included an Act (17 Car. I, c. 11) which repealed the eighth section of the Statute of 1 Elizabeth, c. 1, abolished the Commission, and forbade the erection of any such court in the future. The opposition had at last triumphed; the struggle had been long and sharp; the resistance had been stout, but the victory was none the less decisive. As its final blow, the opposition branded the past history of the Commission with the stain of illegality. It became law, which every judge and lawyer in the land must observe and promulgate, that the High Commission had been abolished because of its illegal exercise of judicial power and its 'great and insufferable wrongs and oppression of the King's subjects'.

[1] The chief evidence now left us is in the *Commons' Journals*. The following are interesting: S. P. Dom. Car. I, 450, no. 94; 461, no. 37; 472, no. 48; 473, no. 71; 474, nos. 7, 68, 69, 70; 476, no. 112. Most of the speeches and petitions rehearse the familiar Puritan complaints or the logic of Fuller and Coke, interlarded with a good deal of vituperative rhetoric. There seems to have been no attempt at investigation; the decision to abolish the Commission was already made, and the petitions, speeches, and arguments were intended merely to provide the necessary formal preliminaries to a judgement.

APPENDIX I

CLAUSES FROM STATUTES AND LETTERS PATENT

A. 26 Henry VIII, c. 1, s. i.
   1 Elizabeth, c. 1, s. viii.
B. The Development of Clause III.
C. The Development of Clause IX.
D. The Development of Clause V.

A

26 Henry VIII, c. 1, s. i

'. . . Be it enacted by the authority of this present Parliament, that the King our Sovereign Lord, his Heirs and Successors, Kings of this Realm, shall be taken, accepted and reputed the only supreme Head in earth of the Church of England, called Anglicana Ecclesia; and shall have and enjoy, annexed and united to the Imperial Crown of this Realm as well the Title and Stile thereof, as all Honours, Dignities, Preheminences, Jurisdictions, Priviledges, Authorities, Immunities, Profits, and Commodities to the said Dignity of Supreme Head of the same Church belonging and appertaining:

'Our said Sovereign Lord, his Heirs and Successors, Kings of this realm, shall have full Power and Authority from Time to Time to visit, repress, redress, reform, order, correct, restrain and amend all such Errors, Heresies, Abuses, Offences, Contempts, and Enormities whatsoever they be, which by any manner spiritual Authority or Jurisdiction ought or may lawfully be reformed, repressed, ordered, redressed, corrected, restrained, and amended, most to the Pleasure of Almighty God, the Increase of Virtue in Christ's Religion and for the Conservation of the Peace, Unity, and Tranquillity of this Realm; any Usage, Custom, foreign Laws, foreign Authority, Prescription or any other things to the contrary hereof notwithstanding.'

1 Elizabeth, c. 1, s. viii

'And that also it may likewise please your Highness that it may be established and enacted by the authority aforesaid, That such jurisdictions, privileges, superiorities and pre-eminences, spiritual and ecclesiastical, as by any spiritual or ecclesiastical power or authority hath heretofore been or may lawfully be exercised or used for the visitation of the ecclesiastical state and persons, and for reformation, order and correction of the same and of all manner of errors, heresies, schisms, abuses, offences, contempts and enormities, shall for ever, by authority of this present Parliament, be united and annexed to the imperial crown of this realm; and that your Highness, your heirs and successors, kings or queens of this realm, shall have full power and authority by virtue of this Act, by Letters Patents, under the Great Seal of England, to assign, name and authorize, when and as often as your Highness, your heirs or successors, shall think meet and convenient, and for such and so long time as shall please your Highness, your heirs or successors, such person or persons, being natural-born subjects to your Highness, your heirs or successors, as your Majesty, your heirs or successors, shall think meet, to exercise, use, occupy and execute under your Highness, your heirs and successors, all manner of jurisdictions, privileges and pre-eminences, in any wise touching or concerning any spiritual or ecclesiastical jurisdiction within these your realms of England and Ireland or any other your Highness' dominions or countries; and to visit, reform, redress, order, correct and amend all such heresies, errors, schisms, abuses, offences, contempts and enormities whatsoever, which by any manner of spiritual or ecclesiastical power, authority or jurisdiction can or may lawfully be reformed, ordered, redressed, corrected, restrained or amended, to the pleasure of Almighty God, the increase of virtue and the conservation of the peace and unity of this realm; and that such person or persons so to be named, assigned, authorized, and appointed by your Highness, your heirs or successors, after the said Letters Patents to him or them made and delivered as is aforesaid, shall have full power and authority by virtue of this Act and of the said Letters Patents, under your Highness, your heirs or successors, to exercise, use and execute all the premisses according to the tenor and effect of the said Letters Patents; any matter or cause to the contrary in any wise notwithstanding.'

B

The Development of Clause III

1550/51. Commissio Regia ad Observandum Librum Precum Communium, &c.

Cardwell, *Annals*, i, 103–4

'De advisamento consilii nostri praedicti vos selegimus, quibus hanc nostram curam, et hoc tam necessarium munus extirpandae et reprimendae haereseos committeremus. Ad inquirendum igitur de omnibus articulis haereseos cujuscunque, et examinandum omnes et singulos subditos nostros, et alios quoscunque infra regnum et dominia nostra residentes et commorantes de et super haeresibus et erroribus quibuscunque, in fide christiana suspectos, detectos, denunciatos, inquisitos, et accusatos, [aut in posterum detegendos, denunciandos, inquirendos vel accusandos,] et quoscunque testes [ubicunque locorum infra regnum et dominia nostra commorantes vel degentes,] aliarumque probationum genera quaecunque, pro veritate praemissorum erudienda quomodolibet requisita, recipienda, et admittenda, testesque hujuscemodi in forma jurandorum testium jurandos et examinandos ac omnibus aliis viis et modis et formis quibus melius et efficacius poteritis, de vertitate praemissorum etiam summarie et de plano ac sine strepitu et figura judicii cognoscendi inquirendi, et investigandi.' [1]

The Letters Patent of 1556/7

Pocock's *Burnet's Reformation*, v, 470

'We minding and intending the due punishment of such offenders and the repressing of such like offences, enormities, and misbehaviours from henceforth, having special trust and confidence in your fidelities, wisdoms, and discretions, have authorised, appointed, and assigned you

[1] The clause of 1549 was the same with the omission of the bracketed portions and the use of the singular instead of plural.

to be our commissioners; and by these presents do give full power and authority unto you, and three of you, to enquire, as well by the oaths of twelve good and lawful men, as by witnesses, and all other means and politic ways you can devise, of all and sundry heresies, heretical opinions, Lollardies, heretical and seditious books, concealments, contempts, conspiracies, and of all false rumours, tales, seditious and clamorous words or sayings, raised, published, bruited, invented, or set forth against us, or either of us; or against the quiet governance and rule of our people and subjects, by books, letters, tales, or otherwise, in any county, city, borough, or other place or places within this our realm of England, and elsewhere, in any place or places beyond the seas; and of the bringers in, users, buyers, sellers, readers, keepers, or conveyors of any such letter, book, remour, or tale; and of all and every their coadjutors, counsellors, comforters, procurers, abettors, and maintainers; giving to you, and three of you, full power and authority, by virtue hereof, to search out and take into your hands and possession, all manner of heretical and seditious books, letters, writings, wheresoever they, or any of them shall be found, as well in printers' houses and shops, as elsewhere; willing you, and every of you, to search for the same in all places, according to your discretions.'

The Letters Patent of 1599

Prothero, *Select Statutes*, 228

'Wherefore we, earnestly minding to have the same Acts before mentioned to be duly put in execution, and such persons as shall hereafter offend in anything contrary to the tenor and effect of the said several statutes to be condignly punished, and having especial trust and confidence in your wisdoms and discretions, have authorized, assigned and appointed you to be our commissioners, and by these presents do give our full power and authority to you, or six of you, whereof you, the said Mathew Parker, Edmond Grindall, Thomas Smyth, Walter Haddon, Thomas Sackford, Richard Gooderick and Gilbert Gerrard, to be one, from time to time hereafter, during our pleasure, to enquire as well by the oaths of twelve good and lawful men, as also by witnesses and all other ways and means ye can devise for all offences, misdoers (sic) and misdemeanours done and committed and hereafter to be committed or done contrary to the tenor and effect of the said several acts and statutes and either of them and also of all and singular heretical opinions, seditious books, contempts, conspiracies, false rumours, tales, seditions, misbehaviours, slanderous words or shewings, published, invented or set forth, or hereafter to be published, invented or set forth by any person or persons against us or contrary or against any the laws or statutes of this our realm, or against the quiet governance and rule of our people and subjects in any county, city, borough or other place or places within this our realm of England, and of all and every the coadjutors, counsellors, comforters, procurers and abettors of every such offender.'

In **1562** the quorum was made three. In 1601 the following change was made. After the clause of greeting, and after the recital of the Act of Supremacy, the Letters Patent proceeded, that 'by force and vertue of our Supreme Aucthoritie and Prerogatyve Royall, and of the said Acts,' do appoint you, &c. (repeating all the names) any three of you, of whom (the quorum) to be one, 'being all our natural borne subjectes, from tyme to tyme and at all tymes duringe Our Pleasure, to exercise use, occupie and execute under Us ; all manner of Jurisdictions, Priviledges', &c., in the exact wording of section viii of the Act of Supremacy. Then followed the recital of 1 Eliz. c. 1, of 5 Eliz. c. 1, 13 Eliz. c. 12, 23 Eliz. c. 1, 35 Eliz. c. 2. It then proceeds as in 1559, 'and whereas diverse seditious and slaunderous persons, do not cease dayly to invent', &c., with no further change except the addition of a word or two here and there. The Commissions of 1605 and 1608 followed this model.

In **1611** further change was made. The repetition of the statute in the clause granting power to the commissioners was omitted, and the following substituted.

The Letters Patent of 1611

Prothero, *Select Statutes*, 425–6

'Know ye therefore that we for sundry good, weighty and necessary causes and considerations us thereunto especially moving, of our mere motion and certain knowledge, by force and virtue of our supreme authority and prerogative royal and of the said Act, do by these our letters patents under our great seal of England give and grant full, free and lawful power and authority unto you the said [commissioners above-named] being all our natural subjects, or any three or more of you, whereof [the Archbishop, the Lord Treasurer, the Lord Privy Seal, ten Bishops and fourteen others] to be one, from time to time to enquire as well by examination of witnesses or presentments as also by examination of the parties accused themselves upon their oath (where there shall first appear sufficient matter of charge by examination of witnesses or by presentments or by public and notorious fame or by information of the ordinary) of all and singular apostasies, heresies, great errors in matters of faith and religion, schisms, unlawful conventicles tending to schism against the religion or government of the Church now established; and also of all persons which have or shall refuse to have their children baptized, or which have or shall administer or procure or willingly suffer the sacrament of baptism to be administered by any Jesuit, Seminary or other popish priest, or which have or shall celebrate the mass or procure the same to be celebrated, or willingly hear or be present at the same, and of their said offences; and also of all blasphemous and impious acts and speeches, scandalous books, libels and writings against the doctrine of religion, the book of Common Prayer or ecclesiastical state or government now established in the Church of England, or against any archbishop or bishop, touching any offence or crime of ecclesiastical cognizance, profanation of the sacraments of baptism and the Lord's Supper and of all other things and places consecrated or dedicated to divine service; wilful and unlawful digging up of buried bodies in any church or chapel, or churchyard; violent and wilful disturbances and interruptions of divine service or sermons in any church, chapel or public preaching place; violent and wilful laying of hands upon the person of any archbishop or bishop; simonies, incests, infamous and notorious adulteries; [1] *(and of all abuses, offences, insolent misbehaviours and contempts being not capital, committed or done unto or against you or any such three or more of you as is aforesaid judicially sitting in our said court of High Commission for ecclesiastical causes; and of all outrageous*

[1] Added in 1613.

offences, abuses and contempts aforesaid against any our officers or ministers in the execution of the process or mandates awarded or made according to the tenour or to the true intent or meaning of these our letters patents ;) and also of all corruptions, contempts and abuses in any ecclesiastical judges, officers, or their deputies or clerks or other ministers whatsoever belonging [1] (*either to our said court of High Commission* (&c.), *or*) to any (*other*) ecclesiastical courts or . . . employed in or by the same, committed in any county . . . or other places . . . within these our realms of England and Ireland and dominion of Wales, and of all the offenders in the premises, and of all their counsellors, procurers and abettors.'

This form obtained until the Letters Patent of 1625/6, when the form of 1601 was substituted with a single change. Instead of the phrase beginning to 'enquire as well by the oaths of twelve good and lawful men', we find, 'to enquire as well by the Examination of the parties themselves as by witnesses, and all other Wayes and Meanes you can reasonably devise, of all offences, Contempts, Transgressions, and Misdemeanours done and committed, and hereafter to be done and committed contrarie to the Tenor and effect of the said severall Acts and statutes and everie or anie of them, and everie or anie parte of them or any of them, and also in like manner as is aforesaid, to enquire of all and singular,' &c. (as before).

C

The Development of Clause IX

1550/51. Commissio Regia ad Observandum Librum Precum Communium, &c.

Cardwell, *Annals*, i, 105

'Caeteraque omnia et singula facienda, exercenda, et expedienda, quae circa dicta inquisitionis et examinationis negotia necessaria fuerint, seu quomodolibet opportuna, vobis triginta et uni, triginta, viginti novem, viginti octo, viginti septem, viginti sex, viginti quinque, viginti quatuor, viginti tribus, viginti duobus, viginti uni, viginti, novendecim, octodecim, septendecim, sexdecim, quindecim,

[1] Added in 1613.

quatuordecim, tredecim, duodecim, undecim, decem, 9, 8, 7, 6, 5, 4, aut tribus vestrum, quorum archiepiscopum Cantuariensem, episcopum Eliensem, episcopum London. episcopum Lincoln. episcopum Norwicen. episcopum Roffen. Nicholaum Wotton, Willelmum Peter, Willelmum Cecill, Richardum Coxe, Jacobum Hales, et Willelmum May unum esse volumnus, et in executione praemissorum interesse; de quorum sana doctrina, fidei zelo, vitaeque et morum integritate, exactaque in rebus gerendis dexteritate specialem in Domino fiduciam obtinemus, vices nostras committimus, et plenam tenore praesentium concedimus facultatem, cum potestate plenissima personas sic detectas, denunciatas, inquisitas, accusatas vel suspectas evocandas coram vobis, et carceri et vinculis, si opus fuerit, mancipandas, ac testes quoscunque pro veritate praemissorum explicandos, et erudiendos quomodolibet requisitos, coram vobis, quibuscunque diebus, et locis vestro arbitrio in hac parte limitandis, evocandos et citandos, eosdemque testes sese subtrahentes omnibus modis et juris nostri remediis quibuscunque compellendos cum omni alia jurisdictionis et auctoritatis nostrae legitima coertione in hac parte et potestate.'

The Letters Patent of 1556/7

Pocock's *Burnet's Reformation*, v, 471

'Giving to you, and every three of you, full power and authority, by virtue hereof, to hear and determine the same, and all other offences and matters above specified and rehearsed, according to your wisdoms, consciences, and discretions; willing and commanding you, or three of you, from time to time, to use and devise all such politic ways and means, for the trial and searching out of the premises, as by you, or three of you, shall be thought most expedient and necessary; and upon enquiry, and due proof, had, known, perceived, and tried out by the confession of the parties, or by sufficient witnesses, before you, or three of you, concerning the premises, or any part thereof, or by any other ways or means requisite, to give and award such punishment to the offenders, by fine, imprisonment, or otherwise; and to take such order for redress and reformation of the premises, as to your wisdoms, or three of you, shall be thought meet and convenient.'

The Letters Patent of 1559

Prothero, *Select Statutes*, 230

'Willing and commanding you or six of you [quorum as before] from time to time hereafter to use and devise all such politic ways and means for the trial and searching out of all the premises, as by you or six of you, as aforesaid, shall be thought most expedient and necessary; and upon due proof had, and the offence or offences before specified, or any of them, sufficiently proved against any person or persons by confession of the party or by lawful witnesses or by any due mean before you or six of you, [quorum as before] that then you or six of you, as aforesaid, shall have full power and authority to award such punishment to every offender by fine, imprisonment or otherwise, by all or any of the ways aforesaid, and to take such order for the redress of the same, as to your wisdoms and discretions shall be thought meet and convenient.' [1]

In 1562 the quorum was made three.

In 1601 the words 'all such politic ways and means' became 'good lawfull reasonable and convenient wayes and meanes'.

In 1611 the following form was substituted:

[XIII] 'And further we give authority unto you (&c.), from time to time during our pleasure to hear all the offences and the offenders aforesaid, and to proceed against them either according to the form of the law ecclesiastical or summarily according to the grave wisdoms and discretions of you (&c.), and likewise to order and determine the same, inflicting such censures and punishments only as are hereafter mentioned and prescribed.

[XIV] And if you (&c.) shall find by confession of the party or other sufficient proof any person to have offended in the premises, or refusing to obey or perform your orders . . ., that then you (&c.) shall have authority . . . to punish the same person so offending by censures ecclesiastical or by reasonable fine or imprisonment according to the quality and quantity of their offence, or by all or any the said means according to your discretions.'

[1] The words 'shall be thought meet and convenient' are wanting in the roll (as well as in that of 1562), and have been supplied from the Commission of 1572.

1625/6, in reviving the form of 1601, inserts:
'Fyne imprisonments, censures of the Church or other lawfull way, or by all or anie of the said waies.'

D

The Development of Clause V

This Clause does not appear until 1559, but was then taken, practically verbatim, from the statutes of 26 Henry VIII, c. 1, and 1 Eliz. c. 1.

The Letters Patent of 1559

Prothero, *Select Statutes*, 229

'And also we do give and grant full power and authority unto you and six of you [quorum as before] from time to time and at all times during our pleasure, to visit, reform, redress, order, correct and amend in all places within this our realm of England all such errors, heresies, crimes, abuses, offences, contempts and enormities spiritual and ecclesiastical wheresoever [sic] which by any spiritual or ecclesiastical power, authority or jurisdiction can or may lawfully be reformed, ordered, redressed, corrected, restrained or amended, to the pleasure of Almighty God, the increase of virtue, and the conservation of the peace and unity of this our realm, and according to the authority and power limited, given and appointed by any laws or statutes of this realm.'

In 1562 the quorum was changed to three.

In 1601 this clause is transported into Clause III and the wording of the statute of 1 Eliz. c. 1 is given, as nearly verbatim as possible, consistent with changing it to read as empowering the commissioners instead of as a grant to the Crown.

In 1611 the clause is omitted entirely from any section of the Letters Patent which confers power on the commissioners.

In 1625/6 it was restored, as in 1601.

APPENDIX II

A LIST OF THE COMMISSIONERS FOR CAUSES ECCLESIASTICAL IN THE PROVINCE OF CANTERBURY, 1549–1641

(This list is believed to be complete, containing the names of all the members who ever had a right to sit, except those of the lost Commissions of 1570 and 1589. The name of the member followed by a title or an office indicates that in the commission of the year named he sat under that title or by virtue of that office. The spelling of the names in the Patent Roll and manuscript copies has been retained; the titles and offices under each are those given in the Roll; no biographical data of any kind have been added; nor have the names or titles been edited. The following abbreviations have been used: 1625 means the Commission of 1624/5; 1626 means the Commission of 1625/6; 1551 means the Commission of 1550/1, &c.; P.C., member of the Privy Council; Kt., Knight, without other office named; Esq., Esquire, without other office named; C.J., Chief Justice; J., Justice; C.B., Chief Baron; B., Baron of the Exchequer; Atty.-Gen., Attorney-General; Solic.-Gen., Solicitor-General; D.D., Doctor of Divinity; D.C.L., Doctor of Civil Law; B.D., Bachelor of Divinity; M.A., Master of Arts; all without other office named.)

Abbot, George. Dean of Winchester, 1608; Archbishop, 1611, 1613, 1620, 1625, 1626, 1629.

Abbot, Robert. Professor of Divinity at Oxford, 1611, 1613.

Ailmer, Theophilus. D.D., 1605.

Alcocke, Robert. B.D., 1572, 1576.

Altham, Sir James. Baron of the Exchequer, 1608, 1611, 1613.

Amye, Sir John. Master of Chancery, 1620.

Anderson, Sir Edmond. C.J., 1601, 1605.

Andrews, Lancelot. D.D., 1601; Bishop of Chichester, 1605, 1608; Bishop of Ely, 1611, 1613; Bishop of Winchester, 1620, 1625, 1626.

Arundell, Thomas Earl of. Earl Marshall, 1620, 1625, 1626, 1629, 1633.

Aubrey, William. D.C.L., 1584.

Ayer, Egidius. *See* **Eyre.**

Aylett, Robert. D.C.L., 1629, 1633.

Aylmer, John. Archdeacon of Lincoln, 1572, 1576; Bishop of London, 1584.

Babington, Gervase. Bishop of Worcester, 1601, 1605, 1608.

Babington, Zacharie. 1611.

Bacon, Francis. 1601; Learned Counsel, 1605; Solicitor-General, 1608, 1611; Attorney-General, 1613; Lord Chancellor, 1620.

Balcanquall, Walter. Dean of Rochester, 1626, 1629, 1633.

Banbury, William Earl of. P.C., 1629.

Bancroft, John. Bishop of Oxford, 1633.

Bancroft, Richard. D.D., 1589 (Additional MSS. 32092, f. 125); Bishop of London, 1601; Archbishop of Canterbury, 1605, 1608.

Bargrave, Isaac. Dean of Canterbury, 1626, 1629, 1633.

Barham, Nicholas. Serjeant-at-Law, 1572, 1576.

Barker, Hugh. D.C.L., 1625, 1626, 1629.

Barlow, William. Bishop of Rochester, 1605, 1608; Bishop of Lincoln, 1611, 1613.

Bates, Roger. D.D., 1620, 1625, 1626, 1629, 1633.

Bayly, Lewis. Bishop of Bangor, 1625, 1626.

Bennet, Robert. Bishop of Hereford, 1605, 1608.

Bennett, Sir John. D.C.L., 1605, 1608; Judge of the Prerogative Court of Canterbury, 1611, 1613, 1620.

Berkeley, Sir Robert. J., 1633.

Bickley, Thomas. Bishop of Chichester, 1584.

Bill, William. Almoner, 1559.

Bilson, Thomas. Bishop of Winchester, 1601, 1605, 1608, 1611, 1613.

Bird, Sir William. Dean of the Court of Arches, 1620.

Bisse, Philip. D.D., 1611.

Blage (Blague), Thomas. Dean of Rochester, 1601, 1608, 1611.

Bonner, Edmond. Bishop of London, 1556.

Bourne, John. Secretary of State, 1556.

Bowle, John. D.D., 1613, 1620; Dean of Salisbury, 1625, 1626; Bishop of Rochester, 1629, 1633.

Bowyer, William. B.D., 1576.

Bowyere, Sir Edmond. D.D., 1625, 1626.

Boyd (Boyes), Sir John. Kt., 1605, 1611, 1613.

Boys, Edward. B.D., 1572, 1576.

Boys, John. Dean of Canterbury, 1601, 1620, 1625.

Bray, William. B.D., 1633.

Brent, Nathanel. D.C.L., 1625, 1626, 1629; Vicar-General to Archbishop of Canterbury, 1633.

Bridgeman, John. Bishop of Chester, 1625, 1626, 1629, 1633.

Bridges, John. Dean of Salisbury, 1584; Bishop of Oxford, 1601.

Bridgewater, John Earl of. Lord President of the Council in the Marches of Wales, 1629, 1633.

Bristol, John Earl of. 1625.

Bromley, Sir Edward. Baron of the Exchequer, 1611, 1613, 1620, 1625, 1626.

Bromley, George. Attorney of the Duchy of Lancaster, 1572, 1576.

Brooke, Fulke Lord. 1625, 1626. *See* **Greville, Sir Fulke.**

Brumley, Thomas. Solic.-Gen., 1572, 1576.

Buckeridge, John. Bishop of Rochester, 1611, 1613, 1620, 1625, 1626; Bishop of Ely, 1629.

Buckhurst, Robert Lord. 1605.

Buckhurst, Thomas Lord. Lord Treasurer, 1601. *See* **Dorset, Earl of.**

Buckingham, George, Marquis of. Lord Admiral, 1620; Duke of Buckingham, 1625, 1626.

Bullingham, John. D.D., 1572.

Bullingham, Nicholas. 1551; Bishop of Worcester, 1572, 1576.

Caesar, Sir Charles. Master of Chancery, 1620, 1625, 1626, 1629; Judge of Court of Audience, 1633.

Caesar, Sir Julius. Master of Requests, 1601, 1605; Under-Treasurer of the Exchequer, 1608, 1611, 1613; Master of the Rolls, 1625, 1626, 1629, 1633.

Calvert, Sir George. Secretary of State, 1620, 1625.

Carew, George Lord. P.C., 1620, 1625.

Carewe, Sir Nicholas. Chamberlain of the Exchequer, 1625, 1626, 1629, 1633.

Carew, Sir Randall. Serjeant-at-Law, 1620, 1625; Chief Justice, 1626.

Carey, Valentine. Dean of St. Paul's, 1620; Bishop of Exeter, 1625, 1626.

Carleton, Sir Dudley. Vice-Chamberlain of the Household, 1626. *See* **Dorchester, Viscount.**

Carleton, George. Bishop of Chichester, 1620, 1625, 1626.

Carlisle, James Earl of. P.C., 1625, 1626, 1629, 1633.

Carye, Sir Henry. Comptroller of the Household, 1620.

Cave, Ambrose. Kt., 1559, 1562.

Cave, Francis. 1559.

Cecil, Robert. *See* **Salisbury, Earl of.**

Cecil, William. Secretary of State, 1549, 1551. (He was never again a member of the Commission.)

Cesar, Sir Charles. *See* **Caesar.**

Cesar, Henry. D.D., 1611, 1613.
Chaderton, William. Bishop of Lincoln, 1601.
Cheke, John. Tutor to the King, 1551.
Chester, William. Kt., 1559, 1562.
Chichester, Arthur Lord. 1625.
Cholmeley, Randolf. Serjeant-at-Law, 1556, 1559, 1562.
Cholmley, Roger. Kt., 1556.
Clark, Bartholomew. D.C.L., 1576; Dean of Arches, 1584.
Cleyton, Richard. Archdeacon of Lincoln, 1611.
Coke, Sir Edward. Atty.-Gen., 1601, 1605; C.J., 1608, 1611, 1613; as Kt., 1620.
Coke, George. Bishop of Bristol, 1633.
Coke, Sir John. Secretary of State, 1626, 1629, 1633.
Coke, William. D.C.L., 1556.
Coldwell, John. Bishop of Salisbury, 1584.
Cole, Henry. Dean of St. Paul's, 1556.
Combes, William. Esq., 1601, 1605, 1608.
Conway, Sir Edward. Secretary of State, 1625, 1626; as **Viscount Conway,** President of the Privy Council, 1629.
Cooke, Sir Anthony. Kt., 1549, 1551, 1559, 1562, 1572, 1576.
Cope, Sir Walter. 1611.
Corbet, Richard. Bishop of Oxford, 1629; Bishop of Norwich, 1633.
Corbett, Thomas. D.D., 1608, 1611.
Cornewallis, Sir Charles. Kt., 1613, 1620.
Cosins, Richard. D.C.L., 1584.
Cottington, Francis Lord. Under-Treasurer of the Exchequer, 1629, 1633.
Cotton, Henry. Bishop of Salisbury, 1601.
Cotton, William. Bishop of Exeter, 1601, 1605, 1613, 1620.
Coventry, Sir Thomas. Solic.-Gen., 1620; Atty.-Gen., 1625; Keeper of the Great Seal, 1629, 1633.
Coverdale, Miles. D.C.L., 1551.
Cowell, John. D.C.L., 1605, 1611.
Cowper, Thomas. Bishop of Winchester, 1584.
Cox, Richard. Almoner, 1549, 1551; Bishop of Ely, 1562, 1572, 1576.
Crane, Sir Francis. 1633.
Cranfield, Sir Lionell. Master of the Court of Wards and Liveries, 1620.
Cranmer, Thomas. Archbishop of Canterbury, 1549, 1551.
Crawley, Sir Francis. J., 1633.
Crewe, Sir Randall. *See* **Carew.**

Crewe, Sir Thomas. Serjeant-at-Law, 1625, 1626, 1629, 1633.
Croke, [Richard]. D.C.L., 1549.
Crooke, George. Serjeant-at-Law, 1625; J., 1626, 1629.
Crooke, Sir John. J., 1601, 1605, 1608, 1611, 1613.
Crowmer, William. B.D., 1576.
Curl, Walter. Bishop of Bath and Wells, 1626, 1629; Bishop of Winchester, 1633.
Curteys, Richard. Bishop of Chichester, 1572, 1576.

Dale, Valentine. Master of Requests, 1584.
Danby, Henry Earl of. P.C., 1629, 1633.
Davenant, John. Bishop of Salisbury, 1625, 1626, 1629, 1633.
Davenport, Sir Humphrey. Ch. B., 1633.
Davill, Sir Henry. Kt., 1608.
Day, George. Bishop of Chichester, 1549.
Day (Dey), William. Bishop of Winchester, 1572, 1576, 1584.
Dayves, Richarde. Bishop of St. Davids, 1572, 1576.
Dee, Francis. Bishop of Peterborough, 1633.
Denham, Sir John. B., 1633.
Digby, John Lord. Vice-Chamberlain, 1620.
Digges, Sir Dudley. Kt., 1613, 1620, 1625, 1626, 1629, 1633.
Dilmer, John. Archdeacon of Lincoln, 1576.
Ditton, Christofer. 1572.
Dixe, John. D.D., 1605, 1608, 1611, 1613.
Dixe, William. D.D., 1601.
Dodderidge, Sir John. Serjeant, 1608; J., 1611, 1613, 1620, 1625, 1626.
Dolben, David. Bishop of Bangor, 1633.
Dorchester, Dudley Viscount. Secretary of State, 1629. *See* **Carleton, Dudley.**
Dorset, Edward Earl of. 1626; Chamberlain to the Queen, 1629, 1633.
Dorset, Thomas Earl of. Lord Treasurer, 1605. *See* **Buckhurst, Thomas Lord.**
Dove, Thomas. Bishop of Peterborough, 1601, 1605, 1625, 1626, 1629.
Draper, Christofer. Alderman of London, 1572.
Drury, John. D.C.L., 1601, 1605, 1608, 1611, 1613.
Drury, William. D.C.L., 1562.
Ducke, Arthur. Chancellor to the Bishop of London, 1633.

Duckett, Gregory. D.D., 1620.
Dunne, Sir Daniel. D.C.L., Master of Requests, 1601, 1605, 1608, 1611, 1613.
Dunne, John. Dean of St. Paul's, London, 1625, 1626, 1629.
Duplyn, George Viscount. Chancellor of Scotland, 1629.

Eden, Thomas. Master of Chancery, 1633.
Edmondes, Sir Thomas. 1625; Treasurer of the Household, 1626, 1629, 1633.
Egerton, Thomas. Solicitor-General, 1584; Lord Keeper, 1601; Lord Chancellor (Lord Ellesmere), 1605, 1608, 1611, 1613.
Elder, John. D.D., 1572, 1576, 1584.
Ellesmere, Thomas Lord. *See* **Egerton.**
Englefield, Frauncis. Master of the Court of Wards and Liveries, 1556.
Exeter, Thomas Earl of. 1613, 1620.
Exeter, William Earl of. P.C., 1629, 1633.
Eyre, Egidius. D.D., 1549; Dean of Chichester, 1551.

Falkeland, Henry Viscount. Deputy of Ireland, 1625, 1626, 1629.
Fane, Sir Henry. Comptroller of the Household, 1633.
Fanshawe, Thomas. Remembrancer of the Exchequer, 1576.
Fanshawe, Thomas. D.D., 1620, 1625, 1626, 1629.
Felton, Nicholas. D.D., 1611, 1613; Bishop of Bristol, 1620, 1625, 1626.
Ferrand, William. D.C.L., 1601, 1605, 1608, 1611, 1613.
Field, Theophilus. Bishop of Llandaff, 1626; Bishop of St. Davids, 1626, 1629, 1633; Bishop of Hereford, 1633.
Finch, Sir Heneage. Recorder of London, 1625, 1626, 1629.
Fisher, William. D.D., 1608, 1611, 1613.
Fleming, Sir Thomas. Solicitor-General, 1601, 1605; Chief Justice, 1608, 1611, 1613.
Fletewood, William. Recorder of London, 1572, 1576, 1584.
Folkland, Henry Viscount. *See* **Falkeland.**
Fortescue, Sir John. Chancellor of the Duchy of Lancaster, 1601, 1605.
Fotherby, Charles. Archdeacon of Canterbury, 1601, 1605, 1608, 1611, 1613.

Fotherby, Martin. D.D., 1608; Bishop of Salisbury, 1611, 1613.
Fowler, Sir Thomas. Kt., 1611, 1613, 1620, 1625.
Freak, Edmund. Bishop of Rochester, 1572; Bishop of Norwich, 1576, 1584.

Gager, William. D.C.L., 1611.
Garret, William. Kt., 1562.
Gawdye, Francis. J., 1601, 1605.
Gayes, Sir John. Kt., 1608.
Gerarde, William. Esq., 1572.
Gerrarde, Gilbert. Attorney-General, 1559, 1562, 1572, 1576, 1584.
Gheast, Edmund. Bishop of Ely, 1562.
Gibson, John. D.C.L., 1601.
Goade, Thomas. D.D., 1620, 1625, 1626, 1629, 1633.
Goche, Barnaby. *See* **Gooch.**
Godwin, Francis. Bishop of Hereford, 1625, 1626, 1629.
Godwin, Thomas. Dean of Canterbury, 1572, 1576, 1584.
Goldman (Gouldman), George. Archdeacon of Essex, 1611, 1613, 1620, 1625, 1626, 1629.
Goldsborough, Godfrey. Bishop of Gloucester, 1601.
Gooch, Barnaby. D.C.L., 1620, 1625, 1626.
Gooderick, Richard. D.C.L., 1551, 1559.
Goodman, Gabriell. Dean of Westminster, 1562, 1572, 1576, 1584, 1601.
Goodman, Godfrey. Bishop of Gloucester, 1625, 1626, 1633.
Goodrich, Thomas. Bishop of Ely, 1549, 1551.
Goodwin, William. D.D., 1611, 1613; Dean of Christ Church, Oxford, 1620.
Gosnold, John. Kt., 1549, 1551.
Gouch, Barnaby. *See* **Gooch.**
Grandison, Oliver Viscount. 1625, 1626, 1629.
Graunte, Edward. D.D., 1601.
Greville, Sir Fulke. Under-Treasurer of the Exchequer, 1620.
Griffith, Edmund. Bishop of Bangor, 1633.
Grimes, Sir Thomas. D.D., 1625.
Grindal, Edmund. Bishop of London, 1559, 1562; Archbishop of Canterbury, 1576.
Gwinn, Thomas. D.C.L., 1633.
Gwyn, Lewys. Chancellor to the Bishop of St. Davids, 1572.

Hackett, John. B.D., 1625, 1626, 1629; D.D., 1633.
Haddington, Thomas Earl of. Lord Privy Seal of Scotland, 1633.
Haddon, Walter. Master of Requests, 1559, 1562.
Hales, James. J., and C.B., 1549, 1551.
Hall, Joseph. Bishop of Exeter, 1633.
Hamilton, James Marquis of. Lord Steward, 1625; Master of Horse, 1633.
Hamond, John. D.C.L., Master of Chancery, 1572, 1576, 1584.
Hanes, Simon. Dean of Exeter, 1549, 1551.
Hanmer, John. D.D., 1611, 1613; Bishop of St. Asaph, 1625, 1626.
Harbert, Sir John. *See* **Herbert.**
Hare, Nicholas. Kt., 1556.
Harsnet, Samuel. Archdeacon of Essex, 1605, 1608; Bishop of Chichester, 1611, 1613; Bishop of Norwich, 1620, 1625, 1626.
Heath, Nicholas. Bishop of Worcester, 1549.
Heath, Robert. Recorder of London, 1620; Solicitor-General, 1625; Attorney-General, 1626, 1629; Chief Justice, 1633.
Heighwarde, Rowland. *See* **Heywarde.**
Herbert, Sir John. Secretary of State, 1601, 1605, 1608, 1611, 1613.
Hesketh, Sir Thomas. D.C.L., Attorney of the Court of Wards, 1605.
Heton, Martin. Bishop of Ely, 1601, 1605, 1608.
Heyward, Sir John. Kt., 1620; Master of Chancery, 1625, 1626.
Heywarde, Rowland. Alderman of London, 1572, 1576.
Hickman, Henry. D.C.L., 1608, 1611.
Hide, Sir Nicholas. C.J., 1629.
Hill, John. D.D., 1611.
Hill, Otwell. D.C.L., 1611.
Hill (Hyll), Rowland. Kt., 1556, 1559.
Hobart, Sir Henry. Atty.-Gen., 1608, 1611, 1613; C.J., 1620, 1625.
Holbeach, Henry. Bishop of Lincoln, 1549, 1551.
Holland, Henry Earl of. P.C., 1626, 1629, 1633.
Hopton, Owen. Kt., 1572, 1576, 1584.
Horne, Robert. Bishop of Winchester, 1572, 1576.
Howard, Sir William. P.C., 1633.
Howland, Richard. Bishop of Peterborough, 1584.

Howson, John. Bishop of Oxford, 1620, 1625, 1626.
Huett, Thomas. D.C.L., 1572.
Huick, Thomas. 1559, 1562, 1572.
Hussey, Sir James. Kt., 1620; Master of Chancery, 1625.
Hutchinson, William. D.D., 1601, 1605.
Hutton, Sir Richard. Justice, 1620, 1625, 1626, 1629, 1633.

Isaac, Edwarde. Esq., 1572.
Ithell, Thomas. D.C.L., 1576.

James, Sir Francis. D.C.L., 1601, 1605, 1608, 1611; Judge of the Court of Audience, 1613.
Jegon, John. Bishop of Norwich, 1605.
Jermin, Sir Thomas. Vice-Chamberlain of the Household, 1633.
Johnson, Philip. B.D., 1576.
Jones, Philip. LL.B., 1572.
Jones, Sir William. Justice, 1633.
Juxon (Jewxson). D.C.L., 1629; Bishop of London, 1633.

Kelley, Thomas Earl of. P.C., 1625, 1626, 1629, 1633.
Kempe, Nicholas. Esq., 1605, 1608, 1611, 1613; Master of Chancery, 1620.
Kenovill, George Earl of. Chancellor of Scotland, 1633.
King, Henry. Archdeacon of Colchester, 1625, 1626, 1629, 1633.
King, John. Dean of Christ Church, 1605, 1608; Bishop of London, 1611, 1613, 1620.
Kingsly, William. Archdeacon of Canterbury, 1620, 1625, 1626, 1629, 1633.
Kingsmill, John. D.C.L., 1572, 1576.
Knollys, William. *See* **Viscount Wallingford.**
Knowles (Knolles), Sir Francis. Treasurer of the Household, 1559, 1562, 1572, 1576, 1584.
Knowles, Henry. B.D., 1572, 1576.
Kyngesmill, William. Kt., 1572, 1576.

Lake, Arthur. Bishop of Bath and Wells, 1620, 1625, 1626.
Lake, Sir Thomas. Secretary of State, 1605, 1608, 1611, 1613.
Lakes, Stephen. D.C.L., 1601.
Lambe, Sir John. Dean of the Court of Arches, 1629, 1633.
Langforde, John. D.C.L., 1572.
Latymer, Hugh. D.D., 1549, 1551.

Laud, William. Bishop of St. Davids, 1625; Bishop of Bath and Wells, 1626; Bishop of London, 1629; Archbishop of Canterbury, 1633.
Lawes, Thomas. Commissary to the Archbishop of Canterbury, 1572, 1576; D.C.L., 1584.
Layfield, John. D.D., 1611, 1613.
Layson, Griffin. Dean of Arches, 1551.
Leicester, Robert Earl of. 1620, 1625, 1626.
Lennox, James Duke of. 1633.
Lewen, William. D.C.L., 1576, 1584.
Lewis, David. Judge of the Admiralty, 1562, 1572, 1576, 1584.
Ley, James Lord. Lord Treasurer, 1625.
Lindsell, Augustine. Bishop of Peterborough, 1633.
Lindsey, Robert Earl of. Chamberlain of England, 1629, 1633.
Littleton, Edward. Recorder of London, 1633.
Lloid, Oliver. D.C.L., 1625.
Lloyd, John. D.C.L., 1605.
Love (Lowe), Nicholas. D.D., 1620; Warden of St. Mary's at Winchester, 1625, 1626, 1629.
Lyell, Richard. D.C.L., 1549, 1551.

Maltravers, Henry Lord. P.C., 1633.
Mandeville, Henry Viscount. President of the Privy Council, 1625; Earl of Manchester, 1626, 1629, 1633.
Manwood, Roger. Justice, 1572, 1576, 1584.
Marleburgh, James Earl of. Lord Treasurer of England, 1626, 1629.
Marre, John Earl of. 1629, 1633.
Marshe, John. Governor of the Company of Merchant Adventurers, 1572.
Marten (Martyn), Sir Henry. Judge of the Admiralty, 1620; Judge of the Prerogative Court, 1625, 1626, 1629, 1633.
Marten, Thomas. D.C.L., 1556.
Marvyn, Henry. 1572.
Mathew, Tobias. Archbishop of York, 1625, 1626.
Mawe, Leonard. Bishop of Bath and Wells, 1626.
May (Mey), William. Dean of St. Paul's, London, 1549, 1551; D.C.L., 1559.
Maye, Sir Humphrey. Chancellor of the Duchy of Lancaster, 1629.
Melrose, Thomas Earl of. 1629.

Meredith, Richard. Dean of Wells, 1611.
Mildmay, Sir Walter. Chancellor of the Exchequer, 1572, 1576, 1584.
Mockett, Richard. D.D., 1611, 1613.
Montague, Sir Henry. Serjeant-at-Law, 1605, 1608, 1611, 1613; Chief Justice, 1620.
Montague, James. Bishop of Bath and Wells, 1605, 1608, 1611, 1613.
Monteigne (or **Mountain,** or **Mountague**), **George.** Dean of Westminster, 1611, 1613; Bishop of Lincoln, 1620; Bishop of London, 1625, 1626.
Montgomery, Philip Earl of. P.C., 1625, 1626, 1629.
Moore, William. B.D., 1572, 1576.
Mordaunt, John. Kt., 1556.
More (Moore), Sir George. Kt., 1613, 1620, 1625, 1626, 1629.
Moreton, William Earl of. Treasurer of Scotland, 1629, 1633.
Morton, Thomas. D.D., 1608; Dean of Winchester, 1611, 1613; Bishop of Coventry and Lichfield, 1620, 1625, 1626, 1629; Bishop of Durham, 1633.
Mounson, Robert. Justice, 1572, 1576.
Mountague, Richard. Bishop of Chichester, 1629, 1633.
Mountford, John. Prebend of St. Paul's, London, 1625, 1626, 1629, 1633.
Mountforde, Thomas. D.D., 1601, 1605, 1608, 1611, 1613, 1620.
Mullins, John. Archdeacon of London, 1576, 1584.
Murray, William. Bishop of Llandaff, 1629, 1633.

Naunton, Sir Robert. Secretary of State, 1620; Master of the Court of Wards, 1625, 1626, 1629, 1633.
Neil, Richard. *See* **Neyle.**
Nettle, Richard. D.D., 1605.
Nevil, Thomas. Dean of Canterbury, 1601, 1605, 1608, 1611, 1613.
Nevill, Henry. Kt., 1572, 1576.
Nevinson, Christopher. D.C.L., 1551.
Newburgh, Edward Lord. Chancellor of the Exchequer, 1629; Chancellor of the Duchy of Lancaster, 1633.
Newell, Robert. D.D., 1633.
Newman, Sir George. D.C.L., 1605, 1608, 1613; Judge of the Court of Audience, 1620.
Newman, Thomas. D.C.L., 1611.

Neyle, Richard. Bishop of Rochester, 1608; Bishop of Coventry and Lichfield, 1611, 1613; Bishop of Durham, 1620; Bishop of Winchester, 1625, 1626; Archbishop of York, 1633.
Nicholls, Sir Augustine. Justice, 1613.
North, Edward Lord. 1556.
Northampton, Henry Earl of. P.C., 1608, 1611, 1613.
Norton, Richard. Kt., 1572, 1576.
Nottingham, Charles Earl of. P.C., 1611, 1613, 1620.
Nowell, Alexander. Dean of St. Paul's, London, 1562, 1572, 1576, 1584.
Nowell, Robert. Attorney of the Court of Wards, 1562.
Noy, William. Attorney-General, 1633.

Oliver, John. 1551.
Osborne, Peter. Remembrancer of the Exchequer, 1562, 1572, 1576.
Ousley, Richard. Clerk of the Duchy of Lancaster, 1562.
Overall, John. Dean of St. Paul's, 1605, 1608, 1611; Bishop of Coventry and Lichfield, 1613.
Overton, William. Bishop of Coventry and Lichfield, 1572.
Owen, John. Bishop of St. Asaph, 1629, 1633.

Parker, Matthew. D.D., 1551; Archbishop of Canterbury, 1559, 1562, 1572.
Parkins, Sir Christopher. Master of Requests, 1605, 1608, 1611, 1613, 1620.
Parry, Henry. Bishop of Gloucester, 1608; Bishop of Worcester, 1611, 1613.
Parry, Sir Thomas. Chancellor of the Duchy of Lancaster, 1611, 1613.
Pasfielde, John. D.D., 1608, 1611, 1613.
Payton, Sir John. Kt., 1601.
Peeres, William. D.D., 1620, 1625.
Peirce, William. D.D., 1626, 1629.
Pembroke, William Earl of. 1613; Steward of the Household, 1620; Chamberlain of the Household, 1625, 1626, 1629, 1633.
Periam, Sir William. Chief Baron, 1601.
Perkins, Sir Christopher. *See* **Parkins.**
Peryn, Sir Thomas. Kt., 1620; Master of Chancery, 1625.
Petre, William. Kt., 1549, 1551, 1562.
Philips, Sir Edward. Justice, 1605, 1608; Master of the Rolls, 1611, 1613.

Pierse, John. Bishop of Rochester, 1576; Bishop of Salisbury, 1584.
Pierse (Piers), William. Dean of Peterborough, 1626, 1629; Bishop of Bath and Wells, 1633.
Pope, Edmond. D.C.L., 1625, 1626, 1629.
Pope, Thomas. Kt., 1556.
Popham, John. Attorney-General, 1584; Chief Justice, 1601, 1605.
Portland, Richard Earl of. Treasurer of England, 1633.
Potter, Barnabas. Bishop of Carlisle, 1633.
Poynet, John. Bishop of Rochester, 1551.
Price, Theodore. D.D., 1625, 1626, 1629.

Randolphe, Thomas. D.C.L., 1576.
Rastell, William. Serjeant-at-Law, 1556.
Ratcliffe, Henry. Kt., 1576.
Ravis, Thomas. Dean of Christ Church, 1605; Bishop of London, 1608.
Reade, Richard. Kt., 1556.
Redman, John. D.D., 1549; Archdeacon of Taunton, 1551.
Redman, William. B.D., 1576; Archdeacon of Canterbury, 1584; Bishop of Norwich, 1601.
Richardson, Sir Thomas. Chief Justice, 1629.
Ridley, Nicholas. Bishop of Rochester, 1549; Bishop of London, 1551.
Ridley, Sir Thomas. Kt., D.C.L., 1611, 1613, 1620, 1625, 1626, 1629.
Rivers, John. Alderman of London, 1576.
Roberts, William. Bishop of Bangor, 1633.
Roper, William. Esq., 1556.
Russell, Thomas. 1572.

Sackford, Thomas. Master of Requests, 1559, 1562, 1572, 1576.
Sackville, Robert. 1601.
Sadler, Sir Ralph. Chancellor of the Duchy of Lancaster, 1572, 1576, 1584.
Saint Leger, Nicholas. B.D., 1576.
Salisbury, Robert Earl of. As **Robert Cecil**, Secretary of State, 1601; Earl of Salisbury, Lord Treasurer, 1605, 1608, 1611.
Salisbury, William Earl of. P.C., 1629, 1633.
Sammes (Sams), William. D.C.L., 1626, 1629, 1633.

Sandes, Miles. 1572, 1576.
Saunderson, Thomas. D.D., 1608, 1611, 1613.
Savile, Sir Henry. Kt., 1605, 1611, 1613, 1620.
Savile, Sir John. Baron of the Exchequer, 1605.
Savile, John Lord. Comptroller of the Household, 1629.
Scamler, Edmund. Bishop of Norwich, 1584.
Scott, John. 1576.
Scott, Thomas. Kt., 1576.
Senhouse, Richard. Bishop of Carlisle, 1625, 1626.
Shilton, Sir Richard. Solicitor-General, 1626, 1629, 1633.
Shrewsbury, Gilbert Earl of. Justice in Eyre, 1611, 1613.
Smith, Miles. Bishop of Gloucester, 1613, 1620.
Smith, Sir Thomas. Kt., 1549, 1551, 1559, 1562, 1572, 1576.
Smith, Sir Thomas. Master of Requests, 1605, 1608.
Southampton, Henry Earl of. 1620.
Southcott, John. Justice, 1559, 1562, 1572, 1576.
Spencer, John. D.D., 1611, 1613.
Stanhope, Edward. D.C.L., 1584, 1601, 1605.
Stanhope, John Lord. Vice-Chamberlain of the Household, 1611, 1613.
Stanhope, Sir Michael. 1613.
Sterlin, William Earl of. Secretary for Scotland, 1633.
Steward (Styward), Nicholas. D.C.L., 1625, 1626, 1629.
Still, John. D.D., 1576, 1584; Bishop of Bath and Wells, 1601, 1605.
Story, John. D.C.L., 1556.
Stradlynge, Thomas. Kt., 1556.
Styward, Nicholas. *See* **Steward.**
Suckett, Lyonell. Alderman of London, 1576.
Suckling, Sir John. Master of Requests, 1620; Comptroller of the Household, 1625, 1626.
Suffolk, Theophilus Earl of. 1629, 1633.
Suffolk, Thomas Earl of. 1611, 1613, 1620, 1625, 1626.
Sutcliff, Mathew. Dean of Exeter, 1601, 1605.
Swale, Sir Richard. Master of Chancery, 1601, 1605.
Syndall, Henry. 1551.

Taillour, Roland. D.C.L., 1549, 1551.
Tailor, James. D.D., 1611.
Talbot, Thomas. D.C.L., 1626.
Tanfield, Sir Lawrence. Chief Baron, 1608, 1611, 1613, 1620, 1625.
Taylor, Frauncis. M.A., 1613.

Taylour, John. Dean of Lincoln, 1549, 1551.
Thirlby, Thomas. Bishop of Westminster, 1549; Bishop of Norwich, 1551; Bishop of Ely, 1556.
Thompson, Giles. Bishop of Gloucester, 1611.
Thornborough, John. Bishop of Worcester, 1625, 1626, 1629, 1633.
Throckmorton, Clemente. 1572.
Tinley, Robert. Archdeacon of Ely, 1607, 1611, 1613.
Tollson, Robert. Dean of Westminster, 1620.
Tonge, —. D.D., 1549.
Totnes, George Earl of. P.C., 1626, 1629.
Townson, Robert. Bishop of Salisbury, 1620.
Trevor, Sir Thomas. Justice, 1633.
Turner, Thomas. D.D., 1629, 1633.

Vaughan, John. D.C.L., 1556.
Vaughan, Richard. Bishop of London, 1605.
Vernon, Sir George. Baron, 1633.

Wade, William. Clerk of the Council, 1601, 1605, 1608, 1611.
Walgrave, Edward. Master of the Wardrobe, 1556.
Walker, John. D.D., 1576, 1584.
Wallingford, William Viscount. Treasurer of the Household, 1611, 1613, 1620, 1625, 1626.
Waltopp, Henry. Alderman of London, 1572, 1576.
Walmesley, Sir Thomas. Justice, 1605, 1608, 1611.
Walsingham, Francis. 1576, 1584.
Walter, Sir John. Attorney to the Prince of Wales, 1620, 1625; Chief Baron, 1626, 1629.
Warner, John. D.D., 1626; Prebend of Canterbury, 1629; Dean of Lichfield, 1633.
Warson, Anthony. Bishop of Chichester, 1601.
Watson, John. Bishop of Winchester, 1576.
Watts, Thomas. D.D., 1562, 1572, 1576.
Wenslowe, Richard. Esq., 1572.
Wentworth, Thomas Lord. Lord Deputy of Ireland, 1633.
Westfeild, Thomas. D.D., 1620, 1625, 1626, 1629, 1633.
Weston, Sir James. Baron, 1633.
Weston, Jerome Lord. 1633.
Weston, Sir Richard. Under-Treasurer of the Exchequer, 1625; Lord Treasurer, 1629.
Weston, Richard. Justice, 1572.
Weston, Robert. D.C.L., 1559, 1562; Dean of Wells, 1572.

Weston, Sir Simon. Kt., 1611.

Westphaling, Herbert. D.D., 1576, 1584; Bishop of Hereford, 1601.

White, Francis. Dean of Carlisle, 1625, 1626; Bishop of Norwich, 1629; Bishop of Ely, 1633.

White, Thomas. D.C.L., 1584.

Whitgift, John. Dean of Lincoln, 1576; Archbishop of Canterbury, 1584, 1589, 1601.

Wilbraham, Roger. D.C.L., 1601; Master of Requests, 1611, 1613.

Wilbraham, Thomas. Attorney of the Court of Wards, 1572.

Williams, Sir David. Justice, 1605, 1608, 1611.

Williams, John. Dean of Salisbury, 1620; Bishop of Lincoln, and Chancellor of England, 1625, 1626, 1629, 1633.

Williams, Lewis. B.D., 1572.

Wilmott, Charles Viscount. 1629, 1633.

Wilson, Thomas. Master of Requests, 1572, 1576.

Wimbledon, Edward Viscount. 1629, 1633.

Winch, Sir Humphrey. Justice, 1620, 1625.

Windebanke, Sir Francis. Secretary of State, 1633.

Winniffe, Thomas (Wynniffe). Dean of Gloucester, 1625; Prebend of St. Paul's, 1626, 1629; Dean of St. Paul's, 1633.

Wirrall, Thomas. *See* **Worrall.**

Wodderidge, John. J., 1605.

Wood, Basil. D.C.L., 1633.

Worcester, Edward Earl of. Lord Privy Seal, 1611, 1613, 1620, 1625, 1626.

Worley, Henry. D.C.L., 1576.

Worrall, Thomas. D.D., 1625, 1626, 1629, 1633.

Wotton, Edward Lord. 1611, 1613, 1620.

Wotton, Nicholas. Dean of Canterbury, 1551.

Wotton, Thomas. B.D., 1572, 1576.

Wren, Matthew. Dean of Windsor, 1629, 1633; and *ex officio* as Bishop of Norwich, and Bishop of Hereford, and Bishop of Ely, 1635–41.

Wright, Robert. Bishop of Bristol, 1625, 1626; Bishop of Coventry and Lichfield, 1633.

Wrothe, Thomas. Alderman of London, 1572.

Wykeham, William. Bishop of Lincoln, 1584.

Wylkes, Richard. D.D., 1551.

Wyndesor, William Lord. 1556.

Wynniffe, Thomas. *See* **Winniffe.**

Yale, Thomas. D.C.L., 1562, 1572, 1576.
Yelverton, Christopher. Serjeant-at-Law, 1601.
Yelverton, Sir Henry. Attorney-General, 1620.
Yong, John. D.D., 1576; Bishop of Rochester, 1584, 1601.
Young, John. Dean of Winchester, 1625, 1626, 1629, 1633.

Zouch, Edward Lord. Warden of the Cinque Ports, 1611, 1613, 1620, 1625.
Zouch, Henry Lord. 1605.

APPENDIX III

BIBLIOGRAPHY

I. A. Letters Patent: General

Province of Canterbury

April 12 (?), 1535. Commission to Thomas Cromwell.[1] (No copy.)

Jan. 6, 1548/9. De Potestatibus ad inquirendum super Haeretica Pravitate. Patent Roll, 3 Ed. VI, part 6, m. 28. Printed by Rymer, *Foedera*, xv, 181.

Jan. 8, 1550/1. Commissio Regia ad observandum librum precum communium. Cardwell, *Annals*, i, 102; Wilkins, *Concilia*, iv, 66; Rymer, *Foedera*, xv, 250; Strype, *Memorials*, II, i, 385.

[1] The original Letters Patent have no title; they begin with the clause of greeting. The titles printed at the head of the printed transcripts usually contain the editor's notion of the High Commission, and have not been reproduced here. The titles quoted are those to be found in the manuscript calendar of the Patent Roll at the Public Record Office, or are the endorsement of some contemporary on some copy. They are important as evidence of contemporary usage. Where no title is quoted, the author is not aware of any applied by a contemporary.

Oct., 1552. A commission 'for the examination and punishment of erroneous opinions in religion', is mentioned by Strype, *Memorials*, II, i, 209; and in the *Privy Council Register, New Series*, iv, 138.

Feb. 16, 1556. A general commission against Lollards, mentioned by Strype, *Memorials*, III, i, 552; and in Wilkins, *Concilia*, iv, 140.

Feb. 8, 1556/7. 'A commission for a severer way of proceeding against heretics.' Patent Roll, 3 and 4 Phil. and Mary, part 2, m. 48. Printed in Pocock, *Burnet's Reformation*, v, 469. In *Ibid.* ii, 556, this is said to have been only the renewal of one issued the preceding year. See also Foxe, *Martyrs*, viii, 301.

March 28, 1558. Cardinalis Poli commissio ad proceden. contra haereticos. Wilkins, *Concilia*, iv, 173.

July 19, 1559. Commissio Matheo Cantuar: Archiepiscopo et aliis. Patent Roll, 1 Eliz., part 9. Tanner MSS. L, f. 5. Printed in full with modernized spelling by Prothero, *Select Statutes and other Constitutional Documents*, 227–32, 2nd edition, Oxford, 1898. Also in Cardwell, *Documentary Annals*, i, 255 (Oxford, 1844). This Commission 'beareth date in July, but was signed in November next after'. 'The Notegatherer,' quoted in Cosin, *Apology*, part i, 114 (1593).

July 20, 1562. 'Commissio Matheo Archiepiscopo et aliis ad puniendum huiusmodi personas qui sunt repugnantes divino servicio.' Patent Roll, 4 Eliz., part 3. A short selection in Prothero, 232–5.

1570. A commission, now lost,[1] is mentioned in the correspondence between Parker and Cecil, S. P. Dom. Eliz., 74, no. 28; *Ibid.* 228, no. 19; and *Parker Correspondence*, 370.

[1] The writer of the list of 1584 appended a list of the renewals of the Commission which establishes the commissions of 1570 and 1589 for the first time. 'Anno primo, Anno Quarto, anno xij when Mr. Doctor Sandes was removed from Worcester to London. Anno xiiij; anno xviij when Mr. Doctor Grindall the Archbishop of York was removed to Canterbury. anno xxvj when Mr. Doctor Whitgift was removed from Worcester to Canterbury; anno xxxj now in being. From anno xviij I am suer yt was not renewed otherwise than here is menconed but I think yt was before in Mr. Doctor Parkers time being Archbishop of Canterbury if euer renewed then as before sett downe.' This lends colour to Coke's charge that the commissions were not enrolled. Three, 1570, 1584, and 1589, and probably one or two others in Parker's time between 1562 and 1570, were not enrolled, and no copies have survived.

June 11, 1572. Commissio directa archiepiscopo Cantuariensi et aliis pro ecclesiasticis causis. Patent Roll, 14 Eliz., part 8. Selection in Prothero, 235.

April 23, 1576. Commission for the Province of Canterbury. The original, signed by the Queen, is in S. P. Dom. Eliz., 108, no. 7, i. There is a copy in Cotton MSS. Cleopatra, F. II, f. 139. Printed in full (with errors), Strype, *Grindal*, 543. Selection in Prothero, *Statutes*, 237–40.

Jan. 7, 1583/4. No copy. An abstract is in Neal, *History of the Puritans*, chap. vi. A correct list of the names of the commissioners, however, seems to be in S. P. Dom. Eliz., 228, no. 19. 'Names of Commissioners Ecclesiastical anno 26 Eliz., who continued by that commission until 31 Eliz. and then renewed with notes of former renewals.' Strype gives the date as Dec. 9, 26 Eliz.: *Annals*, III, i, 260.

1589. No copy: mentioned in S. P. Dom. Eliz., 228, no. 19.

Feb. 3, 1600/1. De Commissione speciali pro Iohanne Domino Archiepiscopo Cantuariensi et aliis. Patent Roll, 43 Eliz., part 16, m. 37, dorso. Printed in Rymer, *Foedera*, xvi, 400. Brief abstract in Prothero, 240.

Feb. 9, 1604/5. Commissio Archiepiscopo Cantuar: et aliis pro ecclesiasticis causis. Patent Roll, 2 Jac. I, part 13, dorso. Copy in Cotton MSS. Cleopatra, F. II, f. 159.

July 1, 1608. Commissio Archiepiscopo Cantuar: et aliis pro ecclesiasticis causis. Patent Roll, 6 Jac. I, part 30, dorso.

Aug. 29, 1611. Special Commission for the Archbishop of Canterbury and others. Patent Roll, 9 Jac. I, part 18, dorso. Printed in full in Prothero, 424–34.

June 21, 1613. Commission directed to George, Archbishop of Canterbury and others for Ecclesiastical causes in England, Ireland, and Wales. Patent Roll, 11 Jac. I, part 15, dorso. Parts printed in Prothero, 424–34.

April 29, 1620. De Commissione speciali directa Georgio Archiepiscopo Cantuariensi et aliis concernente Causas Ecclesiasticas. Patent Roll, 18 Jac. I, part 9, no. 6. Printed in Rymer, *Foedera*, xvii, 200.

Jan. 21, 1624/5. De Commissione Suprema[1] pro Causis Ecclesiasticis. Patent Roll, 22 Jac. I, part 17, no. 3, dorso. Printed in Rymer, *Foedera*, xvii, 648.

March 28, 1625. Warrant renewing the last Commission. Printed Rymer, *Foedera*, xviii, 3.

[1] Note the phrasing used by the Chancery clerk.

Feb. 15, 1625/6. De Commissione directa Georgio Archiepiscopo Cantuariensi et aliis. Patent Roll, 1 Charles I, part 5, no. 4, dorso. Printed in Rymer, *Foedera*, xviii, 293. Concerning which see S. P. Dom. Car. I, 19, no. 47, Jan. 25, 1625/6.

Jan. 8, 1629. A copy is in S. P. Dom. Car. I, 131, nos. 27, 28, 29.

Dec. 17, 1633. Commissio specialis Willielmo Archiepiscopo Cantuariensi et aliis pro Causis Ecclesiasticis. Patent Roll, 9 Car. I, part 1, no. 5, dorso. Printed in Rymer, *Foedera*, xix, 487.

Province of York

March 8, 1557. Commission to the Archbishop of York, the Suffragan Bishop of Hull and others, 'for a severer way of proceeding against heretics.' Mentioned in Pocock, *Burnet's Reformation*, ii, 557.

June 24, 1559. Commissio regia visitatoribus suis in partibus borealibus. Pocock, *Burnet's Reformation*, v, 533. Cardwell's *Annals*, i, 249. Wilkins, *Concilia*, iv, 193.

1568. (No date.) Patent Roll, 10 Eliz., part 2.

Nov. 24, 1599. Commissio specialis de Schismate supprimendo. Rymer, *Foedera*, xvi, 386.

Oct. 24, 1620. Rymer, *Foedera*, xvii, 258. Also S. P. Dom., Jac. I, 117, no. 26.

Jan. 21, 1625. Rymer, *Foedera*, xvii, 648.

Aug. 1, 1625.
Aug. 1627. } Referred to in Hunter's *Illustrations of Neal's History of the Puritans.*

March 25, 1630. Printed in full by Hunter. Long extracts containing all of importance are in *Acts of the High Commission Court within the Diocese of Durham*, 258–65.

Note to the General Commissions

In Grant Book (in R.O.), p. 146, July 18, 1614, is the entry of a commission to the Archbishop of Canterbury, covering 'Ecclesiastical affairs'. It is hardly likely this is a High Commission, and there seems to be no other trace of it.

In the Sign Manual, vol. vii, no. 59, is a note of a commission, dated Westminster, March 21, 1616/7, to the Archbishop and others, to continue during the King's absence in Scotland, which had power, among other miscellaneous duties, of 'perfecting the ecclesiastical commission'. In S. P. Dom. James I, XC, f. 130, is what seems to be a copy of this commission.

B. Letters Patent: Special

England

1535. 'The copy of a commission of visitation granted by the general commission of the Lord Cromwell's in Henry VIII.' Cotton MSS. Cleopatra F. II, f. 131. Pocock, *Burnet's History of the Reformation*, v, 456. Wilkins, *Concilia*, iii, 784.

1538. Commission by Cromwell to Cranmer and others against the Anabaptists. Original in Registrum Cranmer at Lambeth. Mentioned by Strype, *Cranmer*, i, 99.

April 30, 1549. Literae archiepiscopi Cant. et aliorum commissar. regior. de Iohanna de Kente haeretica. Wilkins, *Concilia*, iv, 43.

Sept. 8, 1549. Commissio Thomae Archiepiscopo Cantuariensi et aliis ad examinandum Materiam versus Edmundum episcopum London. Rymer, *Foedera*, xv, 191.

Sept. 17, 1550. Alia Commissio regia Thomae archiepiscopo Cantuariensi et aliis ad examinandum materiam contemptus episcopi London. Wilkins, *Concilia*, iv, 37.

Dec. 12, 1550. A Commission to deprive Bishop Gardiner. Foxe, *Martyrs*, vi, 94.

Sept. 1551. Commission for the trial of the Bishops of Worcester and Chichester. Mentioned by Strype, *Memorials*, II, ii, 204.

Sept. 1552. Commission for the trial of the Bishop of Durham. Mentioned by Strype, *ibid.* 208.

Jan. 28, 1554. A Commission to the Bishops to try heretics, issued by Cardinal Pole. Mentioned by Strype, *Cranmer*, i, 495.

March 15, 1554. A Commission to deprive the Protestant bishops. Wilkins, *Concilia*, iv, 118.

March 16, 1554. Alia Commissio regia de expellendis nonnullis episcopis reformatis. Wilkins, *Concilia*, iv, 119.

March 29, 1554. A commission to the Bishop of Winchester for the removal of Prebends and Canons. Rymer, *Foedera*, xv, 376.

Feb. 16, 1555. A commission for the Diocese of Exeter, 'for repressing of heresies and false rumors.' Wilkins, *Concilia*, iv, 140.

April 26, 1555. A commission for the search and discovery of heretics (Diocese of Canterbury). Mentioned by Strype, *Memorials*, III, i, 476.

Fall 1556. Separate commissions against heresy in Essex,

Norwich, and Suffolk. Mentioned by Strype, *Memorials*, III, i, 553–5.

June 10, 1557. A commission to the Bishop of London 'ad inquirendum de haereticis in suà diocesi commorantibus'. Wilkins, *Concilia*, iv, 152.

June 10, 1557. Commission for the county (?) of Essex from Bonner to Archdeacon of Essex and two Bachelors of Law. Foxe, *Martyrs*, viii, 452–3.

Aug. 17, 1557. Commission to the Bishop of Lichfield 'for reformation of divers heresies'. Mentioned by Strype, *Memorials*, III, ii, 15.

March 28, 1558. Several small commissions against heretics. Mentioned by Strype, *Memorials*, III, ii, 120.

April, 1558. Commission issued by Bonner for the county (?) of Essex, *id.* 125.

July 20, 1562. Commission for the Diocese of Chester. S. P. Dom. Eliz. 23, no. 56.

1567 (?). List of Ecclesiastical commissioners in the Diocese of Chester. S. P. Dom. Eliz. Addenda, 13, no. 123.

1570–2. Certain commissioners named in the General Commissions were to execute their functions only in the dioceses of Canterbury, Winchester, Worcester, St. Davids, or Chichester. This was in reality issuing the special commissions under the general.

Oct. 28, 1573. Commission for the Diocese of Norwich. Harleian MSS. 380, f. 69.

n.d. Summary of a commission for Diocese of Norwich. Cotton MSS. Vespasian F. IX, f. 269.

1588. A commission for the Diocese of Norwich. Lansdowne MSS. 171, f. 267.

June 16, 1596. Commission for the Diocese of Winchester. Patent Roll, 38 Eliz., part 7, m. 12, dorso. Printed by Rymer, *Foedera*, xvi, 291. Copy in Harleian MSS. 171, f. 266.

Same renewed. Patent Roll, 39 Eliz., part 8, no. 5, dorso. Printed by Rymer, *Foedera*, xvii, 324.

Jan. 31, 1598. Commission for Diocese of Chester. S. P. Dom. Eliz. Docquet.

May 17, 1599. Commission for Diocese of Salisbury. S. P. Dom. Eliz. Docquet.

Aug. 26, 1603. Commission for Diocese of Worcester. Rymer, *Foedera*, xvi, 546.

1603. Commission for Diocese of Winchester. Patent Roll, 1 Jac. I, part 13, dorso.

Ireland

Dec. 20, 1578. Letters Patent to Geo. Ackworth, LL.D., and Robert Garvey for ecclesiastical jurisdiction in Ireland. Cotton MSS. Titus. B. XIII, ff. 256–8.

Wales

June 13, 1579. Commissio pro causis ecclesiasticis in Wallia. Patent Roll, 21 Eliz., part 7. Printed in part by Prothero, *Select Statutes*, 241. This covered not only Wales, but the modern English counties of Shropshire, Worcester, Hereford, Gloucester, and Monmouth.

Scotland

Feb. 1610. A High Commission for each province. *Acts and proceedings of General Assemblies of the Kirk of Scotland*, iii, 1078 (Bannatyne Club).

II. Acts and Cases

The greater part of the Act Books, and the great mass of papers belonging to the Registry of the Commission seem to have been lost. There seems to be, in fact, little doubt but that they were destroyed by order of Parliament during the Civil Wars. ' I humbly desire the proceedings of the High Commission may be seen (which are taken out of our hands),' wrote Laud in his ' History of Troubles ' (*Works*, iv, 165). Some books dating between 1633 and 1641 escaped and are now in the State Papers Domestic, CCLXI, Feb. 18, 1633/4 to Feb. 11, 1635/6, ff. 1–320 b; CCCXXIV, Feb. 11, 1635/6 to May 19, 1636, ff. 1–124, rest being blank; CCCCXXXIV, ff. 1–293, Nov. 11, 1639, to December 7, 1640. These great gaps can be filled only, as can the years 1583 to 1641 in general, by a great number of original documents among the State Papers, including sentences, writs, &c. Some of the Act Books and a great mass of original papers of the High Commission at Durham have been preserved and are of the utmost value. Selections have been edited and printed in *The Acts of the High Commission Court within the Diocese of Durham*, edited for the Surtees Society by W. H. D. Longstaffe. Durham, 1858. Burn noted (*High Commission*, 44) a paper book in the Registry of the Bishop of Norwich, called ' Mortimer ', in which 115 pages were devoted to the acts of the diocesan Commission at Norwich from September 1595 to September 1598. The book has, however, since disappeared, and searches at Lambeth, Oxford, Ely, Peterborough, Lincoln, and York, show that no records were there preserved.

Writs and Processes

I. Summons to appear.
S. P. Dom. Car. I, 272, no. 25; 274, nos. 15 and 16.

II. Bond for personal appearance.
S. P. Dom. Eliz. 35, no. 38.
S. P. Dom. Car. I, 162, no. 69 (1630).

III. Warrants.
(*a*) Apprehending priests.
Sign Manual, Car. I, X, no. 14 (1629).
(*b*) Search warrant for Papists, Jesuits, books, relics, &c.
S. P. Dom. Jac. I, 63, no. 53 (1611).
S. P. Dom. Car. I, 265, no. 6 (1634).
(*c*) Arrest of Separatists.
S. P. Dom. Car. I, 314, no. 34.
(*d*) For seizure of books.
S. P. Dom. Car. I, 314, no. 20.
(*e*) Apprehension of an ordinary party (attachment).
S. P. Dom. Car. I, 140, no. 15.
S. P. Dom. Car. I, 277, no. 104.
(*f*) Warrants signed, sealed, but otherwise blank.
S. P. Dom. Car. I, 255, nos. 23 and 24 (1634), 406, no. 57 (1638).

IV. Writs of Commitment.
XII Coke's *Reports*, 45, 5 Jac.
S. P. Dom. Car. I, 140, no. 15.

V. Power to examine witnesses in the country.
S. P. Dom. Car. I, 295, no. 4 (1635).

VI. Articles Original and Additional.
Articuli siue interrogatoria obiecta et ministrata ex officio mero . . . coram . . . Commissariis et Delegatis regiae Maiestatis ad causas Ecclesiasticas . . . [1584]. Strype, *Whitgift*, iii, 81–7.

S. P. Dom. Eliz. 240, no. 140 (against a recusant).
Lansdowne MSS. 1172, f. 97 (Latin) 1607 (Fuller's case).
S. P. Dom. Car. I, 246, no. 13 (1633).
S. P. Dom. Car. I, 280, no. 33; no. 54; no. 71.
S. P. Dom. Car. I, 272, no. 95.
S. P. Dom. Car. I, 388, no. 41 (with answers).

VII. Answers to Articles.
Strype, *Whitgift*, iii, 153 (1585).
S. P. Dom. Jac. I, 157, no. 59 (1623).
S. P. Dom. Car. I, 142, no. 22 (1628).
S. P. Dom. Car. I, 278, no. 65 (1635).
S. P. Dom. Car. I, 278, no. 46.
S. P. Dom. Car. I, 299, no. 85.
S. P. Dom. Car. I, 371, no. 102.
S. P. Dom. Car. I, 388, no. 41 (with articles).

VIII. Examinations.
S. P. Dom. Eliz. 262, no. 25, i (Durham).
S. P. Dom. Eliz. 273, no. 23, i.
S. P. Dom. Jac. I, 97, nos. 73 to 76.

IX. Briefs.
S. P. Dom. Car. I, 281, no. 5.
S. P. Dom. Car. I, 309, no. 25.

X. Complete set of Documents in a case.
S. P. Dom. Car. I, 268, no. 63.
S. P. Dom. Car. I, 290, no. 73.
S. P. Dom. Car. I, 383, no. 47, i to x.
S. P. Dom. Car. I, 432, no. 27.

XI. Sentences:

I. Upon Clergy

(*a*) Deprivation.
S. P. Dom. Jac. I, 168, no. 50 (1624).
S. P. Dom. Car. I, 381, no. 63 (1637).
(*b*) Degradation and Deprivation.
S. P. Dom. Jac. I, 69, no. 2 (1612).
S. P. Dom. Jac. I, 78, no. 78 (1614).
S. P. Dom. Jac. I, 92, no. 38 (1617).
(*c*) Sentence of removal and suspension for non-conformity.
S. P. Dom. Car. I, 168, no. 9 (1630).

(*d*) Sentence of suspension (ecclesiastical irregularities).
S. P. Dom. Car. I, 145, no. 55.
S. P. Dom. Car. I, 251, no. 6.
S. P. Dom. Car. I, 364, no. 44.

II. Upon Laity

(*a*) Adultery.
S. P. Dom. Jac. I, 159, no. 16.
(*b*) Intermarriage within the degrees.
S. P. Dom. Car. I, 191, no. 16.
(*c*) Puritans.
S. P. Dom. Car. I, 420, no. 16; 421, no. 37; 425, no. 18.

XII. Pardons.
Jac. I, Sign Manual, viii, no. 92 (1618).
S. P. Dom. Car. I, 232, no. 40.
S. P. Dom. Docquet, May 2, 1636.

XIII. Fines.
Act of commutation of penance into a fine by the commissioners. S. P. Dom. Car. I, 454, no. 36 (1640).
Grant to courtier of a mitigated fine. Jac. I, Sign Manual, v, no. 88 (1616).
Pardon for a fine of £2,000. Car. I, Sign Manual, i, no. 75.

XIV. List of fees in the Commission since 13 Elizabeth.
S. P. Dom. Car. I, 65, no. 81 (1627).

XV. Certificates of Conformity to the laws of the Church.
S. P. Dom. Car. I, 319, no. 71.

XVI. Form of Submission.
S. P. Dom. Car. I, 445, no. 31.

XVII. Letter of Immunity from ordinary judicial authority.
S. P. Dom. Jac. I, vii, no. 25.

XVIII. Certificates of Contempt of Court.
S. P. Dom. Car. I, 432, no. 54.

XIX. Petitions.
(*a*) For release from imprisonment.
S. P. Dom. Car. I, 255, no. 21.
(*b*) For aid in his distress.
S. P. Dom. Car. I, 280, no. 3.

XX. The Seal of the Commission is on papers in
S. P. Dom. Car. I, 272, no. 25.
S. P. Dom. Car. I, 364, no. 44.
S. P. Dom. Car. I, 406, no. 57.

III. Treatises on Procedure

John Ayliffe. Parergon Iuris Canonici under the various titles, tithes, citation, libel, &c. London, 1726 and 1734.

Bonnier. Traité des Preuves. Paris, 1843.

Practica Iuris Civilis in Curiis Ecclesiasticis; per Franciscum Clarke Almae Curiae Cantuariensis de Arcubus London. Procuratorem in Lucem edita; ac per Robertum Lownes dictae Curiae Procuratoris Clericum rescripta, A.D. 1632. Praemittuntur binae huiusce Operis Censurae. Harleian MSS. 1749.

H. Conset. Practice of the Ecclesiastical Courts. London, 1685.

A. Esmein. Histoire de la Procédure Criminelle en France, et spécialement de la procédure inquisitoire depuis le XIIIe siècle jusqu'à nos jours. Paris, 1882.

Philip Floyer. The Proctor's Practice in the Ecclesiastical Courts. 2nd Edition by Thomas Wright. London, 1746.

Ernest Glasson. Histoire du Droit et des Institutions politiques, civiles et judiciaires de l'Angleterre, comparée au Droit et aux Institutions de la France depuis leur origine jusqu'à nos jours. Volume V covers from 1509 to 1820. Paris, 1883.

William Lambarde. Archianomia, or the Ancient Laws of England. 1644, f°.

C. C. Langdell. A Summary of Equity Pleading. (Chapter I is on Civil Law Pleading in England.) Cambridge (Mass.), 1883, 2nd Edition.

Menochius. De Praesumptionibus, Coniecturis, Signis et Indiciis. One thousand one hundred and sixty-seven folios on the intricacies of presumptions.

Richard Mocket. Tractatus de Politica Ecclesiae Anglicanae. 1st Edition, 1616, burned. 2nd Edition, London, 1638. 3rd Edition, London, 1705.

Thomam Oughton. Ordo Iudiciorum. First part translated with notes by J. T. Law, M.A., Chancellor of Lichfield and Coventry (London, 1831). London, 1728.

Sir Thomas Ridley, D.C.L. A view of the Civile and Ecclesiasticall law and wherein the practice of them is streitned and may be relieved within this land. London, 1607, 4°. 2nd Edition, Oxford, 1634, 4°. 3rd Edition, Oxford, 1662, 8°. 4th Edition, Oxford, 1676, 8°.

Richard Robinson. Treatises on the Ecclesiastical Courts (1588–97). Barrington MSS. 22, f. 667 (at the Inner Temple).

Richard Zouch. Descriptio Iuris et Iudicii Ecclesiastici secundum Canones et Constitutiones Anglicanas. 1st Edition, 1636. 2nd Edition (published with Mocket), 1638. 3rd Edition (published with Mocket), 1705.

IV. Treatises on Jurisdiction

(Besides those quoted in the foot-notes, Chapters VII, VIII, IX)

Prohibitions grounded uppon the Statute de A° 23 Hen. 8. That noe person shalbe cited out of the dioces but in certain cases. Petyt MSS. 518, f. 95 b.

Whether the High Commission may legally proceede to censure men for a breach of decree of Star Chamber made 28 Eliz. for the better ordering of Printers and Stationers. Petyt MSS. 518, f. 68.

Whether the High Commission may fine and imprison by vertue of 1° Eliz. and unless it be in case of heresie or incontinency of ministers. Petyt MSS. 518, f. 68 b.

Precedents in Law French of prohibitions to the High Commission. Petyt MSS. 518, f. 95.

List of arguments on the High Commission (hostile). Cotton MSS. Cleopatra, F. II, f. 171.

A discourse touching Ecclesiastical Jurisdictions (tracing one view in precedent from Magna Carta to James I, and having reference to the debates of 1611). Cotton MSS. Cleopatra, F. II, f. 1.

A collection showing what Jurisdiction the Clergie hath heretofore lawfully used in the Realme of England. Petyt MSS. 511. 16, f. 1.

The proceedings in the court of common pleas concerning Prohibitions and Consultations (the minutiae of Practice). Cotton MSS. Cleopatra, F. II, f. 444.

V. Printed Books

The literature in print about the Commission is meagre. No history of the court seems to have been written in the sixteenth or seventeenth century, and only one has appeared since—John Southerden Burn. *The High Commission, Notices of the Court and its Proceedings.* London, 1865, 8°. This account is very brief, and is in every way inadequate, containing, in fact, as its title admits, merely scattered notices and remarks. A briefer account by Bishop Stubbs in the Appendix to the Ecclesiastical Commission's Report for 1883 (*Parl. Doc.* 1883, xxiv) is the only thing in print worthy of attention, but it does not pretend to be more than an incomplete sketch of certain phases of the Commission's work. The Commission, in fact, has no literature.

The printed books in which some mention of the Commission may be found are legion. Nearly all the source books of the period contain something, and most histories of the period contain at least criticisms and reflections upon the Commission's career. To attempt here a complete bibliography of the period is out of the question, and it is hoped that the foot-notes and manuscript bibliography will inform the reader as to the whereabouts of all contemporary information of which the present writer is aware; and of all subsequent work which seems at all valuable. For aid in further research, the reader is referred to the critical bibliography of the period printed in Usher's *Reconstruction of the English Church*, ii, 370–414.

INDEX

Oxford: Horace Hart M.A. Printer to the University